Regency
HOUSE PARTY

Regency HOUSE PARTY

LUCY JAGO

timewarner
books

A Time Warner Book

First published in Great Britain in 2004 by
Time Warner Books

Copyright © Lucy Jago 2004

A CIP catalogue record for this book
is available from the British Library.

ISBN 0 316 72658 3

Endpapers: wallpaper detail from Kentchurch Court

Design by Andrew Barron @ thextension
Photography by Martin Thompson
Colour reproduction by Radstock Reproductions
Printed and bound in Great Britain by Butler and Tanner Limited,
Frome and London

Time Warner Books UK
Brettenham House, Lancaster Place
London WC2E 7EN

www.TimeWarnerBooks.co.uk

CONTENTS

THE HOST, ELIGIBLE BACHELOR AND POTENTIAL 'MR DARCY', AWAITS THE ARRIVAL
OF THE HOUSE-PARTY GUESTS WITH THE HOSTESS

INTRODUCTION

Nothing was ever half so magnificent.

TOM MOORE, REGENCY POET

ALTHOUGH THE REGENCY lasted for only nine years, from 1811 to 1820, it is an era that has left a particularly brilliant impression on the cultural life of this country. It was an age of war, hedonism, scandal and beauty, an age of magnificent opulence, dreadful poverty and political turmoil. But above all it was an age of glittering individuals. Wellington, Byron, Napoleon, Jane Austen and Beau Brummell all waltzed through it, leaving their indelible marks. And of course there was the Prince Regent himself, whose extraordinary extravagance and self-indulgence did so much to define the times.

In the television series *Regency House Party*, a unique social experiment was undertaken to bring the Regency back to life. For nine weeks, ten young men and women were returned to live and love as their Regency forebears had done. If the popularity of Jane Austen's novels and their screen adaptations is an accurate gauge, it seems we yearn for the lost age of courtship and romance. There were thirty thousand hits on the Regency House Party website, which resulted in

SUMPTUOUS CHAMBERS WITH ALL SIGNS OF MODERNITY REMOVED

1500 applications from which the ten participants were chosen. All were looking for the chance to experience Regency life as they (and many of us) imagined it to be – the refined and fashionable pursuit of pleasure and romance.

'What most of us know about this period,' said Caroline Ross Pirie, the series producer, 'is gleaned from the literature of the time, in particular from its most famous novelist, Jane Austen.' The world Austen created in her books is peopled with dashing heroes and spirited heroines, the Mr Darcys and Elizabeth Bennets of screen adaptation. However, the happy endings often belie the real indignities

AN IMPECCABLE APPEARANCE WAS *DE RIGEUR*
IN REGENCY SOCIETY

and hardship of the Regency 'marriage mart' that she subtly hinted at in her work. The rigid social hierarchies, the love of status and money, the 'pride and prejudice' we find deliciously fascinating today were far less entertaining to those trapped by their restrictions. 'Do you not consider that a connection with you must disgrace him in the eyes of everybody?' snaps Lady Catherine de Bourgh, incensed that her nephew Mr Darcy might 'pollute' his good name by marrying Elizabeth Bennet, with her 'upstart pretensions, a young woman without family, connections, or fortune'. How would modern people, used to the relative equality and freedom of contemporary dating etiquette, cope with the rules and regulations imposed on Regency courtship? Would they find their way through the maze of tradition and restriction, morality and ambition of those times? A man was not even allowed to call a woman by her first name until they were engaged. Would romance flourish in the house, or would it quail under the watchful eye of the chaperones policing every move? Perhaps the house-guests would come to prefer the slow and gentle game of Regency courtship to the predatory immediacy of today? And if romance did blossom, would it be a match of 'sense' or 'sensibility'? Would it be for love (with money and position being irrelevant), or for security and to promote the status quo, as was expected of most Regency marriages?

For two months, cameras followed these young seekers of love, and their four chaperones, as they lived in great style in a beautiful country house in which the Regency world had been recreated down to the smallest detail. Footmen, valets and maids were there to serve them; a specialist chef delighted their palates; quills and sealing-wax awaited their letters; a Regency wardrobe was created to suit each one; carriages were polished and deer roamed in the park. 'We decided to recreate a house party because it was a popular aspect of upper-class life in the Regency and was particularly important for match-making,' explained Caroline Ross Pirie. 'We were inspired by the house party at Netherfield in Jane Austen's *Pride and*

Prejudice and chose volunteers who would not have felt out of place in a Regency country-house drawing room two hundred years ago.' Among them was Christopher Gorell Barnes, who was to act as the host of the party. Taking a break from a successful career as a commercials producer, his good looks, manners and interest for the ladies soon earned him the nickname of 'Mr Darcy'. Fiona Rogers, chosen to be the hostess responsible for the respectable behaviour (or otherwise) of her guests, is in her late fifties and once ran her own estate and staff. She had to ensure that the house-guests behaved in accordance with Regency protocol and manners, and to enforce the rules of 'precedence', in which the highest-born got the best of everything and the lowest had to put up and make do. Their female guests included a beautiful, aloof barmaid of Russian noble stock, a titled lady, a millionairess, a successful novelist and a scuba-diving instructor. Attractive and intelligent, would these women captivate the hearts of the men in the house, maybe even to the point of a proposal of marriage? Among their potential suitors were an ex-dotcom millionaire, a hairdresser, a stage manager, a biology teacher, a musician and a professional artist, all good-looking and all seeking partners.

The setting for the Regency House Party was Kentchurch Court in Herefordshire, ancestral home of the Lucas-Scudamore family. Built in the four-teenth century, and substantially remodelled by the famous Regency architect John Nash, the secluded and romantic house was the perfect setting for a Regency revival. In an extraordinary endeavour of artistic and practical brilliance, all traces of modernity were removed or concealed and the house regained the elegance and grace of two hundred years ago. The guests too had to shed all vestiges of their twenty-first-century lives. Bags, phones, pens, watches, jewellery and make-up were removed as they stepped into the fashions of their Regency predecessors, down to their underwear and up to their hats. No more cleanser, shampoo, hair-dryers, e-mail, television, recorded music, kettles, loos, taps and all the 'essentials' that we take for granted. However, they were also relieved of many of the respon-sibilities of modern life. There was little or no 'work' to do and all the necessities (and most of the luxuries) of life would be provided. Servants would wash their clothes, make their beds, empty their chamber pots, shave their faces, cook their food, and might, if the guest was important enough, make them beauty potions and wax or candle-soot 'make-up'. The guests would be given opportunities to pursue the activities of Regency gentlemen and gentlewomen under the guidance of specialists in the period. In return, they agreed to observe and abide by the strict rules of Regency etiquette, any infringement of which could be punished by expulsion from the house.

From dancing a quadrille at a masquerade ball to bloody, bare-knuckle fist-fighting, from washing hair in rum and rosewater to wielding a sabre while galloping on horseback, the guests threw themselves into their new lives. They were unanimous in declaring the Regency House Party a 'roller-coaster ride'. The joys, pains, luxuries and deprivations were to change them for ever. 'I really am there. I have gone back two hundred years in a time machine. This is mind-blowing.' They also had to adapt to living cheek-by-jowl with each other, not as equals and friends but strictly divided by their position in the social order and their possession, or lack, of wealth. 'I couldn't believe it. A maid helped my chaperone with her clothes but I was just left there looking like a fool!!'

During their stay at Kentchurch, the guests also came to a deep understanding of the fascinations and paradoxes of life under the Prince Regent. The Regency was precipitated by the episodes of 'madness' that rendered the reigning King George III unfit to rule, whereupon his eldest son was appointed to administer the kingdom in his place. It is a late chapter in the Georgian period, the era dominated by the Hanoverian kings, which began in 1714 with George I and ended with the death of William IV in 1837. The nine years in which the spectre of the frugal King haunted the banquets of his prodigal son are a riotous interval between the be-wigged and powdered age of George III and the moralistic, crinolined years of Victoria. The Regency saw the completion of the luxurious and exotic Brighton Pavilion but also the growth of horrific slums around the industrialising cities. The brilliant society hostesses who spent their time planning balls and affairs could watch an eight-year-old hanged for stealing a handkerchief. The intellectuals, wits, poets, dandies and military heroes collected their honours while innocent demonstrators seeking reform were cut down and killed.

This era of extremes produced some of our finest writers, the Romantic poets and novelists Scott, Austen and Mary Shelley all coming to the fore. Never had artists, poets and architects enjoyed such patronage, never had fashion and personal etiquette been so cultivated. Much of the Regent's time was devoted to his tailors,

THE PRINCE OF PLEASURE – THE REGENT BY THOMAS LAWRENCE

boot-makers, jewellers, interior designers, architects, chefs and mistresses, and to creating and endlessly redecorating palaces to indulgence. He elevated fashion above politics and happily spent his mornings watching Beau Brummell perfect the art of tying a cravat while his people rioted against the grinding poverty in which so many of them were trapped. For the first half of his regency the country was at war with France and America; for the second it struggled through poverty and social unrest, yet the prince partied on.

The extraordinary events of the hot and emotional summer at Kentchurch Court, and the fascinating era that inspired them, are the subjects of this book. Wall to Wall TV has already produced three superb and hugely popular series that immersed modern people in the daily life of an earlier age: *1900 House*, *The 1940s House* and *The Edwardian Country House*. *Regency House Party*, like its predecessors, has brought together the most accurate historical research and period detail in collaboration with leading experts. The results are gripping and revelatory about 'the Age of Romance' and the struggles of the guests to live and love as a Mr Darcy or an Elizabeth Bennet. As one of them expressed it: 'This experience has changed our lives. It's been phenomenal.'

KENTCHURCH COURT, A HIDDEN TREASURE AT THE FOOT OF GARWAY HILL

CHAPTER ONE

RECREATING A REGENCY WORLD

THE QUEST TO find the perfect guests for the *Regency House Party* began in December 2002. Adverts were placed in newspapers and magazines and on the Internet, while weekend editions of newspapers carried large editorials promoting the series. At the same time, Caroline Ross Pirie set out to hunt for the house that could host this extraordinary experiment. It needed to be large, set in its own park, devoid of all reminders of the twenty-first century, and well hidden from the prying eyes of curious onlookers. The owners of the house would have to be exceptionally accommodating; the rooms commandeered for the guests would be completely redecorated and refurbished and the rest of the house would be given over to the television production team and the 'servants' – footmen, housemaids, cooks and watchmen. After an extensive (and at times desperate) search across the United Kingdom, during which over one hundred houses were considered, a house that exceeded everyone's dreams was found. Nestled deep in the folds of a Herefordshire valley at the bottom of Garway Hill, Kentchurch Court fitted all the criteria. It is entirely hidden from the road

THE ESTATE GARDENS WOULD PROVIDE
FLOWERS FOR THE HOUSE, PICKED BY THE
LADIES' MAIDS OR GARDENERS

and its secluded location and long history imbue the house with an atmosphere of romance and intimacy. It belongs to the Lucas-Scudamores, one of the oldest-established families in Herefordshire, and is shrouded in tales of ghosts, princes and intrigue.

'I had twelve weeks to transform this house, which had seen seven hundred years of use, into a true Regency dwelling,' said Alan Spalding, the designer chosen to redesign the interiors, gardens and parklands of Kentchurch. The house was originally built in the fourteenth century by the Scudamore family, who had arrived in England with William the Conqueror in 1066. The family, whose name means 'Shield of love', have lived here ever since. The original medieval house and its imposing fourteenth-century tower still remain. Around 1800, the family decided the house needed a major makeover for which they hired the famous Regency architect John Nash. Although Nash is best known today for the beautiful crescents with stuccoed façades that grace Regent's Park in London, he could just as easily turn his hand to the 'Gothic' styles popular in the Regency.

Nash remodelled the interior of Kentchurch, adding a storey to the medieval tower, and a new wing. He also put crenellations around the roof and refaced the building to render it more 'castle-like'. Since the house was about to rediscover its Regency identity, Alan was determined that it should sparkle and fizz just as it had done two hundred years before. Jan Lucas-Scudamore, the current chatelaine of Kentchurch, embarked on the onerous task of packing up the family home, the first time anyone had attempted to do so for nearly seven hundred years. She used several miles of bubble wrap and unearthed many lost marvels as she packed (including a handbag full of letters from Churchill and a pair of Queen Victoria's stockings); then she, her family and her many dogs decamped to a mobile home near by.

The first step for the designer and his construction team was to strip out or hide everything that post-dated the Regency, including electric wires and fittings, plumbing, wallpaper, carpets, fireplaces, furniture and paintings. Alan had to make the house look beautiful while at the same time fulfilling the practical needs of the film-makers and of the family that had to live there afterwards. The house had to function in every way as it would have done during the Regency. The designs should accurately reflect the tastes and financial resources available to the master of Kentchurch Court at the start of the Regency. This was a country residence, isolated from London – would the latest word in fashion have travelled this far? The private rooms (bedrooms, offices and boudoirs) needed to show the different statuses of the people who would be occupying them for the series.

'As the house had been continuously lived in for centuries, many of the rooms contained genuine Regency features, furniture and paintings, while others looked back to an earlier era, particularly Georgian. Others had elements of Victorian,

Edwardian and 1970s design. I went with the feeling of the rooms and tried to keep that atmosphere of a real, lived-in family home that had evolved over time rather than of a film set where every detail was Regency with no reference to the past.'

Meanwhile, hundreds of applications to take part in the series had flooded in within days of the adverts appearing. 'Our "wish list" of guests was loosely based on Mr Bingley's house party in *Pride and Prejudice*,' said Caroline Ross Pirie. 'We were looking for the modern equivalents of the handsome but aloof Mr Darcy, the feisty but impoverished Elizabeth Bennet, the sunny Mr Bingley and his glamorous and competitive sister, and so on. Although the people in Jane Austen's novels were caricatures, the *Absolutely Fabulous* Patsy and Edina of their day, the house party we wanted to create was to be as near the real experience of Regency life as possible.' Caroline and her team had to find five men and five women who were prepared to live and love according to the protocols of Regency country-house society. 'It was like choosing guests for a dinner party without knowing very much about them!' said Caroline. 'And since the series was all about love in the age of romance, at least some members of the party needed to fancy each other. How many times have you tried to match-make and failed, even among people you know quite well?' Gradually, the men and women who were to people the beautiful Regency world of Kentchurch Court emerged from the many hopeful applicants.

'Interior design' was a term first used during the Regency. A passion for redecorating and refurbishing houses in the latest styles became widespread, spearheaded by the most extravagant decorator of all, the Prince Regent. He revolutionised the art of interior design and used as his showcases Carlton House (now demolished), located just off Pall Mall, and Brighton Pavilion.

CARLTON HOUSE, DUE IN LARGE PART TO THE CHANGES IN DECORATION IT PATIENTLY WITHSTOOD AND FASHIONS IN FRIENDSHIP IT WITNESSED, BECAME SYMBOLIC OF THE REGENCY ITSELF AND ENJOYED PRAISE AND DERISION IN EQUAL MEASURE

He was determined to make his various abodes the most opulent in Europe, and gathered around him a circle of friends that ranged from politicians to courtesans, gamblers to scholars, society hostesses to jockeys. The Carlton House Set, as they came to be known, included some of the most brilliant figures of the age, such as Georgiana, Duchess of Devonshire, one of the great hostesses of her day; Richard Brinsley Sheridan, playwright, politician and drunkard; and Beau Brummell, king of the dandies, the man who ruled society for many years and created a revolution in men's fashion. For some, the prince's tastes were a little too rich. 'Not a spot without some finery upon it, gold upon gold – a bad taste', commented one viewer, who said of the apartments that 'they would give an unfavourable idea of the kind of man he was'.

The prince had been given Carlton House by his father in 1783 as a coming-of-age gift. However, aware of his son's lavish tastes and perhaps to remind him who held the purse strings, the King gave him only £50,000 as an allowance. Although the majority of the population lived below the poverty line, the Prince of Wales responded to his father's perceived parsimony by spending more than ever. He often dispatched his chef to make deals with moneylenders and then spent the money on further aggrandising Carlton House. In the course of the next thirty years he transformed the house repeatedly, employing five different architects to scrap the work of their predecessor and start again. He chose the colours, furnishings, paintings, lighting and even the design of the servants' quarters himself.

ACKERMAN'S REPOSITORY IN THE STRAND, WHERE *OBJETS D'ART* AND THE LATEST JOURNAL OF THIS FASHIONABLE INSTITUTION COULD BE ADMIRED

An appreciation of fine design was also a growing trend among the bourgeoisie, particularly in the area of home furnishings, and led to a number of publications which informed 'ladies and gentlemen of refinement and taste' of the latest developments. Printed wallpapers, developed in the mid-seventeen hundreds, became popular at the turn of the century as a new process of producing lighter colours and designs replaced the traditional techniques of stencilling or hand-colouring.

THE VIVID YELLOW AND PAINTED WALLS OF THE GARDEN ROOM WERE VERY FASHIONABLE IN THE REGENCY

THIS PAINTING BY DIANA SPERLING SHOWS THE WOMEN OF THE FAMILY *PAPERING THE SALOON AT TICKFORD PARK. SEPTEMBER 2ND 1816.* ALTHOUGH OF THE LANDED GENTRY, IT WAS CONSIDERED ENTIRELY APPROPRIATE THAT THEY SHOULD REDECORATE THEIR HOUSES THEMSELVES

As soon as the designs were approved, Alan's team began work under the direction of Jo Manser, the art director. As well as ensuring that Alan's designs were beautifully implemented in the house, Jo remained at Kentchurch throughout the filming period and his creative skills and ingenuity were constantly called for in creating sets, conjuring up exquisite decorations for balls and masquerades and making anything from a stuffed dummy used for arms practice to an entire boxing arena. Scenic artists were brought in to stencil walls and paint murals; furniture was hired, bought or borrowed; glasses, plates and serving dishes were sourced or specially made by craftsmen potters working to original Regency designs; prop buyers scoured antiques markets across the country for smaller objects, which needed to be sturdy enough to withstand three months' continual use, including toilet accessories, washbowls, chamber pots, inkstands, linen bedsheets and towels, quill knives and writing boxes. From the Aubusson carpets to the oil lamps, everything had to be found and everything had to be accurate. The deadline of the first house-guests' arrival was fast approaching.

Gradually, an authentic Regency house began to emerge from the chaos. 'I was particularly glad that the house was not the usual classical, columned mansion associated with the Regency,' said Alan, 'because I thought Kentchurch could more accurately reflect the tastes of the time: the love of the exotic, of colour, of fantasy, all coupled with elegance. The Gothic, the Picturesque, the Empire and Georgian styles all feature in different rooms, just as they could have done two hundred years ago.'

The Gothic

The Gothic was a style inspired by the more romantic aspects of Britain's medieval past – by castles, knights, jousts and fair maidens. To recall and express those chivalric values and that mythical past, even the most modest villas began to sprout crenellations, towers, arched and leaded windows and iron-studded doorways. 'One must have taste to be sensible of the beauties of Grecian architecture; one wants passions to feel the Gothic,' declared the famous letter writer and advocate of the Gothic style, Horace Walpole (1717–97). He urged people to let fantasy and emo-

tion break free from the stern laws of balance and order that had dominated Georgian England. The 'passionate' architecture of Kentchurch was thus the perfect backdrop to a series about romance.

'Because the exterior of the house is Gothic,' said Alan, 'I wanted the entrance hall and main corridor of the house to be full of romance and nostalgia for England's heroic past.' The walls were painted to look like stone, and heavy Georgian or medieval pieces of furniture stood against the walls. Suits of armour guarded the entrance and

THE FANTASTICAL AND IMAGINATIVE GOTHIC VILLA BELONGING TO HORACE WALPOLE AT STRAWBERRY HILL

TWO SCENIC ARTISTS SPENT FOUR DAYS
HAND-PAINTING THE LIGHT GOTHIC TRELLIS AND
IVY AROUND THE HOSTESS'S BEDROOM

grandiose paintings of battles and ancestors reinforced the chivalric and heroic themes. At the end of the entrance hall, a flight of steps led up to a landing with a large, stained-glass window. This became the area where house-guests would have morning prayers and perform their amateur theatricals. More armour and medieval weapons added to the military tone.

The men's bedchambers were all located in the medieval tower, and since two of them retained their original panelling Alan decided to leave them as they were. One of them, at the bottom of the tower, was known as the King's Room. This was rumoured to have been the room where the last 'King of Wales', Owain Glyndwr, died, as well as the favourite location for sightings of his ghost. Glyndwr was a Welsh chief who rebelled against Henry IV and proclaimed himself Prince of Wales, establishing an independent Welsh parliament. After his defeat in 1403, he took refuge at Kentchurch and continued to fight for Welsh independence until he died (supposedly in the tower) in 1416. The then owner of Kentchurch, Sir John Scudamore, had married Glyndwr's daughter, Alice, a connection still visible in the Scudamore family's coat of arms.

The room at the top of the tower had been added during Nash's renovations, and Alan decided to use it to reflect the high-Regency fashion for 'chinoiserie'. Chinoiserie is a term used to describe patterns inspired by Chinese designs of the kind used extensively in Brighton Pavilion and in the furniture and pottery of Chippendale and Wedgwood. The chinoiserie furniture that was found for this room was complemented by exotic painted 'tapestries', a Regency affectation that Alan employed in hiding the modern bookcases that lined the walls. The windows

EXQUISITE REGENCY FURNITURE GRACES THE TERRACE ROOM

and dark panelling retained their Gothic feel and, as the sun streamed through them and picked out the dust motes floating in the air, the scene could have come straight from the pen of the Regency's most popular author, Walter Scott. Perhaps the gentlemen guests at the house party would read from Scott's *Marmion* (published in 1808) and be inspired to follow in the footsteps of the young hero, in 'Lochinvar', to be 'faithful in love' and 'dauntless in war'.

Of the ladies' bedrooms, only one, that designed for the future hostess, was Gothic. With views of the deer park, the walls of this room were painted to resemble a gazebo hung with ivy against a peacock-blue sky. The *trompe-l'oeil* trellis formed arches to match those of the window and to create the lightly Gothic touch of the Regency rather than the heavy, ornate Gothic of the Victorians.

Directly below this bedroom was the Terrace Room, which opened on to the gardens. Drawing rooms took on great significance during the Regency and moved away in style and mood from their Georgian antecedents. In the gloomier homes of earlier times, furniture was dressed around the walls to minimise the risk of people falling over it. As more light was introduced into homes in the Regency, a more intimate mood was created by arranging sofas and chairs in small groups. This encouraged cosy conversation and, of course, flirtation. Regency drawing rooms became cluttered with tables displaying curios or books of prints for small groups of guests to discuss or admire. In Jane Austen's *Persuasion*, the decor of one room was described as creating 'the proper air of confusion with a grand fortepiano and a harp, flower stands and little tables placed in every direction'.

'I took my inspiration for the decor of this room from Nash's windows, with their Gothic arch. I used that motif for the wallpaper and chose the particular shade of green because it was very fashionable at the time,' said Alan. 'The green also created the feeling that this room was almost part of the garden, which was a desirable feature for a Regency drawing room.' Mass-produced green and yellow paints had only just become available and their bright, light hues proved irresistible. A gothicised stone fireplace was created out of polystyrene and plaster to cover the existing modern surround, and an original Donegal carpet was found that perfectly matched the green of the wallpaper. The room was furnished with two sofas, games tables, a fortepiano and a harp – indispensable furniture in a Regency drawing room.

The Picturesque

picturesque: *What pleases the eye; striking the imagination with the force of painting; affording a good subject for a landscape*

SUPPLEMENT TO SAMUEL JOHNSON'S *DICTIONARY*, 1801

The 'Picturesque' was a term used in the Regency to refer to landscapes or scenes that looked 'like a picture'. Similarly, real landscapes were picturesque if they were suitable subjects for a painting. To qualify, a landscape needed to be untamed by man's hand, irregular and possessing quirky features such as a rocky outcrop or a blasted oak. Attempts were made to establish the Picturesque as an aesthetic category somewhere between the 'Beautiful' and the 'Sublime', it being not serene like the Beautiful, nor awe-inspiring like the Sublime, but full of variety and interest.

The creation of a harmonious link between a house and its surrounding land was part of the Picturesque sensibility that led to changes in house design during the later Georgian and Regency periods. The principal rooms moved downstairs from the first floor in order to allow immediate access into gardens. 'French windows', such as those in the Terrace Room, allowed greater physical and visual access to the outside and also 'framed' the landscape in a picturesque way.

The rigid layouts of the parterres and formal gardens of earlier periods were dismissed by the new breed of famous garden designers that emerged at this time, who strove to create 'natural' effects. Chief among these was Humphry Repton (1752–1818), who often worked with architects to ensure that house and garden were part of one vision – each lending beauty, interest and perspective to the other. Drawing rooms would often lead to conservatories or garden rooms and then out to shrubberies and pleasure gardens before merging into the more distant landscape populated by farm animals or deer, kept at bay by a ha-ha (a skilfully disguised impassable ditch). Humphry Repton's talent was immortalised in Jane Austen's *Mansfield Park* when Mr Rushworth complains that his country house looks like a prison: ' "Your best friend on such an occasion," said Miss Bertram calmly, "would be Mr. Repton, I imagine." "That is what I was thinking of. As he has done so well by Smith, I think I had better have him at once. His terms are five guineas a day." '

The gardens at Kentchurch had been extensively redesigned during Nash's renovations. The lawns, flowerbeds and gravel paths near the house were framed by sloping woods, a stream and the deer park. Alan put a Temple to Venus at the summit of the park, where secret trysts could be held or from which the master could admire – and congratulate himself on – his estate. A variety of gazebos and sheltered nooks were so cunningly incorporated into the garden that they looked as though they had always been there.

Empire

Je wouldrais, si je couldrais, mais je cannais pas

LORD WESTMORLAND TO KING LOUIS XVIII

The Empire style is the most recognised of Regency tastes. It was in fact a French import, much appreciated and copied despite the fact that Britain was at war with

THE THEATRICALITY OF REGENCY DESIGN IS SHOWN
IN THE 'DRAPED FABRIC' WALLPAPER

France almost continuously from 1793 for twenty-two years. Step back two hundred years and enter the drawing room of a moderately fashionable country house and the conversation would have been in French, or at least peppered with French expressions. The wine and brandy would have been smuggled across the Channel from French ports to accompany French dishes served *à la française*, while guests would have worn the latest French designer garments. Regency society had no intention of letting the small matter of a war interfere with their gastronomic and aesthetic pleasures, and those with the slightest pretension to fashion or taste would have been dedicated Francophiles. Despite the slow-down in trade during hostilities, the Regent himself used French decorative schemes in his houses as well as adding to his collections of Sèvres porcelain and clocks. During the brief fourteen-month peace between the two countries that began in 1802, British aristocrats rushed in unseemly haste to Paris to be presented to Napoleon. They rubbed shoulders at balls with his commanders (whom they had been fighting just a few weeks earlier) and chatted casually with the infamous leaders of the Revolution, whose love of the guillotine was matched only by their hatred of the aristocracy.

The Empire style fused classical stateliness with the foreign influences (especially Egyptian) that percolated through as a result of Napoleon's conquests abroad. At Kentchurch, Alan used it in the rooms that were 'blank canvases' – in other words, those that did not have particularly Gothic or Picturesque features – mainly in the bedrooms. One of the men's bedrooms had white-painted panelling and a bathroom at one end with no dividing wall. 'This room gave me the biggest headache of all,' said Alan. 'I couldn't find any Regency reference for rooms having painted panels and the bathroom was there for all to see!' In the end, Alan decided to make this look like an older room that had been redecorated in high-Empire style. He boxed in the bathroom, placed an Empire-style bed against the false wall and repainted the panels cream instead of white.

Most of the women's bedrooms were also inspired by the Empire style, notably the grandest chaperone's room with its Sphinx-like patterned wallpaper and Empire furniture. The Terrace Room also had some Empire furniture – perhaps to inspire the guests to practise the smattering of French their application forms claimed they had.

Georgian updated

Furniture was of such quality that perfectly good pieces would not have been thrown away on a whim of fashion (except by the Regent, perhaps), and thus many Georgian features of the house were retained and simply smartened up. The dining room, for example, already possessed a handsome Georgian sideboard and plate-warmers and some fine wood-carvings around the large mirror. These all predated the Regency but were allowed to stay. The bright wall colour, however, was replaced with a more subdued pink printed wallpaper.

The library, with its bold wallpaper and fabric designs, created a startling but beautiful effect. The pictures Alan chose for this room were 'Grand Tour' paintings, proudly displaying their continental provenance and heroic subject matter. Such pictures would have been bought before the wars with France rendered travel to the Continent unfeasible. They declared their owner's taste and artistic sensibilities, and of course his wealth. The paintings in the library were there to provide interesting conversation points for the twenty-first-century house-guests, just as they would have done for their Regency forebears. Contrary to modern practice, conversation was encouraged in a Regency library, although books were also provided: two large bookcases were filled with pre-1830s titles.

Any self-respecting Regency house would have had a billiard room; it was a passion among men and occasionally women too. The walls of the Kentchurch billiard room were covered with prints of sporting activities. Alan found his inspiration from Stratfield Saye, the Duke of Wellington's house in Berkshire.

While Alan's team were transforming the house, other details had also to be arranged. The house would require many servants. Footmen, stewards, housemaids,

THE HOSTESS'S BOUDOIR, WITH ITS BEAUTIFUL ADAM-
INSPIRED DECORATIVE CEILING REPAINTED AND GILDED FOR
THE SERIES. THE 'OLD-FASHIONED' GEORGIAN FURNITURE
WOULD HAVE APPEALED TO THE TASTES OF AN OLDER LADY

grooms, dancing masters, musicians, gamekeepers, doctors, physical trainers, gardeners and night-watchmen would all be needed to create an authentic Regency experience. The footmen were recruited mainly from young media and drama students and the maids were trainees in costume and make-up. All were coached in their various tasks and were required to act according to a strict protocol while in the house. They did not, however, have to live the arduous experience of the Regency servitude full time, but returned to their modern-day personas and comforts when off duty. The other servants were chosen to match, as closely as possible, their Regency equivalents: the night-watch-men are all security guards, the dancing teacher is a dancing teacher in real life, and so on. The food was to be prepared by Ian Dowding and his team of cooks according to Regency recipes. Horses, white and blue peacocks, rare-breed chickens and ornamental pheasants were kept in the stableyard until the house and gardens were ready for their ornamentation.

In 1811, Prince George had about six months to prepare for the party to end all parties that was to announce his promotion to regent. 'Start as you mean to go on' is a proverb that might have been written for him. The forty-nine-year-old George, eldest son of King George III, was born to the role of regal impresario – it was his favourite charade and one of the few in which he triumphed.

His father, George III, was fastened into a straitjacket on 2 November 1810 and imprisoned in it for eleven days. He had been on the throne for fifty years and was in his early seventies when he was finally deemed unfit to rule. His first attack

of madness had occurred over forty years before, in 1765, when the King began to talk endlessly, swear horribly and wander around in a white robe, bewildered or melancholic. He spent many hours staring at the floor and when questioned whispered, 'Do not disturb me, I am staring into hell.' The King's 'madness' was in fact porphyria, a rare hereditary disease prevalent among the royal families of Europe. It is probable that the Regent and his only daughter, Charlotte, also suffered from porphyria, if less acutely than King George III.

In January 1811, after much debate, Parliament passed the Regency Bill, appointing the prince as Regent but delaying the bestowal of full power upon him for another year. The prince was already a figure of great notoriety. His extravagance, debts and dissolute mode of life were the prime targets of the age's great cartoonists. His sullied domestic life – the breakdown of his marriage to Caroline of Brunswick and his public liaison with his mistress Mrs Fitzherbert (a Catholic whom he had secretly married as a young man) – were further reasons, if more were needed, for his being the object of the public's ire and ridicule. Parliament hoped he would settle into his role before voting him full powers. They hoped in vain.

THE STAGE IS PERFECTLY SET IN READINESS FOR THE ARRIVAL OF THE HOUSE-GUESTS

At last the morning of 16 June 2003 arrived and the Regency House Party experiment was about to start. The hammering ceased, the paint cans were closed and the dust-sheets were removed. Production cars, security men, generators, lighting lorries and costume vans rolled out of Kentchurch Court. Footmen and maids moved in with quiet professionalism. Regency-recipe shortbread baked in the ovens. The chickens, pheasants and peacocks were let loose and the deer could nibble in the newfound shelter beneath the Temple of Venus. Now it was the turn of the house-guests to begin their metamorphosis into the Regency bucks, beauties and chaperones who would set forth on their journey 'in pursuit of pleasure' in the hot and vivid summer at Kentchurch Court that lay ahead.

The House-Party Guests

Chris Gorell Barnes
Position: Host of the Regency House Party at Kentchurch Court
AGE: 29
Background: Educated privately. In his youth, Chris was well known for organising balls for young people. He is executive producer in his own commercials production company but is considering a move into the more creative side of the business.
Hopes: He thought a few weeks out playing the 'Regency gentleman' would give him time to think about his future career moves, perhaps find romance and have some fun. Chris admitted that he was 'on the prowl'.

Fiona Rogers
Position: Hostess of the Regency House Party and chaperone to Larushka Ivan-Zadeh and Tanya Samuel
AGE: 59
Background: Describing herself as upper-middle-class, Fiona was a debutante and model in her youth and had experience organising charity balls. She married into an old family and managed a large house with servants and horses before divorce left her penniless. She now lives in a tiny cottage and is forced occasionally to rely on the generosity of her son for money.
Chaperone skills: Fiona's two daughters were presented to the Queen as debutantes and the process taught her how to gauge 'the potential eligibility (or otherwise) of suitors!'. She is a woman of direct manners, a commanding presence and an unwillingness to suffer fools gladly.

Larushka Ivan-Zadeh, Countess Griaznov
Position: Highest-ranking female guest
AGE: 27
Background: Of noble Russian descent, Larushka grew up with her own nanny in an affluent family. She studied English Literature at Cambridge University and now writes occasional film reviews and works as a waitress. Claims to be very competitive in love – 'never beaten by prettier girls'.
Hopes: 'A long-term relationship finished a couple of years ago. Since then I have had a string of unsuitable suitors, all of whom are best brushed under the carpet by a disapproving housemaid. If

I'm honest, I'm still clutching on to my dream of Mr Darcy. I work in a pub and always hope that the perfect chap will walk in and sweep me off my feet, away from a life of pints and potatoes and into a massive palace with rose petals strewn before my impeccably shod toes. I am a hopeless romantic holding an inextinguishable beacon for that knight in shining armour. I hope I will find my eligible soulmate at the Regency house.'

TANYA SAMUEL
Position: Woman of fortune
AGE: 31
Background: A hugely dynamic and successful woman who owns and runs her own fashion company, for which she designs accessories and clothes. She is also chairwoman of South Kilburn New Deal for Communities, overseeing a budget of £50 million to regenerate the area over the next ten years. She studied Law at university and lectures on community regeneration across the

country. She comes from a family of high-achievers; her brother is the singer Seal.
Hopes: 'I absolutely love period stuff – clothes and costume dramas – but the parts are limited for a black person. I must be the first black woman in the UK to do something like this and it was an experience I did not want to miss.'

VICTORIA HOPKINS
Position: Woman of fortune
AGE: 28
Background: Born and brought up in Yorkshire and now deputy director of her family's firm, a catering-appliance manufacturer, with a turnover of £3 million a year. She always wears sharp business suits with trousers – 'I don't think I own a skirt' – with heels and immaculate make-up. Ambitious and a self-confessed 'ladette'.
Hopes: 'To find a man. And to learn to live without the delights of modern technology – although I confess the thought of living without my

mobile and e-mail brings me out in a cold sweat. I want to see how I can adapt to the demure way of life and I secretly crave being a girly girl. This would be my chance.'

ELIZABETH, LADY DEVONPORT
Position: Chaperone to Miss Hopkins
AGE: 56
Background: Was a model in London. After a fairly wild youth she settled down to married life and had two daughters, one of whom is severely handicapped. Lady Devonport admits to using

her title when she felt it would help get the best for her children. Now that she is divorced and her daughters are independent, she thought it was time for a fresh start and that a few weeks living the life of a titled Regency chaperone was just what was needed.

Chaperone skills: 'I was married to a peer of the realm so I am familiar with the manners, customs and strange social nuances of the British upper classes. I have good manners in all things but can see the funny side of everything. I have a strong nurturing instinct and want to make life as sweet as possible for the younger generation while protecting them from some of its vagaries.'

JOHN EVERETT
Position: Wealthy gentleman
AGE: 29
Background: Charming, witty and 'in circulation'. Works as a stage manager and master carpenter with the Bush Theatre in London. He went

to boarding school and then to Camberwell College of Art to study theatre design. He is passionate about astronomy and owns his own telescope.
Hopes: Has high expectations of meeting a potential partner at the house and is thinking about marriage. 'I am looking for someone who tantalises me, who finds me attractive and who I know before I've even talked to her. And did I mention that she has to have a rather forgiving personality (and a heaving bosom)?'

JEREMY GLOVER
Position: Gentleman
naval captain
AGE: 41
Background: Built up a successful dotcom business worth £50 million on paper before the bubble burst. He is now comfortably off, rather than rich, and is taking some time out to decide what to do next.
Hopes to gain: 'Gout. An NVQ in fencing and boxing. A wife and one pregnant chaperone.'

ROSIE HAMMOND
Position: Chaperone to
Miss Braund
AGE: 52
Background: Rosie Hammond is a self-made multi-millionaire with a huge landscaping business that she built from scratch after her divorce left her with nothing. She has a son and daughter, both of whom work in her business. Her great passion in life is writing, and she hoped her talents at comic poetry and plays would be useful at the house party.
Chaperone skills: Although single for the past sixteen years, she has been very involved in her children's love lives. 'I have always suspected that good manners are the key to successful relationships and would love to have this proved right.'

LISA BRAUND
Position: Gentlewoman
AGE: 34

Background: Passion for the theatre led her to work in the costume department of *Les Misérables* after leaving school. She left after several years to become a scuba-diving instructor and is passionate about in-line skating (roller-blading to the rest of us).
Hopes: She wanted to join the Regency House because she felt that this was really the era she should have been born into and yearns to be the next Elizabeth Bennet, the heroine of *Pride and Prejudice*.
'I want to know if this is the life I really should have had. I know I should be grateful for the freedom we have in the modern world concerning who we flirt with, date and marry, but I love the romantic game of the Regency, leaving things unsaid, reading between the lines and not just blurting out who you fancy.' At thirty-four, Lisa is the oldest of the charges and wants to meet a long-term partner.

PAUL ROBINSON
Position: Gentleman soldier
AGE: 29

Background: 'Working-class upbringing on the streets of Ashford, Kent. However, I have caddish tendencies associated with the upper class and like to live like a lord.' A hairdresser for the past ten years, he lives in Brighton.
Hopes: Recently split up with a long-term girlfriend and thought that spending some time as a Regency buck was just what was needed. 'The lifestyle appeals to me – to be a man's man, with gambling, drinking and womanising involved.'

HAYLEY CONICK
Position: Gentlewoman
AGE: 25

Background: Born and raised in a small Welsh village. Went to Cambridge University and now works in London as a trainee headhunter.
Hopes: 'To sort out my head and work out who I am and what I want. The opportunity

to actually experience living in another time doesn't come up too often and I might just meet my Mr Darcy.' She admits to being attracted to 'arrogant' types who break her heart.

JAMES CARRINGTON
Position: Gentleman
AGE: 27

Background: After studying drama at university, a career in music beckoned. He became a singer/songwriter and now plays in a band. He has recently secured a publishing deal.
Hopes: To flirt and fall in love.

ROSEMARY ENRIGHT
Position: Chaperone to
Miss Conick
AGE: 56
Background: Born in West
Riding, Yorkshire. Was a
commissioned officer in the
Women's Royal Army Corps –
'a polite, non-combatant'
corps 'which was effectively
a kind of finishing school in
which social skills were taught
and highly valued'. She later
worked as an advertising
copywriter and has published
four romantic novels and one
historical book. Twice
married, twice divorced.
Chaperone skills: Worldly wise
with two marriages behind
her. Possessed of charisma,

elegance, charm and unusual
eloquence, She calmly admits
to a total inability to keep
secrets, all perfect credentials
for a chaperone. 'Many
women have their finest hours
in their later years and I
would hate to miss my
chance.'

MARK FOXSMITH
Position: Gentleman cleric
and tutor
AGE: 32
Background: Has struggled
all his life with severe dyslexia
so left school with no
qualifications but is an
intelligent and interesting
thinker, passionate about
natural history and science.
He is now a Biology teacher.

He writes one page of a diary
every night and has done so
for nearly five years.
Hopes: 'I would like to use my
interest in science to think (or
pretend to think) about the
problems, ideas and theories
of the Regency.' He was also
hoping to meet someone 'able
to put up with my oddities
and who wants to have
children'.

FRANCESCA MARTIN
Position: Lady's companion
AGE: 21
Background: Just graduated
from Bristol University, where
she studied History.
Hopes: Had been single for a

year and a half when her
mother spotted the advert for
the Regency House Party in a
newspaper and encouraged
her daughter to apply. 'I think
my father has designs on me
marrying a Scottish baron and
going to live in a castle. He
jokes that it would raise my
status from middle- to upper-
class but he says it so often
that I'm worried he's serious.'

ZEBEDEE HELM
Position: Hermit
AGE: 32
Background: Zebedee studied
fine art and is now a
successful artist. For the past
few years he has saved money
by spending summers living
in a tepee on people's estates.
Hopes: To get even closer to
nature.

THE MASTER OF KENTCHURCH COURT ADOPTS THE POSTURE AND ATTITUDE OF A REGENCY GENTLEMAN

CHAPTER TWO

PRIDE AND PREJUDICE IN REGENCY BRITAIN

It is a truth universally acknowledged, that a single man
in possession of a good fortune must be in want of a wife.

JANE AUSTEN, *PRIDE AND PREJUDICE*, 1813

'WHEN I SAW the footmen and maids lined up outside to meet me, I realised this was really happening, although it felt like a dream. I am used to grand houses but this was so different. Everything was perfect and I felt like I'd just driven back two hundred years' – Mr Gorell Barnes

The first volunteer to shed his jeans, car and mobile phone for full period dress and the Regency lifestyle was Christopher Gorell Barnes. Chris was to enjoy the most important position in the house – that of master of Kentchurch Court. 'I was really pleased to be the host as I do so much of that in my work: entertaining clients, partying and making sure everyone is enjoying themselves.'

Tall, dark, handsome, well-heeled and with an alluring hint of arrogance, Chris was a veritable Mr Darcy and would surely prove a source of considerable interest for all the female house-guests. How his well-honed techniques for attracting women would work when handicapped by the restrictions of the Regency period, however, was yet to be seen. After all, the Regency gentleman

A WAX JACK, USED TO PRODUCE WAX FOR
SEALING LETTERS. MOST OF THE GUESTS TOOK
SOME TIME TO LEARN THIS ART!

was not even allowed to talk to unmarried ladies alone. A look of incredulity swept across Chris's face on his first perusal of the rulebook he had been given: '*You should be dressed properly in the presence of ladies, stand when they enter a room and be courteous and mindful towards them. You should align yourself to the wishes of your hostess when embarking on a courtship. Once you begin to court a lady you have entered into an agreement and you must not turn your attentions to another . . . so pick the right one! You must not touch a young lady nor address her by her Christian name until you are engaged. Promiscuous behaviour is not tolerated in house society.*'

To aid their metamorphosis into true Regency gentlemen and ladies, all the guests were given the nineteenth-century equivalent of a Filofax – the 'pocket-book'. These were small, leather-bound diaries, usually fastened with a brass clip, that were carried about the person and used for making notes (such as appointments, expenses, fashion tips, details of the latest dance craze), composing poetry, holding money or storing a lock of a loved one's hair. The pocketbooks for the Regency House Party were printed with all the information that the guests at the house party would need – everything from table manners and fan language to the

THE GUESTS

Master of Kentchurch Court:
Mr Christopher Gorell Barnes
Gentleman of commerce: Mr John Everett
Gentleman captain: Mr Jeremy Glover
Gentleman soldier: Mr Paul Robinson
Natural philosopher/cleric:
Mr Mark Foxsmith

Hostess: Mrs Fiona Rogers
Gentlewoman: Larushka Ivan-Zadeh,
Countess Griaznov
Chaperone: Elizabeth, Lady Devonport
Woman of fortune: Miss Victoria Hopkins
Chaperone: Mrs Rosie Hammond
Gentlewoman: Miss Lisa Braund
Chaperone: Mrs Rosemary Enright
Gentlewoman: Miss Hayley Conick
Lady's companion: Miss Francesca Martin

LATER ARRIVALS

Hermit: Mr Zebedee Helm
Woman of fortune from the West Indies:
Miss Tanya Samuel
Gentleman musician: Mr James Carrington

etiquette of duelling at dawn. To help the house-guests to discover the sort of people they might have been had they been born two hundred years ago, their pocketbooks contained a short résumé of their 'Regency lives' based on their current occupations and interests. For example, a modern-day entrepreneur was to become a sea captain, one of the few Regency options affording an opportunity for rapid advancement and the swift acquisition of wealth.

Before entering the house, the women met in Bath for a brief introduction to the Regency 'art of captivation' and to get to know each other. The older women who had been chosen as chaperones instantly took to their charges and two of them even felt the need to apologise to their own daughters for having adopted (temporarily at least) new ones. Since the women had the advantage of meeting up in Bath, it was decided that the men should foregather at the house to enjoy a little gentlemanly bonding before the women descended. Close on the heels of the host was the first guest, Mr John Everett, who came in a beautiful chaise and four.

'There I was, squeezed into this incredibly tight jacket with sleeves that came halfway down my hands,

THE CARRIAGE JOURNEY TO KENTCHURCH COURT TAKES THE
HOUSE-GUESTS BACK NEARLY TWO HUNDRED YEARS

really nervous because there was a camera right beside me and we were trotting
along up the drive. I was peering out of the window and there were two estate
workers tending to a bonfire. They just silently doffed their caps as I went by and
shivers ran down my spine. I suddenly really was a "gentleman".' According to his
pocketbook, he was a rich one.

> *You were born in 1782 and are fortunate enough to have a considerable for-*
> *tune left to you by your father through his importation of luxury goods. You*
> *are known in male circles to have dallied with a fair number of women,*
> *though this has not affected your reputation. You perhaps enjoy the most*
> *freedom in choosing a wife: you do not need money and you have no pressing*
> *duty to marry into a noble bloodline.*

The next man to arrive was Jeremy Glover, who had been given the status of
a naval captain. In the words of his pocketbook:

> *You played a key role as a sea captain in Horatio, Lord Nelson's glorious*
> *victory at the Battle of Trafalgar in 1805, bringing back Villeneuve, the*
> *Admiral of the French fleet, to London. Your success at capturing enemy*
> *vessels furnished you with a large fortune, which, unfortunately, you have*
> *largely lost in unstable financial markets. While your income is no longer*
> *high, you are still a catch. You should attempt to marry money. You have set*
> *aside this year for the express purpose of finding a wife and you have high*
> *hopes of the house party.*

Jeremy Glover could claim a genetic connection to his new identity since one
of his ancestors, Sir Henry Blackwood, really did bring back Villeneuve and was
standing next to Hardy when the great Nelson demanded a farewell kiss. Nelson
was a good example of how a man of fairly low birth in the Regency (he was the

son of a clergyman) could climb to the top of the social rigging in the navy. Although a naval career was considered less aristocratic than a career in the army (for which one needed huge sums to buy oneself a command; to become a major would set you back £2600, the equivalent of over £100,000 today), none the less a man could earn a vast fortune through 'booty' gained by capturing enemy vessels. By displaying heroism and bravery one could rise quickly through the ranks. The navy was not a soft option, however, and not always a noble one either. Recruitment of lower ranks often took the form of abduction. Discipline was maintained with brutal floggings and conditions on board were cramped and insanitary, leading to malnutrition, infection and high mortality rates, even in peacetime. Despite the risks, a young man entering the navy could take comfort in the fact that naval uniforms were the height of fashion.

Army uniforms, even more than those of their comrades at sea, had tremendous pulling power, and Captain Glover's carriage companion, Paul Robinson, was wearing his with some delight. Paul's pocketbook informed him that he was a 'gentleman soldier', although his modern-day occupation as a hairdresser was unlikely to offer him much by way of prior experience. His home town of Brighton, however, was the most fashionable army encampment during the Regency. While the country was at war with France it contained up to ten thousand soldiers, including the Tenth Light Dragoons, of which the Regent himself was colonel-in-chief. The romantic allure of a soldier certainly captivated many Regency ladies, real and fictional, including Lydia Bennet in *Pride and Prejudice*, who spends much of her time imagining 'with the creative eye of fancy, the streets of that gay bathing place covered with officers', and 'herself, seated beneath a tent, tenderly flirting with at least six officers at once'. And even Austen's normally sensible niece wrote to her aunt: 'Captain Austen looks very nice in his red coat, Blue breeches and red Sash, he is now sitting opposite to me and I can hardly write my letter for looking at him.'

OFFICERS DISPLAYING FINE REGIMENTALS AND THE FASHION FOR SMALL WAISTS AND STRONG LEGS

THE HOUSE-GUESTS MEET, STILL CONSTRAINED BY UNFAMILIARITY AND REGENCY FASHION

JACQUES-LOUIS DAVID'S *NAPOLEON BONAPARTE
CROSSING THE ALPS* DEPICTS AN EMPEROR BENT
ON TOTAL MILITARY CONQUEST OF ALL HE SURVEYS –
INCLUDING BRITAIN

The Napoleonic War gave the army an elevated status. With its glamour, élitism, gorgeous uniforms and heroic aspirations, military service became a highly fashionable career. With their social standing and family connections, gentlemen from the upper classes became officers, while those serving among the ranks were, as Wellington so gracefully put it, 'the scum of the Earth'. Rank had to be purchased, and the army remained the profession of choice for many gentlemen, though of course a *real* gentleman was supposed to possess sufficient fortune to alleviate the need to work. However, since only the oldest brother of a landed family could settle back and luxuriate in the knowledge that he would inherit the estates, many younger brothers were faced with the prospect of having to choose an occupation suitable for their station.

The pocketbook informed Paul that in order to maintain the lavish lifestyle expected of his rank he needed to marry a wealthy young woman – his response to which was to guffaw, 'Rock and roll!' Initial impressions suggested that Captain Robinson might struggle to conform to the social niceties and demands of protocol expected of a Regency officer and gentleman.

After the dust whipped up by the carriages had settled, a man in black was seen walking down the driveway. He had no liveried footman to announce his arrival and had to knock at the front door himself. This was Mark Foxsmith. His status in the house was that of a poor cleric and tutor (with a passion for natural philosophy), the closest Regency equivalent to his modern-day job of Biology teacher.

Becoming a cleric was another of the acceptable options open to second sons of the landed classes but, alas, it had none of the fashion or allure of a military career. The 'living' of a cleric was in the power of the local landowner to give, and so they were often bestowed on younger sons – many of whom had little genuine interest in the Church or the hereafter. An ordination exam was required but frequently consisted of being asked nothing more theological than one's age and family background. The Bishop of Salisbury, an old family friend of his father, examined Henry Austen, Jane's brother. Putting his hand on the Old Testament, the bishop said, 'As for *this* book, Mr. Austen, I imagine it is a good many years since either you or I have looked into it.' Many clergymen enjoyed several livings at once (the average was four) and so employed a curate to do the actual ecclesiastical work in the parish. Although interested in finding a suitable partner and very keen to have children, Mark is an enthusiastic scientist and was primarily motivated to join the house out of a desire to recreate Regency experiments. His pocketbook reflected this:

THE HOST AND HOSTESS ARE RESPONSIBLE FOR ENSURING
THEIR GUESTS ARE ENTERTAINED AND HAPPY

Modern scientific thought and experiment fascinate you and you pride your-self on your ability to entertain others with your astounding experiments. Your biggest ambition is to earth a storm and you are intrigued by electricity.

'I heard of a German recently who tried to earth a storm a couple of years ago. That was the last thing he did. Died for science. What a guy!' said Mr Foxsmith. While Mr Foxsmith's profession and small income would have been a handicap in the Regency marriage mart, his experiments might have intrigued Regency ladies, and proved a source of wealth if they had some application in one of the burgeon-ing industries of the time. For some gentlemen, however, even the humble life of a cleric was preferable to the idleness of no profession at all. As Edward Ferrers says in *Sense and Sensibility*:

It has been, and is, and probably will always be a heavy misfortune to me, that I have had no necessary business to engage me, no profession to give me employment, or afford me anything like independence. I always preferred the church, and still do. But that was not smart enough for my family. They recommended the army. That was a great deal too smart for me. The law was allowed to be genteel enough; many young men, who had chambers in the Temple, made a very good appearance in the first circles, and drove about town in very knowing gigs. But I had no incli-nation for the law. As for the navy it had fashion on its side, but I was too old when the subject was first started to enter it – and, at length, as there was no necessity for my having any profession at all, as I might be as dashing and expensive without a red coat on my back as with one, idle-ness was pronounced in the whole to be the most advantageous and honourable.

When they arrived at the house, the men were shown to their chambers in the old tower. Mr Foxsmith and Captain Robinson had been placed together, but Mr Foxsmith refused to share a room. It was common practice during large house par-ties for guests to share or even to sleep in rotation if there were too many people for too few beds, as a letter from the noted Regency author 'Monk' Lewis to Lady Melbourne describes:

Inverary is as full as it can hold. Bed-rooms are in great request and William and Kinnaird being the last comers, are moved about from

chamber to chamber, never knowing one night where they are to sleep
the next. Whoever passes a few hours out of the Castle is certain of finding one of the two new-comers established in his room when he returns;
& a formal complaint was lodged yesterday by a great Russian Count,
that he only stept out for half an hour, and the first thing which He saw
lying on his bed when He came back, were a dozen pairs of Kinnaird's
leather breeches.

To Mr Foxsmith's relief, the situation was resolved by pitching a Regency
tent in the garden, with a camp-bed and a few blankets. That, however, did nothing to solve the issue of how to address the servants. 'I've got absolutely no idea
how to walk past any of the footmen,' he said. 'Do I nod at them, do I say hello,
do I high-five?'

Ensconced in their lodgings and with the ladies yet to arrive, the five men soon overcame their initial reticence and took full advantage of having footmen at their beck and call. 'I went to Ibiza last week and I thought that was pretty crazy, but I think this is going to be totally insane,' said Captain Robinson, as the privileges of the life of a Regency gentleman began to sink in. 'I'm finding it difficult to adjust but I want to grab the opportunity with both hands, especially as I'm supposed to be a bit of a cad. That's cool!' With unlimited access to fine wine, port and Madeira, the gentlemen were soon drunk. And while this would have seemed entirely sensible and gentlemanly behaviour to the Regency forebears in whose footsteps they were so faithfully staggering, it made a less favourable impression upon their hostess when she arrived.

Fiona Rogers was chosen from the multitude of applicants to the series to act as hostess. Her pocketbook described her responsibilities thus:

> *The trustees of the Lucas-Scudamore estates have appointed you social and moral guardian of the house, to ensure nothing occurs that might hazard their property or compromise the family reputation. In this regard you will be expected to act as hostess to Mr Gorell Barnes.*

Mrs Rogers' role at the house was to oversee the women guests, arrange suitable pastimes to amuse them and further romantic intrigue, and maintain a vigilant eye for any unseemly behaviour. 'I do really have a big issue with bad manners,' she declared. 'It knocks me to hell, people who are rude.'

The first major decision that she would have to take, in tandem with the host, concerned the rules of etiquette to which all guests would have to adhere. She could impose the strict rules of the Georgian era, which were still followed to the letter by many great families. Or she could favour the more liberal, bohemian ways of certain fashionable and influential families in high society and the Carlton House Set. By the beginning of the nineteenth century, rules of etiquette had softened as society as a whole became more egalitarian. The old hierarchies were based largely on 'breeding' – a notion that had been severely shaken by the events of the French Revolution. A person's family connections were becoming less important than their fortune, particularly when it came to marriage. Poverty became less of a barrier to social success as long as there was some other distinction to offer, be it brains, beauty or wit. The *nouveaux riches* of the Industrial Revolution were also beginning to make their mark in high society. Although these opulent upstarts were

ONLY THE HIGHEST-RANKING WOMEN ENJOYED THE SERVICES OF A PERSONAL MAID TO HELP WITH THEIR TOILETTE

held accountable for any perceived lapse in standards or taste, their lavish parties were none the less attended by dukes and duchesses. They were even accused by some of driving the aristocracy to impoverishment, by forcing them to compete in their displays of wealth.

Regardless of which 'moral code' the host and hostess chose to adopt, one law of etiquette which persisted from the Georgian era into the Regency was that of 'precedence'. The rules of precedence were founded upon one's 'station in life' and affected every activity, from seating arrangements at dinner to the size and sumptuousness of one's bedroom, from the quality of the horses one could ride to the places one could walk, from the activities one could enjoy to the sort of conversations one was allowed. As the house-guests at Kentchurch were about to discover, one's position in the order of precedence had a huge and wide-ranging impact. Rank was more important than age, so a twenty-two-year-old duchess would pass through a doorway before an eighty-year-old marchioness. It was courteous in such situations to allow the elder lady to pass first, but not obligatory, and was never observed in formal situations when rank always came first. The Regent was one of the few people who dared to ignore the rules of precedence when it suited him – usually to enable him to sit next to his favourite mistress.

It was considered the perfection of fine breeding to know one's place, to be acquainted with that of others, and to fall gracefully into one's station accordingly. *Burke's Peerage* and *Burke's Landed Gentry* were (as they are today) the books that provided the necessary information to place each person on their particular rung of the social ladder.

As well as the role of hostess, Fiona Rogers was also to act as chaperone to the highest-ranking lady in the house, Larushka Ivan-Zadeh, Countess Griaznov. The rules of precedence ordained that as a countess

RANK IN DESCENDING ORDER

Duke, Duchess
Marquess, Marchioness
Earl, Countess
Viscount, Viscountess
Baron, Baroness
Knight

With two people of equal rank, precedence was given to the oldest title, e.g. the Duke of Buccleuch preceded the Duke of Marlborough. The placing of a title is also significant. 'Elizabeth, Lady Devonport', reveals that she has acquired the title through marriage, whereas 'Lady Elizabeth Devonport' would indicate that she is the daughter of, at the very least, an earl. Within the same family, the oldest member comes first – thus Miss Bennet (Jane) precedes her younger sister, Miss Elizabeth Bennet.

Larushka should be given the best guest bedroom, the most influential chaperone, the top seat at table beside the most eligible bachelor, and the greatest licence in her behaviour. Larushka had a terrible secret, however, which she needed to keep from everybody, including her chaperone – she had no fortune. Her poverty would have greatly diminished her chances of finding a titled or wealthy husband at a Regency house party. If her penniless situation were discovered she would be shunned by the hostess, whose first responsibility was to ensure that her host made a good match. Every attempt would be made by the other chaperones to dissuade the eligible men from marrying her, since their own charges would benefit from the countess's fall from grace. Larushka's only attraction (other than her personal beauty, qualities and accomplishments) would be her title, which, since the Tsar was still absolute ruler in the Russian Empire, would be genuine.

Although she would be given jewellery at the house, it would be fake. This situation was not unusual. Many women (often impoverished by their husband's or father's rashness in business or at the gaming table) would have lived on credit and had paste jewels made, or otherwise hired real ones from a pawnbroker for important occasions. For the Prince Regent's party to celebrate the start of his regency, pawnbrokers rented out diamonds for the night at 11 per cent interest. While enjoying her privileges at Kentchurch, Larushka alone would know the precarious nature of her situation and would live in dread of the other guests discovering her secret.

Someone with much less to fear was Elizabeth, Lady Devonport. A very attractive fifty-six-year-old, she gained her title from her husband, from whom she is now divorced. Her Regency provenance, written to match her real life as closely as possible, explained:

> *Your background and education mean that you know exactly how you should behave in society but you do not always conform. Your title has allowed you considerably more licence than your fellow-chaperones enjoy. Your charge is a monied lady of inferior birth. As a titled woman, the family of your charge have engaged you to advise their daughter in the ways of the upper classes and to secure her a match that would complement and add to her considerable fortune.*

In the Regency, titled ladies who had fallen on hard times would advertise

HEAD COVERING WAS A NECESSITY FOR BOTH SEXES, AS WAS A PARASOL FOR WOMEN, IF SUNNY

their services to introduce into society the daughters of those with money but no rank. They would probably have been more astute in their knowledge of finances than Lady Devonport initially seemed to be. 'Ooh, I do hope that she'll be happy,' said Lady Devonport. 'Apparently, the financial gain to be had from a good marriage for my charge has to be in the forefront of my mind – well, I suppose it does, otherwise she's not going to be happy, she's going to be miserable, poor girl. Well, I don't understand that much about the money but I didn't get where I am today by understanding about money. I'm sure it will become as clear as mud.' During 'the Season' (March to early June) a chaperone was bound by honour to secure a husband for her charge. Her duty was to ensure that any unmarried woman younger than thirty was never left alone in the company of a man.

Lady Devonport's charge was to be Victoria Hopkins, whose Regency profile explained:

> *You are the granddaughter of a successful industrialist who founded an esteemed manufacturing business in Yorkshire. You are proud of your family history and all that they have achieved and are suspicious of the old-money classes, who inherit and so do not earn their wealth. However, your bright-*

ness of mind leads you to understand the importance of entering society. You hope your titled chaperone will smooth your entry into society and that you will be accepted for your personal accomplishments, such as playing the pianoforte, without too many whisperings about your lack of rank.

Victoria's first experience of Regency life involved being laced into a tight corset and made to remove all her make-up – quite a challenge for an independent-spirited woman who is used to making her own rules and decisions. With the prospect of nine weeks living under strict Regency protocol, her transformation into a blushing Regency beauty threatened to be far from smooth. However, as she and Lady Devonport drove up to the house in their carriage, all was perfect: 'Victoria and I got in the carriage, which was astonishing; I've never been in a carriage and it was wonderful. Then we arrived in the court and both just burst into tears because it was so beautiful. It was really moving. The house is just fabulous and we could really believe that we were living in the Regency. You can just say to a footman, "Get me a glass of water," and they do. I'll try it with champagne next and see what happens, but a person could get used to this.'

TWO LADIES TAKE AN AIRING IN A PHAETON, FROM NIKLAUS VON HEIDELOFF'S *GALLERY OF FASHION*

Lisa Braund and her chaperone, Rosie Hammond, were the next arrivals. At thirty-four Lisa is the oldest of the charges and wants to meet a long-term partner. In Regency terms she would be considered an old maid, and her pocketbook was not entirely reassuring about her position in the house:

Having neither fortune nor rank to boast of in society, you will have to take particular care to observe the rules of manners and etiquette. Any hostess observing you steal an advantage with the more eligible men of her party will be looking for the earliest opportunity to find fault and diminish your reputation. The mildest social offence could even result in your being asked to leave the house.

Like the impoverished Bennet girls in *Pride and Prejudice*, Lisa would have to rely on her wit, grace and intelligence. And, of course, the skills and schemes of her

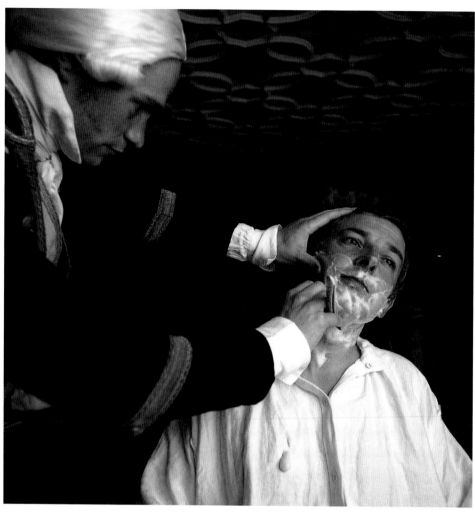

A GENTLEMAN'S VALET AIDED HIM WITH EVERYTHING,
FROM PULLING OFF BOOTS TO ADVICE ON ROMANCE

chaperone, Rosie Hammond. '*Your chaperone is a woman of great experience in all manner of things, with a heart of the highest degree of good nature and generosity. She possesses a sense of fun and a considerable fortune . . .*' Rosie was also a passionate writer of comic verse. Although female poets were thin on the ground in the Regency, Mrs Hammond could take heart in the renown of its women novelists, notably Maria Edgeworth and Fanny Burney, who wrote novels of morals and manners; Mrs Radcliffe, who penned 'horrid' Gothic tales; and most famously Jane Austen. In addition, there were many hundreds of novels written by 'a lady' that were popular at the time but have since been forgotten. Many women wrote for private audiences, often for the delectation of fellow house-party guests. Mary

Berry, for example, wrote her play *Fashionable Friends* for a performance at Horace Walpole's villa, Strawberry Hill. It was thought so good by her friends that she was encouraged to try it out on the public. It was produced at Drury Lane with an excellent cast but was a flop and withdrawn after only three performances on the grounds of its lax morality.

The last chaperone to enter the house, Rosemary Enright, is a writer by profession whose application form showed that she was well prepared for her role: 'It goes without saying that an impeccable Moral Reputation is as essential as Sharp Hearing and Good Eyesight for a Chaperone. A vigilant Chaperone will ensure that no friendship uncongenial to her Charge's family survives the bromide of her glance. The Glance must be perfected. It is the Chaperone's Stiletto, Sabre, Broadsword and Fowling piece.' Rosemary Enright clearly possessed the knowledge and experience that she might need in her capacity as chaperone to the youngest charge, Hayley Conick, who was imbued with the sort of romantic idealism that might well hinder her from making a 'sensible' match. As her pocketbook warned her:

> You should try to secure an engagement that would benefit you financially, but those who know you well worry that you will be swayed by your impulsive and romantic nature. They fear that you do not know what it is to be an old maid and that your pride may prevent you from agreeing to the abject necessity of an advantageous alliance. Your impetuousness and disregard for etiquette means that you should listen to your chaperone and perhaps learn a little patience.

As the women settled into their new abode, the men indulged in yet another bout of drinking, this time accompanied by wagers on who would 'bed' whom first. As Mr Everett explained: 'The excitement about the girls just built up. We went up on the hill to the Venus Temple with a telescope and our ale so we could spy on the women as they arrived. It was completely useless of course – you can't see a thing through those old telescopes – but we talked about them a lot, and what might happen, and it was great fun.'

The first meeting between the male and female house-guests was to be that evening at dinner. It proved a more dramatic and scandalous event than perhaps anyone expected.

THE HOUSE-GUESTS GET TO GRIPS WITH REGENCY DINING

CHAPTER THREE

LE REGENCY EST ARRIVÉ!

It was amazing, wearing these incredible clothes, seeing the footmen
in their wigs, with a whole train of Regency people following behind.
I really thought I had died and gone to heaven.

LARUSHKA IVAN-ZADEH, COUNTESS GRIAZNOV

EXPECTATIONS OF THE first dinner at Kentchurch were high. The dinner hour
was established at 6 p.m. This was in accordance with Regency convention, but not
fashion. The most fashionable people in London would never have dreamed of sitting down as early as six. For dandies such as Lord Alvanley, eight o'clock was the

preferred time and the *haut ton* often lingered at
table until midnight. As Victoria Murray notes in
her illuminating book *High Society*, in Georgian
times dinner was served at around four o'clock,
although in Scotland it was usually at two or three
o'clock. It became fashionable around the middle
of the eighteenth century in London to eat later,
and gradually the habit crept into the provinces.
The peregrinations of the dinner hour were limited to high society, since such fashionable considerations surrounding mealtimes could rarely be
afforded by those who worked for a living.

MRS ENRIGHT PREFERS SPLENDID HATS TO
'FOOLISH' MOB CAPS

The usual dinner hour in Scotland is 3.00,
which in time but not without groans and
predictions, became four, at which it stuck
for several years. Then it got to five, which
however was thought positively revolutionary; and four was long and
gallantly adhered to by the haters of change and as 'the good old hour'.
At last even they were obliged to give in. But they only yielded inch
by inch and made a desperate stand at half past four. Even five however
triumphed, and continued the average polite hour from (I think) about
1806 or 1807 till about 1820. Six has at last prevailed, and half an hour
later is not unusual. As yet this is the furthest stretch of London

imitation . . . – Henry Cockburn, *Memorials of His Time*, Edinburgh, 1856

Dinner was often the first time in the day that men and women came together. Breakfast was usually an informal affair, a buffet-style meal that many women skipped or had brought to their rooms. Luncheon or 'nuncheon' (pronounced 'noonshine'), was a recent introduction in Regency houses and consisted of a few sandwiches and small cakes for the ladies at midday. The men rarely attended, as they would be enjoying outdoor pursuits. So the gathering of guests in the drawing room before dinner was, for all its formality, often the first opportunity men and women had of jostling for position, conversing and flirting.

Dinner was an occasion for displaying one's finest raiment. Women could devote the majority of the afternoon to their *grande toilette* and certainly by four o'clock most women would have retired to their chambers to dress. A maid was sent out of courtesy by the hostess to help Mrs Hammond dress but she was not obliged to help Miss Braund unless instructed to do so by Mrs Hammond (and for this she could expect a tip).

'I felt really stupid when the maids helped Mrs Hammond off with her coat and gloves and I stood waiting and no one helped me. It was then that I realised what my place in the house would be. Mrs Hammond has to ask the maids to help me??!! How bloody annoying,' wrote Miss Braund in her diary. 'I'm finding the status thing really hard. In the twenty-first century you can be friends with anyone but here I am completely restricted by my status.'

Being a notch down the social pecking order meant that Mrs Enright and Miss Conick got assistance only when there was a maid to spare. This was a source of some irritation. As they were quick to point out, a maid was not a luxury in the Regency but a necessity. The corsets and dresses of the period required lacing and fastening at the back and the complication of the hairstyles made hairdressing a two-person operation. The women of 'lower consequence' were beginning to feel the impact of their situation, and the younger ones were becoming aware of their dependence upon the good will and generosity of their chaperones. In addition, Miss Braund was mourning the loss of her contact lenses, which had been replaced by Regency-style glasses. 'When I first came, I didn't wear glasses at all, especially when talking to the guys. But now I'm putting them on more because otherwise I can't see their expressions across the table. If something's happening at the other side of the room I need to see but when I have got my glasses on I feel ugly. It's a bit difficult.' Having wallowed in the attentions of a personal maid and hairdresser or suffered the ignominy of trying to put up their hair themselves, the ladies and their chaperones descended for dinner at the appointed hour.

Waiting for them in the drawing room were the five eligible young men who were to be their companions for the next nine weeks. Regency etiquette demanded that no girl was to talk to a man unless he had first been introduced. Since it was considered an honour for a man to talk to a lady, it was incumbent upon him to make the introduction, usually through her chaperone or a mutual acquaintance. However, as the hostess was busy organising the procession into dinner and the host was not acquainted with the girls, introductions were left to the chaperones, who did their best to smooth over the awkwardness of this meeting. Their pocket-books had informed the guests that talk before dinner was expected to be subdued: riotousness at such an early hour was considered inelegant. The hostess informed the gentlemen which lady they were to take in to dinner. Protocol dictated that they took the arm of the lady who was their closest social equal. This would be the first time that the men and women would be made unequivocally aware of their relative social positions – the procession into the dining room was 'precedence' in action. The elder chaperones took precedence over the younger girls, with the exception of the countess, whose title put her at the head of the troop. She was escorted by the host, followed by Lady Devonport on the uniformed arm of Captain Glover. Mrs Hammond was accompanied by Captain Robinson in his smart regimentals, and Mr Foxsmith took Mrs Enright. The three young ladies without beaux were herded out of the drawing room by the hostess and Mr Everett, who were bringing up the rear. In most large houses the dining room was separated from the drawing room by one or more rooms to allow for the procession (and also so that the noise of the men drinking, smoking and carousing would not disturb the ladies in the drawing room after they had retired). This was the case at Kentchurch, a route that was lined with bowing footmen.

Dinner was served *à la française* in most grand houses, which meant that the majority of dishes were arranged in the middle of the table and people were supposed to help themselves from the nearest dish and then offer it to their neighbours. If someone wanted a dish at the other end of the table they had to ask a fellow guest to serve them. If the dish was too distant, they would hand their plate to a footman, who would then take it to the guest nearest the dish before returning it to the original guest – always moving anti-clockwise around the table and never in reverse. It was extremely difficult to conduct a conversation in the midst of such a profusion of requests, and diners often missed out on many dishes entirely. One unhappy diner wrote: 'Confusion arises, and whilst the same dishes are offered two or three times to some guests, the same unhappy wights have no option of others.'

The best dishes – the roasts and the finest puddings – were always placed near the host or the principal guest, and those further down the pecking order often had to make do with whatever was left. The first range of dishes to be placed on the table usually consisted of a choice of entrées, side dishes and several roast joints. These would then be cleared but guests would retain their plates for the second course – consisting usually of fish, pies, plum pudding, vegetables, small birds, chicken and a variety of puddings. These would all be served and eaten together, apple pie sitting happily next to roast trout, pheasant next to blancmange.

The challenges to conversation created by dining *à la française* meant that, in smaller households, hostesses were beginning to adopt the new method of serving *à la russe*. In this form of dining, the dishes were handed round in turn to the guests, which imposed a limit on the number of dishes that could be included on the menu but led to more peaceful and equanimous dinners. The cult of gastronomy and *haute cuisine* was as strong in England during the Regency as it had been in Paris during the reign of Louis XV, when the principles of *haute cuisine* emerged. According to one of the famous French 'fathers of the table', Grimod de la Reynière, there was a direct link between the new gastronomic culture of *haute cuisine*, sex and the desire of the *nouveaux riches* to show off their recently acquired wealth – all factors which became apposite to English society during the Regency. The upper classes took their lead from the Prince Regent, whose indulgence (prandial and post-prandial) knew no restraint.

The splendid dinner at Kentchurch Court overwhelmed the guests. Few of them had ever enjoyed such a quantity of fine dishes served with so much aplomb. Some items, however, caused consternation. The worst offender was a roast hare, made to appear as life-like as possible with its ears sticking straight up and with fur still on the paws, head and tail. Miss Conick's vegetarian constitution rebelled,

LADIES OF LOWER STATUS ARE SEATED TOGETHER, WITH LITTLE ACCESS TO THE ELIGIBLE GENTLEMEN

ROASTED HARES LOOKING SOMEWHAT STARTLED TO FIND THEMSELVES ON A DINNER TABLE

while Mr Foxsmith's sense of moral indignation soon surfaced. 'The meal tonight was excellent with the exception of what I can only say is the most barbaric dish of hare,' he remarked. 'To kill an animal and to get his ears to stick up and to make it look as alive as possible before eating it is just horrible. How could these Regency people have lived with themselves, making it so plain that this thing was hopping around and enjoying being a hare moments before it got its ears stuck up and bits pulled off its body? It seems that every time they saw an animal they wanted to kill it. It's difficult to describe how much meat they give you here,' he continued. 'Dish after dish after dish of meat and then more meat and then another bird and another animal and another mammal. It's meat heaven in here. Occasionally they slip up and a plate of vegetables turns up.'

SWEET CHICKEN PYE

SERVES 4–6
Equipment: 2-litre-capacity pie dish

FOR THE PASTRY
250 gm / 9 oz plain flour
75 gm / 3 oz butter
50 gm / 2 oz lard
1 egg and 1 egg yolk (large eggs)

To make the pastry, rub the fat into the flour, then form it into dough with the egg and egg yolk. Allow to rest in the refrigerator.

FOR THE FILLING

4 chicken breasts	1 strip of lemon zest
100 gm / 4 oz smoked bacon	125 mg / 4½ oz of prepared chestnuts
1 onion, chopped	1 eating apple (Cox)
5 cloves	10 dried apricots
2 bay leaves	4 egg yolks
4–5 sprigs of thyme	50 ml / 2 fl. oz double cream
1 stick cinnamon	50 gm / 2 oz butter
salt and pepper	50 gm / 2 oz plain flour
mace and nutmeg	1 tsp sugar

Preheat the oven to gas mark 5 / 375°F / 190°C. Put the chicken, bacon, cloves, bay, thyme, cinnamon and lemon zest in a saucepan, cover with water, season with the salt and poach gently until the meat is cooked. Melt the butter in a shallow pan and fry the onion gently. Tip in the flour and cook for a couple of minutes before adding enough of the chicken stock to make a thick sauce. Drain the chicken and bacon, cut into pieces and place in a bowl. Discard the herbs, cloves and cinnamon. Add pepper, and a pinch each of mace and nutmeg.

Peel, core and chop the apple, cut the apricots into quarters and the chestnuts in half. Add these to the chicken and bacon. Add as much of the sauce as will bind the ingredients together. Whisk together the egg yolks, cream and sugar and mix in with the other ingredients. Line the pie dish with the pastry, leaving enough over for a lid. Spoon the filling into it, wet the edges of the pastry and cover with a pastry lid, crimping the edges to seal it. Glaze the top with egg wash and bake for 45 minutes to one hour.

A sweet Chicken Pye.

TAKE five or six small chickens, pick, draw, and truss them for baking; season them with cloves, mace, nutmeg, cinnamon, and a little salt; wrap up some of the seasoning in butter, and put it in their bellies: and your coffin being made, put them in; put over and between them pieces of marrow, *Spanish* potatoes and chesnuts, both boiled, peeled and cut, a handful of barberries stript, a lemon sliced, some butter on the top; so close up the pye and bake it, and have in readiness a caudle made of white wine, sugar, nutmeg, beat it up with yolks of eggs and butter; have a care it does not curdle; pour the caudle in, shake it well together, and serve it up hot.

Ideally this pie should be served cold. To serve hot it is best finished in a slightly different way. When making the mixture, leave out the egg yolks and add the cream and the sugar on their own. Then spoon it into a deep pie dish without a pastry base. Wet the edges of the dish and put a pastry lid on it. Bake for the same amount of time and send it to the table hot.

CHEF IAN DOWDING DEVISED NEW CREATIONS BASED ON RECIPES
FROM *THE COMPLEAT HOUSEWIFE* BY ELIZA SMITH, 1758

The extravagance of the dinner at Kentchurch would have been quite normal in Regency times. A hostess was expected to provide far more food than the company could possibly consume. While today it would be thought mean and lazy to serve fewer than three courses at a formal dinner party, in the Regency the same criticism would have applied to any host or hostess who offered fewer than fifteen dishes.

Of course, such gourmandism was only enjoyed by a small élite. It is one of the sad ironies of the Regency that while the tables of the wealthy groaned with rich and lavish fare, bread and potatoes (occasionally augmented by a small piece of cheese or bacon) were the staple food for the working classes, a large proportion of whom lived on or below the poverty line. A semi-skilled worker earning about fifteen shillings a week was able to afford a few more items such as meat, porter (a dark brown malt liquor probably so named because of its popularity with London porters), tea and a little sugar. Compare this with the bill for the kitchens at Carlton House. The accounts of August 1819 reveal that the prince bought sixty-seven loaves of bread at 11d. each and ninety loaves at 1s. ½d. He spent over £258 on meat, including 1854 lbs of beef, 1625 lbs of mutton and 1785 lbs of veal. The poultry bill came to £323, for 385 pullets, 232 chickens, 88 quails, 31 large capons, 12 geese and 10 rabbits. The fishmonger's bill was a mere £118, which included 61 lobsters and expensive turbot and sole – he must have had lobster twice a day. In the same month a demonstration by 60–80,000 people demanding a repeal of the Corn Laws (iniquitous tariffs that kept the price of imported corn as high as that of British corn in order to protect landowners and large farmers) was savagely repressed. At least eleven people died and nearly six hundred men, women and children were badly wounded. The proportional equivalent for today's population would be 250 deaths. This horrific event came to be known as the Peterloo Massacre and caused great consternation among those liberal ruling families who wanted reform of the Corn Laws and were determined to improve the lot of the poor.

During the first formal dinner of the Regency House Party, conversation flowed, as did the drink, and a congenial atmosphere was quickly established.

'It is literally like going back in a time machine,' said Miss Hopkins. 'I don't

know how to behave just yet. I want to be me and I'm not me – the way I'm dressed, the surroundings, the people and the way they're talking to me. But Lady Devonport, my chaperone, is putting me at ease. She's as mad as I am, so that's good. I think we might get up to a little bit of mischief.'

However, such was the length of the ritual that by eight o'clock many of the party were, in modern parlance, completely sozzled. Mrs Rogers suggested that the ladies retire to the drawing room, leaving the men to drink port and discuss the merits of the young women they had just met. 'A lot of people are terribly nervous,' said Mrs Rogers of the company, 'because they don't perceive themselves as being the right strata of society to be here. I think it's very indicative of the society that we live in nowadays that people are frightened of the upper classes in this country. Wasn't it Shylock or someone who said, "If you prick us, do we not bleed?" '

DIANA SPERLING'S DEPICTION OF THE SCENE AFTER DINNER AT DYNES HALL SHOWS THE
TEA URN ON THE TABLE TO THE LEFT. 'PAPPY' AND 'MUM' BATTLE IT OUT OVER A CHESS SET.
THIS PICTURE ILLUSTRATES THE CUSTOM FOR 'OLD MAIDS' TO WEAR CAPS INDOORS.

However, several of the guests were more interested in the game of romance
than issues of status. 'Mrs Rogers has taken me under her wing. She thinks I'm a
nice gal,' said the countess. 'She said to me, "Are you an owl or a lark?" and I
looked at her and thought, Is this some sort of test to see whether I'm posh
enough?, but she meant am I a late riser or an early riser! She asked me what my
income is and I wanted to tell her because I think we make quite a good team but
then I realised that the host, who is obviously the prize catch of the men, is also her
charge. Her loyalties might be split.'

As the women assembled in the drawing room, an urn of hot water and tea-
making equipment was brought in by a footman. Although the drawing room was
used by both sexes, it was the mistress of the house who held sway here (while the

dining room was very much a male preserve). This was due to the custom of ladies retiring from the dinner table after the dessert course, a decidedly English idea which probably emerged in the eighteenth century, when drinking tea became hugely fashionable. After dinner, a tray loaded with a spirit lamp and an ornate urn would be brought in and the hostess would leave the table to brew tea for her guests. Gradually, the ceremony moved into another room entirely.

The appeal of the tea urn had faded somewhat by the time the gentlemen rejoined the women, an hour and a half after they had withdrawn, and the port had made several circuits of the table. Mr Foxsmith promptly engaged Mrs Enright in conversation, only to spoil the effect by keeling over backwards mid-sentence. He remained there, too inebriated to move. Thus were first impressions formed.

This behaviour would have been far from unusual in the Regency. At one party, the Regent himself fell over drunk in the middle of dancing a quadrille and was then sick in front of the guests. After evenings of such excess, Regency men were often in no fit state to join the women in the drawing room. As one of the most perspicacious diarists of the Regency, the dandy Captain Rees Gronow, recalled: 'Female society amongst the upper classes was most notoriously neglected; except by romantic foreigners, who were the heroes of many a fashionable adventure.' Alas, there were no glamorous romantic foreigners to distract our ladies from the men's behaviour. Miss Braund spoke for the women when she said, 'I was really disgusted with them. It was so childish and they were *so* drunk. It was really rude and I sat there thinking, What am I doing here? This is ridiculous. I don't like *any* of them.'

> *Man, being reasonable, must get drunk;*
> *The best of life is but intoxication . . .*
>
> LORD BYRON

Although bottles were smaller in the Regency (approximately two-thirds modern size), the level of drinking considered acceptable amongst all echelons of society would raise eyebrows today. As one dandy wrote of a dinner party he attended, 'A perpetual thirst seemed to come over people, both men and women, as soon as they had tasted their soup; as from that moment everybody was taking wine with everybody else, till the close of dinner; and such wine as produced that class of Cordiality which frequently wanders into stupefaction.' 'Drinking was the fashion of the day,' wrote Gronow, and indeed it was considered rather a dashing quality in a gentleman to be permanently tipsy. 'The Prince, Mr Pitt, the Lord Chancellor and many others who gave the tone to society would appear at an evening party fit for nothing but bed. A three-bottle man was not an unusual guest at a fashionable table; and the night was invariably spent drinking bad port-wine to an enormous extent.'

Sheridan was known to drink as much as twenty bottles of port while watching rerun after rerun of his great play *The Rivals* at Drury Lane, the theatre of which he was manager. When the theatre was gutted by fire, an acquaintance found him outside, glass in hand, staring at the blazing building. The acquaintance expressed surprise at seeing Sheridan there. 'Why?' said Sheridan. 'Can't a man take a glass of wine at his own fireside?'

Others were less witty about their drinking, but none the less provided good fodder for the satirists and wags of the time. The Regent was prince among these, as Charles Lamb reminds us:

> Not a fatter fish than he
> Flounders round the polar sea.
> See his blubbers – at his gills
> What a world of drink he swills . . .
> Every fish of generous kind
> Scuds aside or shrinks behind;
> But about his presence keep
> All the monsters of the deep . . .
> Name of title what has he?
> Is he Regent of the sea?
> By his bulk and by his size,
> By his oily qualities,
> This (or else my eyesight fails),
> This should be the Prince of Whales.

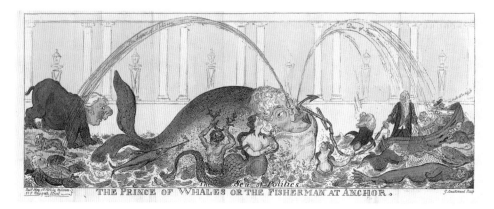

THE PRINCE OF WHALES OR THE FISHERMAN AT ANCHOR.

Pubs never closed and gin was cheap: 'drunk for a penny, dead drunk for twopence'. There were fifty thousand pubs in Britain at the beginning of the nineteenth century, catering to a population of just under 12 million rising to 14 million by 1821. That meant one pub for every 240 people, including children. In society, ale or claret was served with breakfast, or perhaps a glass of hock and soda to cure a hangover; mid-morning Madeira or sherry was served with biscuits and a glass of ratafia (a very light liqueur flavoured with fruit or almonds) for the ladies. Those who went hunting or shooting took silver hip-flasks of brandy to sustain them; at dinner, champagne and wines were followed by port and brandy and yet more champagne at supper. Water was never drunk on its own (it was often contaminated and therefore unsafe), except at spa towns for constitutional purposes. Upper-class women, although they drank during meals, confined themselves mainly to 'ladies' drinks' at other times of day, such as orgeat, a non-alcoholic drink made of barley or almonds, orange-flower water or ratafia.

Drinking etiquette was also very different from today. A gentleman would 'invite' his neighbour to drink and each would then fill a glass and down it in one. The glass was then washed by a servant in a bowl kept behind a screen, or by the diners themselves in a personal cooler on the table. It was common practice to share glasses, and drinking another's 'leavings' was a good opportunity for men and women to display a sense of intimacy with each other. Although the guests at Kentchurch Court were aware of the habit of 'knocking it back in one', few were able to do so, even the most enthusiastic of the drinkers.

The women, meanwhile, had provided their own entertainment prior to Mr Foxsmith's gymnastics display. A mighty row erupted between Miss Hopkins ('a lady of fortune but inferior birth') and the hostess. 'All evening she'd been saying things about my class and my accent, implying I'd never have been accepted at a real Regency dinner and that I was inferior to everyone else, common, because I have an accent. I'm the only one here with an accent so I felt really isolated and much more homesick than I thought I'd feel. It was so rude and so snobby I just lost it. I think I actually swore at her, which I know I shouldn't do but I'm a really independent girl and used to being a boss and I'm not going to be talked to like that, by anybody,' was Miss Hopkins' view of the row. She did not mention the fact she was also suffering from severe nicotine withdrawal, as were many of the guests.

Smoking was not allowed in the house and was considered the ultimate in vulgarity during the Regency. It was a vice frowned on in men, forbidden to young women and scarcely tolerated in wives, who could only indulge their pleasure in private. Miss Hopkins ended the evening by storming off to her room, threatening to quit the house, leaving Mrs Rogers looking furious and, later, tearful.

Not all the women were finding the adjustment to Regency life quite so painful. 'Miss Conick is an altogether delightful young woman,' said her chaperone, Mrs Enright. 'And very, very good-looking, and in the most unusual style too. I should think that she will take the eye of all the young men. And here we must be very careful because she is so engaging that some hackles may rise, if the young men with the most to offer in terms of fortune were to take a fancy to her too early in the proceedings. So we shall have to be very cautious. I do already feel myself rather fond of Miss Conick.' An astute observer, Mrs Enright gave her first impressions of the gentlemen from whom she had to pick a suitable match for her charge. 'Most of them were very much the worse for wear for drink. Mr Everett behaved himself beautifully and rather redeemed the rest of the party. I asked my charge, Miss Conick, if she had any initial thoughts on the desirability of the gentlemen, and my own choice for her so far, who turns out to be the richest member of the party, but she says he is too thin. Too thin, for heaven's sake! There are worse faults in a man than thinness, as I shall have to point out to her. Mr Gorell Barnes, although appearing amazingly gauche on first meeting despite his good looks, is improving on acquaintance. Mr Foxsmith, who disgraced himself thoroughly, seems like a nice chap when you get to know him. He's sober this morning, which amazes me; I thought he would be in hospital having his stomach pumped. Captain Robinson is a rough diamond whose heart is in the right place – and who else is there? Oh yes, the very interesting naval captain, Glover, who tells me he made an amazing amount of prize money with his ship. He's an Irishman. He has possibilities as long as he keeps off the drink. Our hostess delivered a long lecture on deportment this morning, which was perhaps a little redundant but never mind; it is her house and we do all want to stay in it very much.'

Staying in other people's houses took up a large part of the year for the upper classes. Visits to country estates were not an occasional treat but rather a way of life, designed to engage guests in the pursuit of pleasure and, for many, romance.

MRS ENRIGHT RECORDING HER INITIAL IMPRESSIONS OF HER FELLOW HOUSE-GUESTS
IN THE BEDROOM SHE SHARES WITH MISS CONICK

IAN DOWDING WITH A SPECTACULAR DISH OF ROASTED PEACOCK,
A FAVOURITE OF THE REGENT

Entire families would be welcomed at short notice, even though they would often bring with them a retinue of maids, valets, nannies, governesses, secretaries and quite often the family doctor. Take for example the annual peregrinations of the Bessborough family (friends of the Regent and whose daughter was Lady Caroline Lamb, lover of Byron). During the summer of 1807 they made a tour of the north, staying at the grand estates of Bolton, Wentworth, Howick, Castle Howard and Alnwick. They wintered in Cornwall, spent the Season in London in a rented mansion and then travelled around the country again, staying at the great estates of

Petworth, Chatsworth, Holywell, Hardwick, Wentworth and Woburn before returning in time to spend Christmas in London.

The house parties that arose from these spontaneous visits (or were arranged in advance by invitation) often lasted for weeks. Every kind of entertainment would be provided and no demands were made upon the visitors other than that of amusing the company. Guests of all ages were expected to 'sing' for their supper – either literally or by showing off the brilliance of their wit and charm. Conversation was considered an art and was highly cultivated during the Regency; after all, it was the main source of amusement.

One of the most important functions of the house party, beyond that of entertaining wealthy and idle aristocrats, was to promote match-making. Since the decline of the arranged marriage in the course of the eighteenth century, ambitious parents had to engineer marriages, by seeing that their daughters met the right sort of young men in the right circumstances. Balls and assemblies provided opportunities for striking up an initial acquaintance, but it was the relaxed atmosphere of a house party that enabled all the participants to put together the last pieces of the jigsaw that led to a formal proposal.

Some of Kentchurch's chaperones were quick off the mark in promoting the interests of their charges. 'The wonderful Captain Robinson and I have reached an agreement,' whispered Mrs Hammond. 'He will promote my charge and tell all of the other chaps what a wonderful girl she is and how he is delighted with her fair looks and her manner and how he wishes that she could be his, because it is very important that the other chaps see her as very desirable. For that great favour he has agreed to accept twenty whole pounds to help him with his gambling endeavours while here in this glorious house. That's what Jane Austen had to live on for a year. And he's taking the money on the strict and firm understanding that he will not divulge this to the chaps and he will not take any other bribes from any of the other chaperones at all . . . ever!'

The bad moods and hangovers induced by the excesses of the previous evening were dispelled the following day by the intriguing sight of a pretty young lady walking up the drive. The new arrival was shown into a small, plain room next to Mrs Rogers' and told that the hostess would call for her soon. This was Francesca Martin, the lady's companion. As her pocketbook revealed:

You were brought up in genteel society but you have no fortune and must rely on the charity of others. Your stay at Kentchurch is entirely dependent on the beneficence of Mr Gorell Barnes. Your duty is to attend to the needs of his hostess, Mrs Rogers, and you will abide by her wishes in all matters.

As Lady's Companion your status is not equal to that of a house-guest. You will only be invited to dine at table and enjoy the household entertainment when required to make up numbers or when invited by Mr Gorell Barnes. The privileges of the lady guests do not apply to you. Should you require any modest addition to your wardrobe, you will have to hope the other ladies pass their cast-offs your way.

A lady's companion is not an eligible prospect for any gentleman visiting the house. However, it is not completely unknown for women of your status to marry.

'Gosh, I wasn't expecting that!' she exclaimed. 'I knew that I must be pretty low-grade in the house as I had to walk up the drive and it was so hot. I was sweating like mad. I didn't realise I would be this lowly, though. Still, it doesn't matter, I'm just fascinated to see how everything works.' That evening, after a briefing from Mrs Rogers about her status and a reminder of the need to maintain correct standards, Miss Francesca (always referred to by her first name to denote her inferior position) was left to eat a cold supper in the hostess's boudoir. 'I was lying on my bed, in my beautiful undergarments, and the bell went downstairs for dinner. I suddenly realised it would be my first night and I was going to have dinner by myself in my room. I don't normally get emotional but I heard that bell and realised that it would be quite difficult to hear everyone outside having a good time or people downstairs singing by the piano but not actually being invited to join them.'

Meanwhile the others enjoyed what was to be one of the grandest events of their stay at Kentchurch. The date was 19 June 2003, 192 years to the day since George, Prince of Wales, was officially declared Regent. During his time as Prince of Wales his personal expenditure had to some degree been controlled by Parliament, but now that he was regent, and sovereign in all but name, the shackles were loosened. Naturally, he decided to celebrate in style. Two thousand guests – the men wearing court dress or uniforms – were invited to Carlton House for 9 p.m. on 19 June 1811 for the grandest and most extravagant party ever seen in Europe.

An hour before the appointed time of arrival, the queue of carriages formed a solid block stretching back from Carlton House to Bond Street. The Regent made his entrance at 9.15 wearing the uniform of a field marshal, not because he had ever graced a battlefield but because he had recently appointed himself to that position. His outfit was resplendent – even the seams of his coat were embroidered – and it was said to have cost as much as it weighed: £200, equivalent to £10,000 in today's money. He was joined by the exiled French royal family, the Bourbons, who were received in a room specially hung with blue silk and stitched golden fleurs-de-lis. His estranged wife, Princess Caroline, was pointedly not invited and his mother and sisters refused to attend, upset that the Regent was so openly flouting the rules of precedence on a public occasion, especially at a time when his father was so ill.

'Nothing was ever half so magnificent. It was *in reality* everything that they try to imitate in the gorgeous scenery of the theatre . . . assemblage of beauty, splendour and profuse and magnificence . . . women out-blazing each other in the richness of their dress,' raved Tom Moore, the poet. This beauteous crowd were largely members of the aristocracy. 'It is they who have given the Regency its raffish air and rather gamey smell,' noted J. B. Priestley, one of the best modern writers about the era. These were not the grave and magnificent aristocrats of the earlier eighteenth century who had felt so secure in their positions. The French Revolution, the waves of *émigrés* who fled to London, the march of the Industrial Revolution and the war with Napoleon had all combined to change their comfortable lives for ever. 'This was a ruling class nearing the end of one stage of its development, blazing in an Indian Summer and over-acting in a series of farewell performances.'

The main supper table at the Regency party filled the two-hundred-foot length of the Gothic conservatory. In front of the Regent's seat was a large circular basin feeding a stream, filled with goldfish, that meandered between banks of moss and flowers, past three picturesque bridges all the way to the far end of the table. The less important guests had supper served to them at tables in specially made canvas tents dotted about the garden, linked to the main house by canvas corridors. The tableware and serving dishes were of solid gold and silver. The fare consisted of hot soups and roasts and a surfeit of cold dishes and puddings, and iced champagne for everybody. Peaches, grapes, pineapples and other out-of-season fruit were piled up everywhere. Thousands of lights and flowers created an effect which 'was inexpressibly delightful and even magically impressive', according to *The Times*. 'There was no crowding, hurry or bustle in the waiting: everything was done as in a private house.'

MENU FOR THE GRAND REGENCY CELEBRATION DINNER AT KENTCHURCH

FIRST COURSE

Leek and ham soup
Salmon baked in pastry
Fricassee of chicken
Cabbage and spinach cake
Roast saddle of mutton
Asparagus with butter
A boiled neat's (beef) tongue
Port-wine sauce
Potato pudding

SECOND COURSE

Salmagundi (a dish composed of
chopped meat, anchovies, eggs, onions
with oil and condiments)
Raspberry cake
Boiled turkey with crayfish
Braised beefsteaks
A raised game pie
Syllabub
Wine and butter sauce

The guests at Kentchurch were also served a most sumptuous dinner to celebrate the start of the Regency and afterwards were ushered on to the lawn by footmen carrying candelabras to watch a Regency fireworks display. An arch had been built which blazed with the roman candles, rockets and Catherine wheels popular in the period.

'The sound was huge and the light was brilliant,' wrote Mr Foxsmith in his diary. 'I hoped lots of people would be able to see them from the village but to have it all to ourselves made it more special. I was so thrown by the experience. Speechless. Almost embarrassed that I wasn't worthy of it.' 'Absolutely brilliant,' exclaimed the host. 'They were probably the most awesome, unsurpassable thing I have seen in my entire life,' said Miss Conick.

The guests all felt humbled by the beauty and magnificence of the event and the setting, and proud of their role in this extraordinary experiment to live and love in the Regency. For most of them, it was a heady concoction of emotions: anxiety, doubts and fears mingled with excitement, curiosity, high hopes and romantic longings.

But what was that? Two guests, one male and one female, were clearly seen moving off alone towards the woods. An extraordinary breach of etiquette and decorum. How perfectly Regency!

THE REGENCY BEGAN IN MAGNIFICENT STYLE ON 19 JUNE 1811, AND IN HEREFORD ON 19 JUNE 2003

A DANCE MISTRESS INSTRUCTS THE YOUNG LADIES IN AN ESSENTIAL ACCOMPLISHMENT

CHAPTER FOUR

REGENCY REALITY

WHAT CAN A WOMAN DO?

———

Good breeding demanded that outward conventions should not be violated,
but asked few questions as to what went on beneath the surface.

LADY AIRLIE

GOSSIP, OF COURSE, was much indulged in at house parties, since they provided
the perfect setting for anything from light flirtation to adulterous love, although the
latter was only really acceptable among those high-born enough to flout convention. At Kentchurch, only Lady Devonport and the countess enjoyed sufficient
status to be outrageous. Scandals in the upper
echelons of society were usually glossed over by
the silent acquiescence of all involved. The subject on everybody's lips at Kentchurch concerned
the identity of the couple spied leaving the fireworks party together. Were they the same people
who had been seen by the gardener kissing pas-
sionately on the lawn in the early hours of the
morning? Narrowing down the 'guilty' parties
was difficult, since no one was above suspicion,
not even the chaperones, possessing as they did as
much charm and intelligence as their charges.
Would they stand by their promise of promoting
the younger women's interests, or seduce the men
themselves? It was commonplace during the
Regency for chaperones to distract the attention of

THE COUNTESS HOPES THAT HER SKILL WITH
THE FAN MIGHT WIN HER THE NOTICE OF THE
MOST ELIGIBLE GENTLEMAN

unmarried men, even to have full-blown affairs, although it was frowned upon if
the chaperone's behaviour injured the chances of her charge.

Was Lady Devonport fulfilling the non-conformist behaviour noted in her
pocketbook? Was she following the example of Lady Bessborough, who had two
children by the young Lord Granville although he was destined to be her niece's
husband? Or should suspicion fall upon the heads of the younger women of the
party? Had Miss Hopkins returned the attachment Mr Everett had made apparent

after they first met and before he could even remember her name? Was the host pursuing his suit with the countess or Miss Conick, both of whom had been singled out for his particular attention?

With these questions buzzing in their heads, the house-guests set about the task of getting used to the daily routines of Regency life. Between breakfast and dinner, guests were left to a considerable degree to do what they liked and usually the men and the women remained separate. The Duchess of Leinster described the normal course of events when she wrote to a friend about a recent house party given by her husband at Carton in Ireland:

> The house was crowded – a thousand comers and goers. We breakfast between ten and eleven, though it is called half-past nine. We have an immense table – chocolate – honey – hot bread – cold bread – brown bread – white bread – green bread – and all coloured breads and cakes. After breakfast, Mr Scott, the Duke's chaplain, reads a few short prayers, and then we go as we like – a back room for reading, a billiard room, a print room, a drawing room, and a whole suite of rooms, not forgetting the music room . . . There are all sorts of amusements; the gentlemen are out hunting and shooting all the morning. We dine at half-past four or five – go to tea, so cards about nine . . . play till supper time – 'tis pretty late by the time we go to bed.

As the duchess's letter makes clear, with the gentlemen out hunting and shooting all the morning ('morning' being the period from breakfast to dinner time), the women had to amuse themselves. For the most part, this meant indoor activities. Reading was acceptable, although novels were considered potentially dangerous to a young woman's sensibilities and morals if not carefully chosen. 'I declare after all there is no such enjoyment as reading!' said Miss Bingley, in the hope of attracting Mr Darcy's approval. 'How much sooner one tires of anything than of a book! – When I have a house of my own, I shall be miserable if I have not an excellent library.' Uplifting, moralising or educational texts (historical and literary) were considered appropriate for younger women in order to improve their conversational skills. The art of conversation was increasingly nurtured from the turn of the nineteenth century, as women came to be seen not merely as decorative adjuncts and housekeepers but as companions to men, able to converse with them on certain

MISS BRAUND, MISS HOPKINS, MISS FRANCESCA AND MISS CONICK ENJOY
A RELAXED BREAKFAST BALL WHILE THE MEN ARE OUT

topics with the same level of competence. In 1791 the bookseller James Lackington commented: 'There are some thousands of women who frequent my shop, that know as well what books to choose, and are as well acquainted with works of taste and genius, as any gentleman in the kingdom.' The library at Kentchurch contained a rich variety of pre-1830s titles, but, as the women were still getting to know each other, closeting themselves with a book was not what was required.

A woman's education (which might take the form of a governess, home study or a few years at school) would also emphasise the skills of needlework, dancing, deportment and dress. Sewing and embroidery were considered laudable activities

SKETCHING A COTTAGE. DIANA SPERLING'S DEPICTION OF A
FAMILY'S ARTISTIC OUTING, 29 SEPTEMBER 1816

and even high-born ladies of the Regency, married or not, spent many hours sewing (making and mending clothes, trimming bonnets and dresses in the latest manner) or embroidering decorative pieces. Lady Bertram in *Mansfield Park* 'spent her days in sitting nicely dressed on a sofa, doing some long piece of needlework, of little use and no beauty'. It was customary for young girls to complete their education by stitching a sampler embroidered on to woollen cloth called a 'tammy', although those who had enjoyed an expensive education may have stitched their samplers on to silk cloth and tinted it with watercolour. Most women would also be taught a smattering of French, and perhaps Italian, history, spelling and rudimentary geography. To learn to budget personal and household accounts, a young woman could turn to *The Young Ladies' New Guide to Arithmetic* by John Grieg (1803), which showed them 'the Method of Making out Bills of Parcels, Book-debts, Receipts, Promisory Notes, and Bills of Exchange'. According to Jane Austen, many schools were institutions 'where young ladies for enormous pay might be screwed out of health and into vanity'.

The ladies at Kentchurch sat together and embroidered designs on the theme of love, but this could not pass the whole day from breakfast to dinner. Two other drawing-room accomplishments they could perfect were art (in particular, water-colours) and music. Drawing classes abounded and gave employment to thousands of drawing masters. Although there was interest in portraiture, there was more enthusiasm for reproducing picturesque landscapes, and few young ladies would travel anywhere without a box of watercolours. Other artistic pastimes included draughtsmanship, sculpting in wax, paper-cutting (creating profiles of a subject, usually a friend or relative), shellwork and japanning (a hard black lacquer used on wood then decorated with gilt).

THE COUNTESS TAKES REFUGE IN THE SOLITUDE OF READING

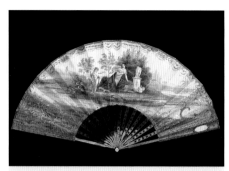

FAN LANGUAGE

The young ladies of Kentchurch were
instructed in the art of using a fan to
pursue their romantic interests.
There were several methods of using
it for silent 'conversation'.
The elegant manner of holding a fan
was to place it between the third finger
and forefinger with the thumb on the pivot
end, to show off a well-groomed hand.

Carrying in right hand in front of face:
FOLLOW ME

Carrying in left hand in front of face:
DESIROUS OF ACQUAINTANCE

Placed on left ear:
I WISH TO GET RID OF YOU

Twirling in left hand:
WE ARE WATCHED

Carrying in right hand:
YOU ARE TOO WILLING

Twirling in right hand:
I LOVE ANOTHER

Drawing across the cheek:
I LOVE YOU

Gazing pensively at shut fan:
WHY DO YOU MISUNDERSTAND
ME?

Shutting the fully opened fan very slowly:
I PROMISE TO MARRY YOU

Women would also be expected to obtain a certain level of proficiency on an instrument – enough to plonk out a few country tunes on the fortepiano for dancing after dinner at least. Younger women would be motivated to practise not only for their own enjoyment, or that of others, but also to attract the notice of an eligible young man. A lady needed to be 'accomplished' in order to display her sense of taste and refinement, but also to advertise her matrimonial qualities, since her level of achievement was seen to correlate directly with her latent talents as wife and mother. Playing an instrument also allowed for a potential suitor to hold a candle over the music and turn pages for the graceful player. Miss Hopkins and Miss Francesca were both able to play a little and the former enjoyed the occasional lesson from a music mistress. However, Miss Francesca's status excluded her from this privilege.

Lessons from a dancing mistress did pass some of the time. A 'breakfast ball', during which the girls could practise their steps in the 'freedom' of their nightgowns (corsets and full underwear still had to be worn, of course), was organised by Mrs Rogers. The Duchess of Devonshire started the fashion for these balls, during which young ladies could learn the complicated steps of dances before they 'came out' into society. The ball would be followed by a breakfast to which young men might be invited, thereby providing a useful opportunity for the older ladies to vet potential suitors. Only those girls with exemplary deportment were allowed to engage in the new craze sweeping Europe, the German waltz, which was seen as a highly immodest dance as it allowed men to touch women and hold them closely. These breakfast balls gradually evolved into grander occasions and eventually gave birth to the 'garden party'.

Letter-writing was another popular occupation for women. It was an important part of the daily routine and many wrote to their favourite correspondents every day. 'I have now attained the true art of letter-writing,' wrote Jane Austen in 1801, 'which we are always told, is to express on paper exactly what one would say to the same person by word of mouth.' Another school of letter-writing favoured the use of exaggerated prose and some aristocrats even chose deliberately to spell badly as a mark of their superior status – only clerks or others who had to work (and write) for a living needed neat

DISPLAYING MUSICAL TALENT WAS ONE OF THE FEW WAYS A LADY'S COMPANION COULD MAKE AN IMPRESSION ON MALE HOUSE-GUESTS

writing and correct spelling. Wafers (small disks of gum and flour that were licked and then stuck on the letter) were available for sealing unimportant notes, but most letters – and certainly any containing information, gossip or scandal – were sealed with wax melted over a small desk taper and applied to the paper. Red wax was used for business, black for mourning and any other colour for social correspondence. By the Regency period, post was delivered by mail coaches protected by armed guards and following strict schedules. By 1812 the cost of a letter was fourpence for fifteen miles or less, eightpence for eighty, rising to seventeen pence for seven hundred miles. Any enclosures in the letter, including a second sheet of notepaper, doubled the price of postage; therefore plenty of abbreviations were used and letters were often 'crossed', the page being turned at right-angles once filled and written over again. The recipient paid the cost of postage, although a friendly or needy coachman might be persuaded or bribed to take the letter some of the distance before posting it for a small fee. For many of the guests of Kentchurch, however, used as they were to e-mail and text messaging, writing with quills and ink was a laborious business.

The younger women's freedom was also curtailed by the fact that they needed to be chaperoned at all times. 'If Mrs Enright has to go and do something privately I'm in no man's land, because I can't go anywhere without her,' explained Miss Conick in frustration. 'We were just downstairs talking to Mr Foxsmith having a very nice, civilised conversation but then she needed to go upstairs and of course I couldn't be left with him. There was nowhere for me to go; the other girls had gone out for a walk all together, but I couldn't go and find them because I can't go out by myself.'

As the women were discovering, however, even outdoor pursuits for Regency women were somewhat tame. According to the 'Lady of Distinction' who penned the Regency's definitive guide to the art of 'captivation', *The Mirror of the Graces*, outdoor exercise for ladies was to be of a gentle sort, obtained on horseback or on foot in fine weather and in a carriage otherwise:

> Country air when breathed at proper hours, is the finest bracer of the nerves, and the surest brightener of the complexion. – But these hours are neither under the midday sun in summer, when its beams scorch the skin and set the blood in a boil; nor beneath the dews of evening, when the imperceptible damps, saturating the thinly-clad limbs, sends the wanderer home infected with the disease that is to lay her, ere a return-ing spring, in the silent tomb! – Both these periods are pregnant with danger to delicacy and carelessness.

Riding was one of the few outdoor occupations women could indulge in, and they were even allowed to ride unchaperoned, provided they kept within the boundaries of the deer park. Regency gentlewomen would have been proficient on horseback or on mules, although only the more important ladies at Kentchurch were able to ride as they alone had the correct dress as required at a reasonably fash-ionable house party. Lady Devonport had been on a horse nearly every day of her life and thoroughly enjoyed the opportunity to learn side-saddle and dressage. The countess had never ridden before. 'I'm loving learning to ride but when I leave here and want to go riding I'll have to find out if they have a side-saddle!' The others were limited to 'battledore and shuttle-cock' (hitting a shuttlecock backwards and forwards with a simple bat as many times as possible without letting it touch the ground) or walking, chaperoned, in the gardens. 'Can I have my skates?' asked Miss Braund, optimistically. 'I'm really missing them. The paths here are gravel . . . but I could skate indoors.'

The restrictions that dominated women's activities extended as far as their clothing. 'Sunday was boiling hot and spent reading *Sense and Sensibility* in my *new dress*,' noted Miss Francesca in her diary, whose wardrobe of two

LADY DEVONPORT FOUND HER RIDING HABIT, COMPLETE WITH CORSET AND UNDER-TROUSERS, DASHING BUT RATHER HOT

dresses accounted for her enthusiasm at the new addition. 'Green and short-sleeved – I feel so much cooler. Sadly, also feel like a twelve-year-old girl as it's all puffy sleeves and floral patterns.' Many of the women noted that their Regency dresses made them feel unattractive. 'I'm becoming this polite, demure, completely obedient little girl. These dresses are so childish and yesterday I did two really naughty things – I went running in the rain and took my hair down for five minutes in front of two gentlemen. How ridiculous is that? I feel genuinely guilty about it!' bemoaned Miss Conick. 'In the house I don't feel sexy or attractive because I have reverted to being a little girl and the restrictions on me make me a little girl,' said Miss Hopkins. 'Therefore the idea of being attractive doesn't feel right, it infringes on the little girl I have become.' As Mrs Enright observed in her diary:

> The actual, babyish forms of the clothes worn by Regency girls of marriageable age are infantilising. Light, filmy materials, a 'waistline' just under the bust suggesting less a true bodice than the yoke on a very young child's garment, short, puffed sleeves emphasising the 'chubby' or 'rounded' upper arm that was so much acclaimed – and the narrow silhouette (which *is* attractive) all tend to suggest a female who is not fully formed and perhaps never will be. She is by nature (the sartorial message

MISS BRAUND IS LACED INTO HER CORSET,
DESPITE THE SOARING SUMMER TEMPERATURES

seems to say) a permanently immature entity and therein lies her attraction to the opposite sex. She will be obedient, manageable, unchalleng-
ing, compliant in every way.

Although Regency fashions were light, colourful and comfortable in comparison to the stiff, boned, brocaded and panniered styles of the Georgian era, they
still required rigid corseting for the women, which the author of *Mirror of the
Graces* condemns:

We see immodesty on one side, unveiling the too redundant bosom; on
the other, deformity, once more drawing the steeled boddice upon the
bruised ribs. A vile taste and stupid approval by a large majority of

women, have brought the monstrous corset into a kind of fashion; and in consequence we see, in eight women out of ten, the hips squeezed to a circumference little more than the waist; and the bosom shoved up to the chin, making a sort of fleshy shelf, disgusting to the beholders, and certainly most incommodious to the bearer.

All the women in the house, including maids, had to wear corsets at all times. Any lady wishing to be free of one had to remain in her chamber. Corsets were largely used to keep the line of the stomach flat so that the dresses could fall freely from the high waist to the floor without the disfiguring bump of the belly. There were many different sorts of corset, including the 'improved long stay, pregnant stay, divorces etc. etc.'. The long stay emphasised the bosom, the pregnant stay attempted to disguise the condition, while the 'divorce' separated the bosoms and pushed them up and out.

Rosalind Ebbutt, costume designer for the Regency House Party, Bafta winner and veteran of many famous costume dramas such as *Vanity Fair*, *Oliver Twist* and *Tom Jones*, explains, 'Most women wore some form of corset during this period and they gradually became more and more constricting until we end up with the full Victorian corset which caused so much damage to women's bodies.' Ros used paintings, drawings, fashion plates, original costumes in museums and her extensive library of fashion manuals to design the costumes for the series. She visited the house to make sure the costumes would suit the interiors and the status of the place and to devise suitable liveries for the footmen and dresses for the maids. Many of the costumes were direct copies of originals or made from fashion plates. 'I particularly love the military-style coat I made for the countess from a Regency drawing. She has this design for her riding habit and it looks wonderful. The military references were all the rage in the early Regency while we were at war and men's

RECIPE FOR
ANTI-FRECKLE LOTION
UNCTION OF MAINTENON
The use of this is to remove freckles.
Wash the face at night with elderflower water, and then anoint it with the unction.
In the morning, cleanse your skin of its oily adhesion, by washing it copiously in rose water.
FOR THE UNCTION:
Take of Venice soap an ounce, dissolve it in oil of bitter almonds and deliquated oil of tartar, each a quarter of an ounce.
Let the mixture be placed in the sun till it acquires the consistence of ointment.
Add three drops of the oil of rhodium, and keep it for use.

military dress was so gorgeous – this was long before camouflage was invented.' The only difficulty was in finding shoes to fit the girls, who were much bigger in all dimensions than their Regency sisters. Regency shoes were similar to modern-day ballet shoes: made of very soft leather or silk, with a thin leather sole, lined with kid, completely flat or with a very low heel, and tied around the ankle with thin ribbons. Rich women would often take two or three pairs to a ball and discard them if they became slightly soiled, just as the men would their kid gloves. On the rare occasions that wealthy Regency ladies ventured out in the rain, leather ankle boots would have been worn. Regency footwear was so delicate that modern women would find it uncomfortably unsupportive. Ros equipped the house-party guests with ballet-style pumps and slip-on ankle boots for outdoors.

According to their status, the women were provided with formal evening or ball wear, regular evening wear, day dresses of various sorts ranging from the formal to simple cotton 'wraparounds', coats, pelisses, short jackets, bonnets, turbans, caps for the chaperones to wear indoors, shawls, fans, reticules (for carrying small items), parasols, gloves and underwear. The underwear alone consisted of a loose linen 'chemise' that was put next to the skin, over which was fastened the corset, over which went a petticoat, on top of which was finally placed the dress. The only garment that was slightly altered to suit modern women were the knickers. 'Western women did not wear knickers because skirts were long – there was no need for them,' explained Ros. 'Only in the Regency, with the fashion for figure-hugging and almost transparent dresses, did the need for something like knickers come in. At the time, in direct contrast to today, knickers were seen as very racy. They were associated with Parisian dancers and actresses and no polite Regency lady would wear them. In Paris, with the Empire fashion for sheer dresses, women had a sort of body-stocking made out of peach silk which would go under the dresses and look as if the wearer was naked underneath. Peach knitted silk leggings, cut to any length, were also worn. In the house we did give all the ladies these fitted knickers as modern women are used to wearing underwear. They also have loose cotton drawers, which were far more usual among Regency women, which simply had a waistband but had no gusset, so did not need to be removed when visiting the chamber pot.'

As well as acquiring the necessary accomplishments, young women were

REGENCY WOMEN COULD SPEND ENTIRE AFTERNOONS, EVEN WHOLE DAYS,
IN PREPARATION FOR THEIR APPEARANCE AT DINNER

expected to devote much of their time to 'beautification'. The women at Kentchurch were all keen to do this, perhaps even more so because of their discomfort at wearing pretty, 'puffy' dresses, but it proved a challenge without the products and plumbing they were used to. Hair-washing *à la* Regency required a certain amount of ingenuity. In the end, the women realised that it had to be a communal event – one washed her hair, the other poured over the water for rinsing. Miss Conick was particularly delighted with the feel and smell of her hair after using a 'Wash for the Hair: This is a cleanser and brightener for the head and the hair and should be applied in the morning. Beat the whites of six eggs into a froth, and with that anoint the head close to the roots of the hair. Leave it to dry on; then wash the head and hair thoroughly with a mixture of rum and rose-water in equal quantities'.

For cleaning teeth there were commercially produced powders, bright pink in colour, and brushes or rags with which to rub the powder on to the teeth. Numerous products could also be bought for whitening teeth. Home remedies sufficed for the most common medical complaint of the Regency – toothache – which, if ineffective, was followed by a visit to the dentist, where the tooth was extracted or hand-drilled and filled with molten lead, tin or gold. By 1800 Wedgwood was supplying paste for making china teeth, but it is unlikely that Regency mouths were a thing of great beauty.

The complexion was among the chief marks of a person's beauty in this pre-foundation era. A clear, pale complexion was much prized, and the Georgian use of white lead-based paint and heavy rouge and lipstick was frowned upon. Our Lady of Distinction writes: 'It is complexion that lends animation to the picture; it is complexion that gives spirit to the human countenance. Even the language of the eyes loses half its eloquence, if they speak from the obscurity of an inexpressive skin.'

During the Regency, the famous Gowland's Lotion was the panacea for blemished skin. As Sir Walter Elliot effused in *Persuasion* on seeing the improved looks of his daughter (actually brought

CRÈME DE L'ENCLOS
This is an excellent wash, to be used night and morning for the removal of tan.
Take half a pint of milk, with the juice of a lemon, and a spoonful of white brandy, boil the whole, and skim it clear from all scum.
When cool, it is ready for use.

about by love, the other great complexion improver), 'He thought her less thin in her person, in her cheeks; her skin, her complexion, greatly improved – clearer, fresher. Had she been using anything in particular? "No, nothing." "Merely Gowland," he supposed. "No, nothing at all." "Ha! He was surprised at that," and added, "Certainly you cannot do better than continue as you are or I should recommend Gowland, the constant use of Gowland, during the spring months."'

REGENCY BEAUTY ESSENTIALS: SOAP, TOOTHPOWDER AND BRUSH

There was no Gowland's Lotion at Kentchurch, however. 'I actually bribed a maid for a small bottle of foundation but she said she had never heard of such a preparation and had no idea where to acquire it!' said Mrs Hammond.

'We're left with natural beauty, of which I'm not a fan, quite frankly,' quipped Miss Francesca. 'A woman in my lowly situation needs to grab a man but you've got to be pretty fit to do it without make-up. It's very annoying because you spend hours getting into your dress and doing your hair and you still look pretty gross! The deodorant thing doesn't affect me, though. Half a lemon seems to be working.'

'I'm feeling really quite unattractive,' said Miss Braund. 'If I was at home I would be able to wash my hair, blow-dry it and put my make-up on and make myself feel better.'

At least Miss Braund did not have to worry about freckles, which were considered hugely unattractive. Home recipes abounded for their reduction – or a liberal splashing of the ubiquitous Gowland did the trick. Miss Conick, being so 'blemished', was advised to try an anti-freckle remedy by Captain Glover. 'I told him that I certainly would not! I love my freckles and if he doesn't that's his problem.' If all else failed, the unfortunately freckled maiden should cover herself from the neck down and not expose her imperfections to others.

The Regent himself had an afflicted complexion, though his complaint was not freckles but floridity. To cure this complaint he regularly applied leeches (to reduce the 'inflammation') and then dusted his face liberally with white powder. He must have made a pretty sight after a few turns of a quadrille. Fortunately for the house-guests, none of them suffered from floridity except when under the influence of drink or exercise, and so leeches were not called for at this point.

Although the fair Regency maiden was best advised to keep herself above cosmetics, a little rouge was allowable for older ladies or those a little pale. *The Mirror of the Graces* is strict on this point: 'A little vegetable rouge tingeing the cheek of a delicate woman who, from ill-health or an anxious mind, loses her roses, may be excusable, *however* a violently rouged woman is one of the most disgusting objects to the eye which transforms the elegant lady of fashion into a vulgar harridan.' As for any other make-up, the guide is quite definite: 'Nothing but selfish vanity could prevail upon a woman to attempt the clumsy deceptions of Nature. These only excite in the beholder a contempt for the bad taste and wilful blindness which could ever deem them passable for a moment. There is a lovely harmony in nature's tints which is seldom attained by our attempts at chromatics.'

Ingenious attempts at 'chromatics' were, however, attempted by the ladies of Kentchurch. Those of their Regency forebears not blessed with a perfect complexion would have distracted attention from their faults by using candle soot to emphasise eyebrows and lashes. Francesca was soon wandering around with what looked like a couple of shiners, so enthusiastically had she applied the 'soot' eyeliner. The ladies also made liberal use of the vegetable rouge on their cheeks, lips and cleavages, and various experiments at Regency-style 'foundation' were soon under way. 'I use lots and lots of face powder for my skin and my watercolour paints double up as mascara and eyeliner for myself and Miss Braund,' Mrs Hammond divulged. The results were surprisingly effective. 'I have been cruelly robbed of all the things I depend on,' said Miss Hopkins, who nevertheless had an interesting view of the benefits of a beauty-aids cold turkey. 'But it is actually quite nice to learn to love yourself in a raw state. Putting on make-up is like putting on a mask. I never walk out of the door without it in my modern life and I hadn't realised how dependent I am on it. The men here have to like you as you are, and it's liberating.'

While the female house-party guests were trying to come to terms with the restrictions imposed on their activities and bodies, one particular reality of life at the beginning of the nineteenth century was a source of consternation for all the guests. On the first day Rosemary Enright cried, 'A most beautiful house but oh dear, oh dear, the sanitation arrangements are of the most primitive!' Later she observed that

> During the first few weeks at the house we were all obsessed with the 'chamber pot experience'. All we seemed to talk about was whether we had been able to 'go' or not. Talking about poo is hardly the stuff of high romance. As my charge and I were sharing both pot and room, we developed a sort of code. 'I need to use the room now' meant that the other person should stay away for a while, quite a long while usually, after this new diet of meat that we consume here. We can transform ourselves into
>
> Regency ladies and gentlemen but we can't transform our digestions.

Miss Conick was equally appalled. 'I'm still trying to work out how to deal with no running water and a chamber pot. What would happen if you didn't eat or drink for nine weeks? Would you die? I might try because I'm not sure me and chamber pots mix.'

While Regency sanitary provisions were roundly condemned by the houseguests, the bathing facilities were considered little better. For most people during the Regency, personal cleanliness was limited to a daily washing of the hands and face and a bath every few weeks, or even months. This was an improvement on the early eighteenth century, when immersing oneself fully in water was considered extremely dangerous to one's health. Perfume was used to mask offensive odours and this continued, though to a lesser degree, into the Regency – the Regent's perfume bill was £263 in 1822 and double that six years later. Lighter perfumes were

THE 'POT' SO FEARED BY ALL THE GUESTS, SOURCE OF MUCH EMBARRASSMENT AND HILARITY

coming into vogue at the turn of the century, such as 'sweet waters' scented with lavender, rose, honey or orange blossom, as personal hygiene improved and the stench to be covered was less intense. The most influential promoters of personal hygiene were the dandies of the day, Beau Brummell in particular. He was a keen advocate of the daily bath and in fact took three or four himself most days. He detested the use of perfume and recommended instead that linen be laundered daily on Hampstead Heath. Some French followers of fashion took his word so much to heart that they sent their laundry to England. By the Regency, rather than being a sure method of hastening one's end, immersing oneself in water (i.e. taking a proper bath) was being promoted as an aid to health and beauty, even for ladies. As *The Mirror of the Graces* advises: 'The frequent use of tepid baths is salutary to health, and to beauty. By such ablution, the whole surface of the body is preserved in its original brightness, many threatening disorders are put to rout. The generality of English ladies seem ignorant of the use of any bath larger than a wash-hand basin. I strongly recommend to every lady to make a bath as indispensable an article in her house as a looking glass.'

For anyone used to power showers and plumbed-in baths, a small china bowl, minuscule natural sponge and round ball of lavender or carbolic soap seemed totally inadequate after a day imprisoned in corsets, undershirts, petticoats, stockings and full-length dresses (with a camisette to cover the chest and neck for the older ladies) or full walking dress for the gentlemen (including waistcoat, coat, boots, cravat and hat) in baking-hot weather. (The summer of 2003, of course, was one of the hottest we have ever known.) How was cleanliness to be achieved with a jug of cold water?

A bathroom did in fact exist in the house, but none of the guests had discovered it. This room was one of the designer's many triumphs. 'There was already a bath and basin in this small room but they were Edwardian. I couldn't rip them out so I boxed in the bath and made a platform on which I placed the Regency tin bath. Steps were built up to the level of the bath and the whole was decorated in a Roman style. The window in the ceiling was swagged with pale muslin and the walls painted a deep red with a classical relief.' Eventually the guests' clamourings led the footmen to reveal the bathroom to them and a bath rota was drawn up. Two baths a day were allowed, and these were allocated among the fourteen guests, making an

average of one bath a week each – 'whether they needed it or not', as Lady Devonport commented drily. The countess was first, followed by the chaperones, then Miss Hopkins, Miss Braund and Miss Conick. 'It was rather strange bathing under my chemise,' noted Miss Hopkins, 'but to submerse yourself in hot water after a week of sponge-washing was just bliss.' Having to wait her turn, Miss Braund wailed in frustration, 'Forget the status thing! Give us all a bath!' Miss Francesca was only allowed to bathe in the water left by others. 'Oh God!' she moaned when she saw the milky water that had been left for her by Mrs Hammond. 'Here goes. I need a bath, even if it is in someone else's water.'

The abrupt change from their hectic and well-travelled modern lives drove many of the female house-guests to desperation in the first few weeks. They were both frustrated by the limits imposed on their movements and envious of the freedom allowed to the men. While the men were out hawking, shooting pistols and being trained in an array of physical exercises, the chaperones were discussing whether their charges could leave the house at all without them and whether both a bonnet *and* a parasol were necessary when outdoors. Mrs Rogers shouted at Miss Conick for being outside alone and Miss Hopkins was ticked off despite being only twenty yards from Lady Devonport. Only the lady's companion, Miss Francesca, seemed to have plenty to do. She was sent on errands by Mrs Rogers and her guardian, Mr Gorell Barnes, some of which involved long walks delivering messages and invitations around the estate. She could go alone or accompanied by a footman if she had much to carry. 'At first I was worried about being the lowest of the low but now I am pleased. Firstly it means that I don't have any privileges so I don't have to feel guilty – which I think the countess feels sometimes – and also it means I have the freedom to go where I like, unchaperoned.'

The other younger ladies, however, were beginning to feel that certain chaperones wanted to control their charges too much. Miss Braund in particular was so desperate to get some exercise and to escape her chaperone that she resorted to running around the garden in the dark, dodging the night-watchmen. She had been roller-blading around Hyde Park in shorts with her friends only a few days before, but was now instructed to stay by her chaperone's side at all times. That these sorts of restrictions were commonplace in the Regency is shown in numerous examples of literature of the period; that it was unacceptable to a liberated, twenty-first-century, scuba-diving, roller-blading, working girl was equally obvious from Miss Braund's dejected air. 'I wanted to do what was right for the project. I knew that chaperones were powerful and that Mrs Hammond in particular was powerful over me because she had money and I had none. But I liked the girls and wanted to be allowed to be with them. The other chaperones let their charges congregate together, but Mrs Hammond really wanted to play the game to the letter so I had to remain by her side in splendid isolation. It was *so* difficult.'

The unfortunate Miss Braund also had to put up with poor sleep. The short-
ness of her bed and the lumpiness of the mattress, coupled with a chronic back
problem, rendered a good night's rest almost impossible. The problem came to Mr
Gorell Barnes's attention and he immediately called a footman to order a new bed
for Miss Braund. No guest of his was to suffer pain caused by the furnishings. Miss
Braund blushed when she spoke of this kindness and it seemed that her earlier
assessment of the uselessness of all the men was being gently modified. Touched
though she was by the host's kindness, it was another of the men who was in the
process of stealing her heart.

The beauties of nature are occasionally dimmed by the etiquette controlling women's behaviour and dress

CHAPTER FIVE

ET IN ARCADIA EGO
THE PICTURESQUE REGENCY

WHILE THE WOMEN learned to curb their modern expectations and content themselves with long and languorous days with little to do, the men were propelled into Regency life at a furious pace. They spent their first days acquiring some of the skills and attainments that were considered vital to increase one's attractiveness to the opposite sex. A sensitivity towards nature, a good knowledge of poetry, art,

music and literature, plus well-reasoned discourse and lively conversational skills, were all prerequisites of being a Regency gentleman. He should display his wealth conspicuously yet elegantly, provide lavish entertainments for his guests and pay zealous attention to the latest fashions in dress. That was the 'gentle' part. The 'man' part involved dexterity with a weapon, equestrian skills, mastery of 'the ribbons' (a carriage), elegant and masterful deportment and skill on the dance floor. Would any of the gentlemen master the qualities of a true gentleman, as enumerated by Jane Austen in *Persuasion*?

THE HOST AND HIS GUESTS ENJOYING THEIR
FREEDOM TO THE FULL

Everything united in him; good understanding, correct opinions, knowledge of the world, and a warm heart. He had strong feelings of family-attachment and family-honour, without pride or weakness; he lived with the liberality of a man of fortune, without display; he judged for himself in every thing essential, without defying public opinion in any point of worldly decorum. He was steady, observant, moderate, candid; never run away with by spirits or by selfishness, which fancied itself strong feeling; and yet, with a sensibility to what was amiable and lovely, and a value for all the felicities of domestic life . . .

Of course, a true Regency gentleman would have started absorbing and learning these skills from childhood. If he came from a wealthy family, he would have received a grounding in Greek and Latin from a private tutor before going on to Eton, Harrow, Winchester or some other eminent institution, or otherwise continuing his education at home. It was only in the early nineteenth century that practical subjects such as English, Writing and Arithmetic joined Classics, French and Geography on the curriculum. For an extra fee, dancing, military exercises, 'wine daily, by desire', 'pure milk', 'Windsor soap' and 'Chaplain' could also be included. During the holidays, boys would hunt, shoot and fish – sports developed as part of a country squire's traditional attachment to his land and to nature. Cricket was also popular, played by men and watched by ladies.

By the time a young man went to university he would already be an excellent horseman, well versed in 'military exercises', fond of his hounds and the countryside in all seasons. He would speak French, dance well and write a good letter, possibly in Greek.

While at Oxford or Cambridge (the only two universities in England at the time), a gentleman would continue his study of the classics. To be educated was to be genteel. Some students cared less for Virgil than for their horses, carriages, clothes and drink, but for all gentlemen the cultivation of an aristocratic *manner* was as important as the cultivation of taste and intellect. The reality for the aristocracy at this time was that many newly prosperous merchants in Britain were buying vast tracts of land and building houses as grand as those of established aristocratic families. It became increasingly difficult to distinguish a 'genuine' aristocrat from a *nouveau* impostor and therefore an elegant (or fashionably inelegant) manner was a sign of true gentility. Judging by the performance of the men during the first dinner at the Regency House Party, they had much to learn before they could aspire to 'gentleman' status, aristocratic or *nouveau*.

OXFORD UNDERGRADUATES BY THOMAS ROWLANDSON

*THE LORD OF THE MANOR GOING OUT TO A DINNER PARTY AT 5 O'CLOCK WITH
A TREMENDOUS STILE BEFORE THEM.* DIANA SPERLING

The first and most crucial attribute to acquire was the ability to handle a
horse. It was inconceivable that any Regency gentleman (or -woman) would be
unable to ride unless infirm. If you could not ride, you would have been a virtual
prisoner in your house. As the charming watercolour of Diana Sperling shows,
walking to a neighbour's house for dinner meant carrying shoes in a special bag,
taking a lantern for the return journey and risking losing footwear in the mud.
Relying on a carriage for transport, however, required significant wealth. They
were expensive to buy and maintain, needing as they did stabling for the horses and
liveries for the coachman and grooms. Even renting a carriage and pair (two horses)
with a coachman cost £200–300 a year (£10,000–20,000 today). The two-wheeled
carriages with one horse (the Ferraris of their day) were called 'bankrupt carts' by
the Chief Justice 'because they were, and are, frequently driven by those who could
neither afford the Money to support them, nor the Time spent in using them, the
want of which, in their Business, brought them to Bankruptcy'. Stabling your own
horse, particularly in a city, was harder than finding a parking space today. Just
feeding a horse cost £30 a year – more than feeding the groom, in fact – while the
coachman's liveries cost more than his annual salary. On a practical level, coaches

also took some time to prepare and had to be ordered several hours before they were needed. They were therefore more useful for displaying one's wealth than for surveying one's estate. They were necessary on long journeys, of course, or when carrying large loads, but otherwise riding a horse or mule was much the quickest and cheapest option.

Kentchurch Court enjoyed the services of a master-at-arms, whose job it was to teach the men to ride, wield sabres, fence, and shoot pistols and rifles. 'Only the host had ever ridden before and three of them had never even sat on a horse,' said master-at-arms Hamish Macleod. 'However, our gentlemen were determined to look the part, so what they may have lacked in skill they made up for in enthusiasm.'

The grooms were on hand to take them out whenever they liked, but going riding was not simply a case of wandering into the stable and leaping on to a horse. The correct etiquette was to order a horse through a footman, who then informed a groom to tack up the animal. The footman would then help his master to dress (even in hot weather, full riding dress, gloves and hat were required) and then bring him ale and water before he rode and even during riding exercises if he was near the house. Mark Foxsmith said of the experience: 'I thoroughly enjoyed going horse-riding although I've only had a donkey ride on a beach before. What struck me most was how knackering it must be to cover a long distance on a horse. I wouldn't fancy spending twelve hours on a horse – I suppose you got used to it but it would still be tiring. And according to my pocketbook I've tied my cravat completely wrong for riding.'

The 'military exercises' that upper-class Regency boys learned as a matter of course at school, particularly

Mr Everett finds his Regency clothes restrictive, but a gentleman must never be seen in his shirt-sleeves by a lady

LIGHT RELIEF FROM AN ARDUOUS TRAINING REGIME

the art of wielding a sabre, also had to be taught to the men in the house. 'Sabre' is the term for any flat-bladed sword, as opposed to an épée, a fencing weapon, which has a triangular blade. During the Regency, all military personnel carried a sabre as a matter of course – there were forty thousand of Napoleon's troops massed across the Channel for much of the period and the threat of invasion was a daily worry. Britain had been at war on and off since 1775 and so great emphasis was placed on military skills. Sabre fighting became a popular form of exercise and in the army it would have been taught like a PE lesson, with an instructor.

Instruction for our guests began with learning the basic moves – 'cuts' (attacking) and 'parries' (defensive) – and their accompanying footwork, the 'lunge', the 'retreat' and the 'attack'. These moves could then be combined into endless, choreographed sequences. Eventually the men would need to combine riding with sabre-wielding, since to serve in the British Army a man had to be able to attack with his sword while charging into battle on horseback. The men decided to work towards giving a display of their horsemanship and handiness with a sword to the ladies – nothing could be more appealing, they thought. However, much work would be needed if they were to appear 'dashing' rather than dreadful.

Violence was widespread during the Regency, at home as on the battlefield, and all gentlemen (non-military as well as military) were armed, since highwaymen and street robbers were rife. At the beginning of the nineteenth century thieves and robbers, bandits, highwaymen, 'wreckers' (coastal dwellers who lured ships on to rocks, then plundered the wreckage), pickpockets, con-men and cut-throats roamed the lanes, roads, heathlands, woodlands, coastal paths and city streets virtually unchecked. A man took a serious risk if he walked alone at night. The Prince of Wales (before he became Regent) and his brother the Duke of York were attacked and robbed while walking near Berkeley Square one night; soon afterwards, two young ladies returning from the opera in their own carriage were held up and robbed by a single footpad in St James's Square. There was no police force during the Regency: the Metropolitan Police Act was passed in 1829 and it was even later before the rest of the country was required to maintain a regular constabulary. A Regency gentleman was expected to defend himself, his family and his property against any threat from without. He was also expected to defend his 'honour' in response to any insult or innuendo directed against him personally or any threat to his pursuit of romance. Although illegal, duelling was common. The playwright Sheridan fought two duels with the same man over the same girl. He was nearly killed but survived to marry her. The dandy Alvanley tipped his jarvey (hackney-cab driver) a whole sovereign after he drove him to a duel. When the driver exclaimed at being tipped so much just for going to Wimbledon the wit replied, 'No, my good man. I give it to you for bringing me back.' The rule of honour was so rigid that the smallest infringements could lead to a duel. 'If you looked at a man it was enough; for without having given the slightest offence, cards

REGENCY GENTLEMEN WOULD HAVE BEEN FAMILIAR WITH HUNTING IN ALL ITS GUISES

were exchanged and the odds were that you stood a good chance of being shot, or run through the body, or maimed for life,' wailed Gronow, a perceptive Regency observer.

Alongside learning the skills of the Regency gentleman, the men needed to adopt his attitudes too. For this, a 'professor' was called upon. Peter Radford, Professor of Sport Sciences at Brunel University, won two medals in the Olympic Games of 1960, and over the years he has researched and written exhaustively about the world of Regency sportsmen. His presence proved hugely inspiring for the men.

The Regency was a time of huge tensions. For the first half of it the country existed under threat of invasion by Napoleon's forces. For the second, social unrest meant that the country was virtually at war with itself. Men needed to be stable, to hold it all together. The women couldn't take on that role as the men owned everything and made all the decisions, which seems very peculiar to us now, of course. I had to get our gentlemen thinking as a Regency gentleman would have done, and that began with walking. Regency gentlemen walked knowing that they owned the land they were walking upon. They would have their heads in the air, firm shoulders and a 'manly tread' of about five miles an hour. There was to be nothing timid or apologetic in their manner. On a Regency street the lower orders would make way for a gentleman to pass. They really did hold their heads so high they looked down their noses – this was not a mark of snobbery, it was just how the world was.

It was time to forget about slouching around in jeans and start being 'manly'.

Many of the men at Kentchurch, and in particular Captain Glover, were especially taken with the notion of the 'third eye', introduced by the professor. 'The "third eye" is about the world looking at you and you constantly being aware of, and responsible for, your actions,' explained the Captain: 'behaving and carrying yourself as a gentleman all the time, no matter what company you're in and even when you're on your own. The lifestyle of a Regency gentleman has got much more emotional range, I've found, so you can be picking flowers and making little love tokens one minute but fighting with a sabre and trying to knock melons off posts the next.'

Professor Radford's teaching influenced other areas of the men's self-awareness as well. 'Everything I'm learning seems to fall into place, everything's relevant to my modern life,' said Captain Glover. 'I've been shown that holding a sword correctly is all about having trust. If you hold it too tightly – and some of us might have been holding on too tightly to things in 2003 – something's going to break. If you hold it too loosely, it disappears. You have to hold it just right. I think I'm becoming wiser because of the experience.'

After teaching the men how to carry themselves, the professor put them through rigorous exercises – throwing logs, lifting dumb-bells, boxing and sparring, and (last but not least) shovelling muck. To live as a Regency gentleman and indulge the vigorous lifestyle that it entailed, one needed to be extremely fit: hard-playing, hard-drinking and always being on call to risk one's life in defence of honour, property and country. There was nothing soft or effeminate about Regency man, despite his attention to dress and knowledge of poetry.

Self-styled sporting 'professors' (whose titles did not relate to any academic institution) were celebrities during the Regency. The most famous of them was Gentleman Jackson, a prize-fighter who went on to start a 'Boxing Academy' in Bond Street to which the *haut ton* went for physical training. Jackson was said to

RECEIVING TUITION IN THE ART OF BOXING AT GENTLEMAN JACKSON'S ROOMS
IN BOND STREET BY GEORGE CRUIKSHANK

have been 'the finest-formed man in Europe' at just under six foot and fourteen stone. He could write his name on a wall with an 84lb weight suspended from his little finger. One eye-witness wrote his impressions of Jackson as he walked down Holborn Hill: 'It was impossible to look on his fine ample chest, his noble shoulders, his waist, his large but not too large hips . . . his limbs, his balustrade calf and beautifully turned but not over delicate ankle, his firm foot, and peculiarly small hand, without thinking that nature had sent him on earth as a model. On he went at a good five and a half miles an hour, the envy of all men, and the admiration of all women.'

Jackson's manners were impeccable and he possessed the dignity and gentility that made his nickname stick. Although the son of a builder, he was granted the status of a 'gentleman' by his pupils, who were his social superiors but allowed him to tell them what to do. The rooms where he trained men were so popular it was said that more than a third of the nobility frequented them, including the Prince of Wales. They were the focus of all debate on fighting, cricket, pedestrianism, horse-racing and wagering and remained so until his retirement in 1824. Men could mingle and bond there with fewer class constraints than in other public places, or even at home. He would put his pupils through severe physical ordeals – not only exercises but also starvation diets, purges and bleeding. To be attractive and alluring to women, it was an advantage to have a physique similar to Gentleman Jackson's and, however handsome the men at the Regency House Party might be, they were none of them Chippendales.

Sports, gambling and trials of strength and stamina were woven into daily life at every level of society. One of the great sports of the day was 'pedestrianism', or walking wagers. These were competitions between two or more individuals or challenges accepted by one man, for example Captain Barclay's famous (and successful) feat of walking a thousand miles in a thousand hours for a thousand guineas.

The professor explained to the men the extraordinary level of wagering and betting in a Regency gentleman's world. The Earl of March, for example, set up a wager that he could get a letter to go fifty miles in one hour. As the fastest horse could travel at around only thirty miles an hour over a short distance, this feat seemed impossible and an easy wager to win. Articles of agreement were written up; the earl then put the letter in a cricket ball and persuaded his local cricket team to throw it in a circle between themselves. It was an incredible feat of skill, for the ball could not be dropped if it was to travel exactly fifty miles in one hour. They achieved their goal and the earl was richer by ten thousand guineas. Captain Barclay achieved his pedestrian wager by creating a well-lit, protected walking track with a good surface, security guards and a team of supporters next to a small house in which he slept for brief periods. Every hour he would complete a circuit of the ring. He overcame extreme mental and physical fatigue and then went off to sea to fight a naval battle just one week later.

To give the men a taste of this test of physical endurance so beloved of Regency gentlemen, the professor had them soak their feet in vinegar and dry them seven times to harden the skin. He marched and ran them around the deer park until they were nearly dropping. He then set them the challenge of working out a pedestrian wager for a week's time that the entire household could place bets on. His parting shot was to give some of the men emetics and sweating treatments, which put them out of action for twenty-four hours. 'I was so sick. I had no idea I would feel that bad. I got dressed to go down for dinner but I just collapsed on my bed and couldn't move till the following afternoon,' remembered Mr Everett.

While the men were throwing themselves zealously into becoming Regency bucks, 192 years earlier the Prince of Wales was acclimatising himself rather gingerly to his new role as regent. His first task was to appoint a prime minister. It is doubtful that the prince had any genuine political convictions of his own; his life of cards, dancing, actresses and Madeira was hardly fertile ground for the development of political acumen. It was quite typical that the heir to the throne, on reaching 'maturity', should side with whichever political party stood in opposition to the incumbent king (or queen). The Prince of Wales should not be a blurred replica of his father or mother but should lay claim to his own political opinions. King George's chosen ministers were Tories, so his son backed the Whigs while he was Prince of Wales. The prince held frequent parties for them at Carlton House after he came of age in 1783. Two prominent Whigs in particular became his friends, Charles James Fox and Richard Brinsley Sheridan. Sheridan, although rising magnificently to any occasion he deemed worthy of the effort, was otherwise lazy, extravagant and dissolute. Fox, while charming and a genuine statesman, would

often sit night after night at the gaming tables, throwing away his money and sinking disastrously into debt. He lived openly with a mistress and both he and Sheridan were very heavy drinkers. With such friends as these, it is hardly surprising that the prince saw little reason to moderate his own wild behaviour and follow the example of his frugal father. However, by the time he had to form a government himself, the two great leaders of the previous decades, William Pitt for the Tories and Fox for the Whigs, had both died. Without Fox the Whigs were divided among themselves, and after much dithering the prince asked the Tories to form his first government, under Prime Minister Spencer Perceval. The Whigs, who had been the prince's staunch supporters while he was in the political wilderness, were furious at this betrayal. However, the prince deemed 'their liberal and anti-monarchical sentiments unfavourable to good government'. He also worried that they would sue for peace with France just as British forces were making headway. The Regent was not one to reject a heroic role, provided it required no personal sacrifice on his part.

The Regent's appointment of a Tory government was headline news in *The Times*, a mocked-up newspaper delivered weekly to the house which contained genuine articles from the paper of the time as well as 'planted' items about Kentchurch Court. It was not politics, however, that caught the house-guests' eyes, but two intriguing adverts. The first was from 'Thomas Thirkell of Bristol, A Patented and Improv'd Water-Closet Maker, New invented Hydraulic Pumps, Engines Etc.' available for 'ready money'. The guests pounced upon this small box at the bottom of the front page as if their lives depended upon it. 'I decided that, as I was the richest in the house, I would buy a flushing loo for us all to use,' said Mr Everett. 'The advert warned that they were quite expensive and required payment with "ready money" and so Mr Gorell Barnes, in order not to be outsmarted by me, said he would buy a second one if they were too much money. I wrote to the manufacturers immediately, requesting one of their new machines.'

The Regency house offered its inhabitants a number of technological advances that made it far more commodious than its Georgian predecessors. Developments in heating, cooking and lighting were accompanied by improvements in sanitation, such as the invention of the 'shower-bath' and the object of so much excitement at Kentchurch, the flushing water closet. The latter were first patented in 1778 by Joseph Bramah and within twenty years he claimed to have sold six thousand. They became common in country houses by the early decades of the 1800s. Water was piped or pumped to the upper floors to service them, although some used rainwater and the force of gravity. As early as 1813 the Earl of

Moira had two bathrooms in his Leicestershire home and at least six water closets on two floors, while his wife could boast to her friends of a bathroom, water closet and gilded wash-hand stands.

For the occupants of Kentchurch, such luxurious sanitation was still a pipe dream. Their new flushing loo was situated at the bottom of the medieval tower and was for the use of both men and women. Beside the loo was a basket of rags, a jug and bowl for hand-washing, and a small linen towel. It would remain to be seen whether a single loo whose flushing system was highly innovative two hundred years earlier could adequately service the needs of fourteen people.

Of equal interest (though less urgency) to our house-guests was the second advert: 'A young man, who wishes to retire from the world and live as a hermit in some convenient spot in England is willing to engage with any nobleman or gentleman who may be desirous of having one. Any letter directed to Z. Helm (post paid), no 6 Coleman Lane, Plymouth, mentioning what gratuity will be given, and all other particulars will be duly attended.'

'We should have a hermit,' declared the master of the estate, who wrote off at once to offer the use of a small hermitage that he had been informed existed at the top of a hill to the east of the house. Hermitages were not unusual on the great estates of Britain and, although their heyday was the eighteenth century, many still existed during the Regency. They varied from being single-roomed rustic huts, often woven out of the roots of upturned trees, to rather grand temples. 'Hermits' were also a varied lot, ranging from genuine ascetics seeking an escape from worldly distractions to joyously worldly 'hangers-on' who earned their keep by looking nobly savage for visitors, behaving bucolically and even joining guests in the big house to furnish them with unusual conversation.

The notion of housing a hermit on one's estate was symptomatic of the changes that occurred in house and garden design over the course of the eighteenth century. As the bourgeoisie expanded and travel improved, public rooms for entertaining guests became increasingly important. A 'circuit' of rooms such as a library, grand dining room, drawing room, billiard, music and garden rooms was considered essential for the enjoyment of one's guests. Similar circuits outside the house soon became popular. One famous example was at Stourhead. Besides the ubiquitous pleasure gardens and deer park, it boasted a re-erected market cross from

Bristol, a Turkish tent, a Temple of Flora, a Chinese bridge, a grotto (one portion of which contained a cold bath), a rustic cottage, a pantheon, a temple of the sun, a Palladian bridge and numerous inscriptions for guests to read and ponder upon. These circuits might also include other picturesque features, such as a ruin, a fallen oak or a hermitage. A ruin was symbolic of man's art overshadowed by the forces of nature, a 'fallen' oak hinted at the passage of time, while a hermitage epitomised the idea of man's return to nature.

The enthusiast for rustic follies could choose what he wanted from useful books of designs such as William Wright's *Grotesque Architecture or Rural Amusement*: 'consisting of plans, elevations and sections for Huts, Retreats, Summer and Winter Hermitages, Terminaries, Chinese, Gothic, Natural grottoes, Cascades, Baths, Mosques, Moresque Pavilions, Grotesque and Rustic Seats, Green houses etc. Many of which may be executed with Flints, Irregular Stones, Rude Branches and Roots of Trees.'

The Lake District visited by an admirer of the picturesque, from The Tour of Dr Syntax

Dedicated followers of the picturesque and the romantic went further afield than the artfully created gardens of country houses and ventured into the countryside itself. With the Continent out of bounds due to the war with France, the appreciation of home-grown landscapes took off. William Wordsworth's *A Guide Through the District of the Lakes*, published in 1810, brought tourists flocking to the area, while Walter Scott's *Lady of the Lake* did the same for the Scottish Highlands. This fashion for 'nature' and romantic scenery was widespread enough to provoke a rather jaundiced reaction among some. The poet Southey wrote, 'A taste for the picturesque has sprung up; and a course of summer travelling is now looked upon to be essential. While one of the flocks of fashion migrates to the sea-coast, another flies off to the mountains of Wales, to the lakes of the nothern provinces, or to Scotland . . . all to study the picturesque, a new science, for which a new language has been formed, and for which the English have discovered a new sense in themselves, which assuredly was not possessed by their fathers.'

Two years later, the famous Regency cartoonist Rowlandson collaborated with William Combe to produce *The Tour of Dr Syntax in Search of the Picturesque*. When Dr Syntax is invited to join a hunt he replies:

> Your sport, my Lord, I cannot take,
> For I must go and hunt a lake;
> And while you chase the flying deer,
> I must fly to Windermere.
> Instead of hallowing to a fox,
> I must catch echoes from the rocks.
> With curious eye and active scent,
> I on the *picturesque* am bent.

To distract the ladies from the confines of their corsets and the claustrophobia of their lives, Mrs Rogers decided it was time for them to get out of the house and enjoy the 'picturesque' at first hand. A picnic was therefore organised. Accompanied by a footman, the women strolled through the little wooded valleys, over a footbridge, across a stream and through the long grass and wild flowers of a meadow until they reached a little copse, where they came upon a rustic cottage. Strewn across the grass were rose petals and hanging in the trees were streamers and ribbons of pink and white.

'I'd never been on a picnic before in my life. Never. And here I was walking on rose petals with a breeze blowing the ribbons – it was one of the most beautiful settings I had ever seen,' breathed Miss Hopkins. The cottage had two floors and a surprise was waiting for them upstairs: two shepherdess costumes, complete with crooks, were laid out for their amusement. Miss Braund and Miss Hopkins, despite claiming to be the least girly girls of the lot, put them on with delighted giggles.

'A BO-PEEP OUTFIT WAS JUST PERFECT FOR THE SCENE,' GIGGLED MISS BRAUND

'I call her "boo-boo" now, and she calls me "lou-lou",' giggled Miss Braund. 'Normally I wouldn't be seen dead in a Bo-Peep outfit but they were just perfect for the scene.'

The footmen and maids laid out a resplendent picnic with cooled champagne, wine and lemonade. The ladies played games, read poems, talked of the men and drank in the rustic beauty and splendour.

'It was the most romantic experience of my life. I can feel myself changing here. I was such a hard-nosed businesswoman and now I am discover-

A GAME OF BATTLEDORE AND SHUTTLECOCK WAS ONE OF THE
FEW WAYS FOR WOMEN TO GET SOME EXERCISE

ing a whole side to myself that I never knew I had – or if I knew it I ignored it. I am becoming more feminine. I am really enjoying the dresses although I wouldn't be seen dead in one before. I love putting my hair up and finding flowers and jewellery to decorate it with. I have never felt so free. And this place is so quiet and the surroundings so beautiful, I think we are all going through huge changes every day,' noted Miss Hopkins.

Throw any group of people together who don't know each other (or even who do) and tensions will arise. Put them in a setting with which they are unfamiliar, give them rules of behaviour which they do not fully understand and set them a competitive goal involving love and seduction, and you have a heady concoction. The house-guests, successful and adventurous in their daily lives, had never taken time out to contemplate who they were rather than what they wanted. For the first time they were forced to abandon the identities they had created for themselves in their twentieth-century lives and survive without the mod cons and luxuries to which they had become accustomed. Suddenly they were truly alone with themselves and it was no surprise that for many of them this was a period of self-reflection, self-doubt and sometimes tears. Miss Hopkins, while delighted at being a 'girl' one moment, was outraged by the way she was patronised at another; her chaperone, Lady Devonport, was distressed by her charge's mood swings; Mrs Rogers felt that the guests did not understand the difficulty of her position; Mrs Hammond felt 'so old and ugly' she claimed to be 'losing the will to live'; Miss Braund felt belittled and constricted by her status as a 'gentlewoman' of no fortune; Mrs Enright was taxed with listening to the complaints of others; and the countess, while maintaining a cool exterior, was worried about seeming to enjoy her privileges too much. Miss Francesca enjoyed the freedom of being lady's companion but was shocked and nervous at being so inconsequential.

The men were not immune to these changes either. Mr Gorell Barnes was frustrated by his hostess and found it difficult to enjoy the house as he wished while she kept rigid command of the women and determined to make everyone conscious of their place in the social hierarchy (as any Regency hostess would have been expected to do). Mr Everett was obsessed with his coldsore and felt at times inadequate in the company of these beautiful and sophisticated women. Captain Robinson was on the verge of leaving the house because he felt too much of a 'rough diamond' and was more interested in being friends with the footmen than with the other guests. 'It's just crazy here,' he exclaimed. 'I mean, after just a few days everyone's walking round as if they can't see the footmen any more. They've just got used to being served by these invisible people. It's mad. I just don't feel like I fit in here at all.' Mr Foxsmith seemed to be revelling in everything, was already entranced by a certain lady and was only really worried about animal rights. And Captain Glover? He alone seemed to the manor born.

Perhaps because they were both near the bottom of their respective hierarchies, Miss Francesca and Captain Robinson were naturally drawn to each other. Since Mrs Rogers did not chaperone her closely, Miss Francesca had plenty of opportunities to converse intimately with the captain. And it was during one of these private trysts that they hatched an audacious and scandalous plan that they would spring upon their unsuspecting fellow guests. With tumultuous effect.

'Engaged? Engaged? How can that be!?' spluttered Mrs Rogers when the host informed her that her charge had accepted a proposal of marriage from Captain Robinson.

'It's great,' said Robinson. 'Francesca is lovely and now that we are engaged she is allowed to go to dinner whenever she wants and doesn't have to do errands all the time and might even get to have a bath in clean water. I got drunk last night and woke up engaged.'

'I'm very nervous,' said Miss Francesca. 'Mr Gorell Barnes is going to write to my father. My poor parents are going to be pretty shocked. He might refuse when he realises it's an engagement of convenience, of course. I just didn't want him to leave and getting engaged seemed a good way of making him stay.' Once it was pointed out to the couple that an engagement made at the house party was as real as any made outside, their doubts as to the wisdom of the move grew, and many hours were devoted to earnest discussion of their situation.

In the mean time, the lessons in 'picturesque' that the ladies were receiving were enhanced by the arrival of the hermit. Zebedee Helm, a successful artist who had spent the past twelve summers living in a tepee in aristocratic gardens across the country, was attempting to make himself comfortable in the hermitage. He had use of a small hut devoid of all furniture except a thin straw pallet for a bed. For cooking he had an outdoor pit with coals, a trivet, a spoon and a few pans. His pet duck, suffering from bad gout in its left leg, sat quacking companionably beside him. Tall, handsome, with a gentle and very amusing way of speaking, Zebedee appeared to be an utterly charming and picturesque hermit. Whether he would prove to be a romantic hermit too, only time would tell. 'I think I represent the total contrast to the strict rules the house-guests are having to live by,' said Zebedee. 'The role of the hermit could have been to make people living such a contrasting life to mine feel even more refined and elegant. But I think it can work the other way too. They're all tied up in their corsets and their fancy boots and frilly bonnets and things and that's not comfortable. I expect they'll be up here mucking around with me a lot,' he prophesied.

'Up here there's hardly any protection from the outside, so the whole atmosphere of the place enters you daily and I expect I'll turn quite green and rolling by the end of this experience because it's quite a green and rolling place.'

The day of the grand wager arrived, when the men would pit themselves against each other in a series of tests before the watchful and appraising eyes of the ladies in the house. Captain Glover and Mr Everett formed the Eclipse team, named after a famous Regency racehorse. The host, Mr Foxsmith and Captain Robinson formed the Goths. The wager was to be in five parts and each team had to win one of the first four parts to compete in the final. From eleven in the morning until seven at night, the men pitted themselves against each other and against

ZEBEDEE HELM AT HIS RUSTIC HERMITAGE, HIGH ABOVE KENTCHURCH COURT

their own physical limits. 'It was incredibly hard. I have never exerted myself like that before,' said Mr Everett.

The first test was to run backwards for quarter of a mile. The second was a Regency version of the sack race: a man from each team was tied in a large sack, right up to the neck, and they raced each other over a forty-four-yard distance, ten times. Once down, it was very difficult to get up and this was a particularly thrilling race. They were allowed to cross and jostle each other and such sack races were often quite violent in the Regency. The third race was to cover a quarter of a mile walking backwards on every fourth step. The competitors had seconds who shouted out, 'One, two, three, back!' to them but the Eclipse team were so cunning they deliberately shouted out confusing commands to fox their rivals. Any mistake resulted in going back ten paces. It was wonderful mayhem and throughout it all the women were laying bets – on who would win, who would fall over the most, who would collapse – for 'chicken stakes' (small sums) or for privileges and forfeits. The latter was a modern variation on a Regency gambling debt. Instead of paying money, a woman who lost a bet would give her victor a privilege – for example, Miss Braund won a riding lesson from the countess.

The fourth race was the '100 Stones' test, famously hard in the Regency and almost beyond the capabilities of our modern young men. A hundred stones were laid out in a line with an empty basket at one end. The competitor had to run to the first stone, put it in the basket, run to the next, and so on, until all the stones had been collected. This meant running for nearly six miles, bending down frequently. Any stones that missed the basket had to be replaced and fetched again. It was a huge physical challenge and a very tense race. The final wager was for one man from each team to cover a quarter of a mile every quarter of an hour for four hours. Any turns missed or late finishing would result in disqualification. Whoever won three of the last five laps won the race and won the day. As it turned out, Captain Glover was unable to complete this challenge as he had hurt his leg, and so it was that Captain Robinson won the day for the Goths. That night at dinner he was toasted as the hero of the hour. It was a bittersweet occasion, since he had already taken the decision to leave the house, his new fiancée and the Regency party the following day.

'I won the sports day for the chaps and that's a good way for me to go,' he said.

'I've made some friends in here that I'll see again but I believe in the spirit of rock and roll – live fast, die young – and I've fitted so much into the ten days I've been here but now I think I've done all I can.'

Although Miss Francesca and her fiancé had been torn asunder, other possible unions were beginning to form. Love tokens and *billets doux* had been left on pillows or delivered by maids and footmen around the house. Passions had been declared, gentle flirtations started, and several diaries were filling up with details of encounters with particular members of the opposite sex. 'I think the romantic game has started to take off,' said Captain Glover. 'We're also beginning to understand what Regency gambling was all about as well as taking up more sporting activities so I think things will become a little bit more competitive from now on.' From her lonely end of the table Miss Francesca made perceptive observations about the Regency relationship game:

I never thought that the status situation, having the same people sitting next to each other every night at dinner, might affect relationships. I thought if a guy looks at a girl and thinks, She's quite lovely, just because he doesn't sit next to her at dinner doesn't mean that nothing will happen. But I was looking round last night and I think people have become very close to the person who has been on their right for the last six nights! This nineteenth-century status stuff really works. I wonder if they're forming attachments simply because they haven't spoken to other people they might really like but haven't got to know. I didn't expect that from twenty-first-century people. Someone like myself or Miss Conick or Miss Braund are just not getting access to the right people.

It now transpired that the couple seen leaving the fireworks display together had been Mr Foxsmith and Lady Devonport. Their secret was out, but they seemed unperturbed by the gossip. Would Lady Devonport's status and popularity save her from being thrown out of the house for such gross flouting of protocol? And was Mr Foxsmith, poor and inconsequential as he was, protected by the status of his *objet d'amour*? Could their passion survive the strictures of Regency protocol and would the other burgeoning relationships in the house soon be conducted as openly as the *coup de foudre* enjoyed by the chaperone and her young admirer?

MISS CONICK IN DRAMATIC MOOD FOR THE HOUSE-GUESTS' GOTHIC REVUE

CHAPTER SIX
A VERY HORRID TALE
THE GOTHIC IMAGINATION
IN REGENCY BRITAIN

Emily turned to look within the dusky curtains, as if she could have seen the countenance of which Dorothee spoke. As her eyes wandered over the pall itself, she fancied she saw it move. Without speaking she caught Dorothee's arm who, surprised by the action and Emily's look of terror, turned her eyes to the bed where she too saw the pall slowly lifted and fall again . . . and in the next moment the apparition of a human countenance rose above it.

Screaming with terror they both fled, and got out of the chamber as fast as their trembling limbs would bear them.

KENTCHURCH COURT IS HOME TO SEVERAL GHOSTS WHO MADE THEIR PRESENCE KNOWN OVER THE SUMMER

IT WAS LATE. Darkness had fallen at Kentchurch Court and Mrs Enright was in bed, peering at her book by the light of a sputtering candle. Miss Conick was not in the room, despite the lateness of the hour, but Mrs Enright was too absorbed in supernatural terrors to worry about her earthly duties. The page-turner in her hands was one of the most popular books of the Regency, *The Mysteries of Udolpho* by Mrs Radcliffe ,'the greatest master in the art of freezing the blood' and the best-known exponent of the 'Gothic romance'. Ann Radcliffe, daughter of a London tradesman, wrote five novels, plenty of romantic verse and a non-fiction account of her travels in Holland, Germany and the Lake District. Her most famous work, *The Mysteries of Udolpho*, was published in 1794 and remained popular for decades. The 'Gothic novel' formed part of the Gothic revival noted in the architecture and decor of Kentchurch. Just as the arched windows and crenellated battlements of the house were designed to evoke the chivalric medieval past and inspire emotion – 'You need passion to appreciate the Gothic,' wrote Walpole – so Radcliffe and her myriad imitators dwelled entirely on the passions. Indeed 'common sense' in general was spurned by Gothic novelists, who left such dull fare to the well-mannered classicism of authors such as Jane Austen.

Romanticism and the Gothic revival challenged the rationality of the Enlightenment, which seemed to some to 'standardise men and beliefs' and suppress individuality. The Romantic movement fought for individual expression rather than universal reason. As the influential thinker Burke wrote in 1757 in his *Philosophical Enquiry into the Origin of Our Ideas of the Sublime and the Beautiful*, it was necessary to go beyond the rational to create great art. Every creative individual's goal should be to seek out the 'immeasurable', in solitude, darkness, death or 'tranquillity shadowed with horror'. Doing so led to 'delight'; delight could lead to the 'sublime'; the sublime led to the transportation of the self to other, higher realms of feeling. This theory allowed for inspiration to come from other-worldly sources – imagination, visions, dreams and so on. Indeed, the first novel described as 'Gothic' was written as the result of a vision. 'I had thought myself in an ancient castle, and that, on the upper banister of a great staircase I saw a gigantic hand in armour,' wrote Horace Walpole of the vision that inspired *The Castle of Otranto*. 'In the evening I sat down to write, without knowing in the least what I intended to say.'

Such aesthetic concerns were doubtless far from Mrs Enright's mind, gripped as she was by a young heroine's flight from the ghost of a murdered countess. Radcliffe's novels lay at the 'blockbuster' end of the Gothic genre,

THE NIGHTMARE BY HENRY FUSELI, OF WHOM BLAKE WROTE: 'THE ONLY MAN THAT E'ER I KNEW / WHO DID NOT MAKE ME ALMOST SPEW.' FUSELI'S ARTISTIC ASPIRATIONS TO THE SUBLIME WERE HIGHLY INFLUENTIAL IN THEIR DAY

JAMES WYATT'S PAINTING OF FONTHILL ABBEY, AN EXTRAORDINARY GOTHIC 'ABBEY' WITH AN
ENORMOUS TOWER, BUILT FOR WILLIAM BECKFORD, AUTHOR OF *VATHEK*, IN 1796–1806

awash with cliff-hanger chapter endings and supernatural phenomena. Although
they contained long passages of moralising, the principal action usually followed
the trials of persecuted heroines imprisoned in wild and isolated castles, often set
against a patchily evoked medieval backdrop. So influential was Radcliffe, both on
readers and her fellow writers, that Jane Austen gently pokes fun at the susceptible
young girls and the 'horrid novels' which gave them so much titillation. The delicious terrors which a reading of *Udolpho* provokes in Catherine Morland in
Northanger Abbey are mocked by another character, Henry Tilney, who cannot
resist the temptation to tease Catherine about the Gothic horrors she so eagerly
anticipated as she made her way to the medieval abbey where his family lived.

'*The Mysteries of Udolpho* are actually rather good,' said Mrs Enright, her
eyes wide in the flickering candlelight of her gloomy bedroom. 'And they are genuinely scary. There is supposed to be a ghost in this house.' At that very moment
a scream pierced the night. Mrs Enright dropped her book in fright and lay as still
as a corpse, unsure what action to take. What could it be? A ghost? A murderer, a

COUNTESS DRACULA SINKS HER TEETH INTO HER VAMPIRIC ROLE FOR
MRS HAMMOND'S HOUSE OF HORROR

rapist? A tortured lover? A gang of local ruffians? A lecherous monk? All these would have been possibilities (indeed, probabilities) in a Gothic novel.

Having heard about the ghost that allegedly haunts the medieval tower of the house, Captain Glover had decided to play a trick on the girls. He had found a mysterious trunk outside his door containing costumes for a monk, a vampire and a ghost, and, since the House Ghost had yet to honour the guests with an appearance, he decided to haunt the women's corridor himself. He showed the costumes he had found to the other men and they hid them in Mr Foxsmith's tent while thinking up other ways to frighten the girls. Captain Glover's aim was to scare the young ladies (clad in their diaphanous nightgowns, of course) out of their chambers one night, whereupon the men would rush to their aid, catch their fainting forms and (if at all possible) calm their palpitating bosoms. It was a good plan, but sadly for Captain Glover it didn't quite work out as intended. Two of the young women had caught sight of the costumes in the tent during an evening stroll, and immediately suspected that a mysterious nocturnal figure might soon be making an appearance. The scream that so shocked Mrs Enright came not from a petrified female, but from Captain Glover himself. He had been pounced upon during his 'haunting' by the lady's companion, Miss Francesca, and the poor man was frightened out of his wits. It took several minutes for him to regain his composure, and his humiliation was compounded by the fact that all this took place under the amused gaze of the young women, who had been lying in wait for him in Miss Hopkins' room. The ruse failed, his 'romantic' aims were thwarted, and all in all the girls were just too clever for him.

The following day, a carriage arrived at Kentchurch bearing a stranger. His card was delivered to Mr Gorell Barnes with a request that he be shown around the court. This sort of nosiness was perfectly acceptable in the Regency, when parties of the well-to-do would make a day out of visiting each other's houses and gardens with a picnic and their sketchpads. The card was that of Mr Kim Newman, well-known author of *Anno Dracula* and *Dracula Cha Cha Cha*, horror-film writer, critic and expert on the Gothic. On his arrival he sat drinking red wine with the host and discussed the 'Gothic imagination' and the close connection (admirably expressed by Captain Glover in his escapade) between horror and sex.

> I think people in the Regency were not very different to us. Their actions had different consequences but their feelings and lustiness were probably the same. Most young girls wanted a nice, handsome young man then as they do now. Judging by the number of men and women indulging in affairs, the desire for sex was no less than it is today. One of our main influences in picturing the Regency is Jane Austen, but I don't think she's typical of the period. She was clearly under-sexed and so are the so-called romances in her books. The Gothic novels are far more illustrative of the desire for excitement and titillation that existed then as now.

Although Radcliffe's novels were fairly subtle in their sexual content, sex and sensuality underscored much of the horror in her books – potential rapes, poisonings, affairs, deaths and murders were all caused by sexual urges. In the most sensational Gothic novel of the era, *The Monk*, these urges and inclinations give way to explicit acts. Written by Matthew Lewis, *The Monk* was an overnight success. And scandal. It was published in 1796 when Lewis was only twenty-one and serving as attaché at the British Embassy at The Hague, and for ever after he was referred to as 'Monk' Lewis. Whereas Ann Radcliffe was credited with chilling the blood, Monk Lewis might have been credited with raising the blood pressure. The central plot of the book details the sexual corruption of an Italian friar by a young novice who was in fact a woman in disguise. With her help, he uses witchcraft to gain the support of the devil in abducting and eventually raping a virtuous young girl he has taken a fancy to. Much of the action takes place in the crypt of the monastery, which is of course filled with decaying bodies. And for good measure the villain then stabs the heroine in the heart and leaves her to die in the arms of the man she loved. The lover makes a swift recovery from his broken heart and goes on to marry a woman who has been rather more careful with her virginity.

> With every moment the friar's passion became more ardent, and Antonia's terror more intense. She struggled to disengage herself from his arms. Her exertions were unsuccessful; and finding that Ambrosio's conduct became still freer, she shrieked for assistance with all her strength. The aspect of the vault, the pale glimmering of the lamp, the surrounding obscurity, the sight of the tomb, and the objects of mortality which met her eyes on either side, were ill calculated to inspire her with those emotions by which the friar was agitated . . . He treated her with the rudeness of an unprincipled barbarian, proceeded from freedom to freedom, and, in the violence of his lustful delirium, wounded and bruised her tender limbs.

The Monk transgressed all the Regency boundaries of literature and taste. Whether the success and credibility Lewis gained justified the offence his work caused was as hotly debated then as similar disputes about the purpose and meaning of modern art today.

The Monk is set abroad, as were the majority of Gothic novels and romances. France or Italy were favoured locations, since their continental settings allowed the characters to indulge in the sort of immoral or violent behaviour that would never have been countenanced at home. In the words of Henry Tilney in *Northanger Abbey*, when he finds Catherine Morland so influenced by the Gothic novels she is reading that she suspects his father of having murdered his mother: 'Dear Miss Morland, consider the dreadful nature of the suspicions you have entertained.

MISS BRAUND SINGING FOR HER SUPPER AND A NEW SILK DRESS

Remember the country and the age in which we live. Remember that we are English.'

This notion that the 'continental character' was different – and decidedly inferior to that of the British – was underlined by a vehement strain of anti-Catholicism. 'Anti-Catholic feelings were very strong in Britain,' said Mr Newman when asked about this, 'but that was just part and parcel of being "anti-foreigner" and particularly anti-French. The average person's attitude to France then was not unlike now, that sort of "ooh la! la!" approach in which we might credit them with being sexier and better dressed than us but also feckless, opportunistic, vulgar, with ridiculous dietary habits and so on. France had been Britain's enemy for the past five hundred years and we were once again at war with them.'

To most British people, who had never been further than their local market town, 'Boney's' conquests in Europe and Africa would have seemed like world domination. He enjoyed supreme power over almost all of western Europe; he had crowned himself Emperor of France and King of Italy and installed members of his family on the thrones of the other kingdoms he conquered. Napoleon's troops threatened the British coastline and battles on the Continent were costing British lives. However, his insatiable ambition was beginning to cloud his powers of judgement and the great Regency hero, the Duke of Wellington, took full advantage of the change.

Although not as brilliant a leader as Napoleon, Wellington had a cool head and was able to profit from his opponent's mistakes and his own advantages. The armies he led, the British expeditionary forces, had the best-trained infantry in Europe, the most lethal musketry and a good supply line from the sea. And although Wellington's numbers were usually smaller, his opponents rarely enjoyed a unified command. The

The Royal Navy reigned supreme in the world after the French and Spanish navies were defeated at the Battle of Waterloo. On 20 October 1805 Admiral Villeneuve sailed out of Cadiz harbour with thirty-three ships-of-the-line. Admiral Nelson gave battle the following day with a fleet of twenty-seven ships off Cape Trafalgar. Eighteen of Villeneuve's ships were captured or destroyed and none of the others could fight again. French and Spanish casualties numbered 5,860 killed and wounded and 20,000 taken prisoner. British losses were just 1,690 – including Nelson. He was shot by a French sniper who identified him by the military decorations on his coat. Captain Hardy had tried to persuade Nelson to change his coat earlier in the battle but Nelson replied he was not afraid to show his military decorations to the enemy. He had already lost an arm and an eye in previous battles. 'Thank God I have done my duty' were his final words, and three hours after receiving the fatal wound he was dead. Standing beside Hardy was Captain Blackwood, an ancestor of Captain Glover's.

French *maréchals* were quarrelsome and divided and by 1812 Wellington had outfought most of them in the Peninsular War. By the summer, he was about to enter France. Napoleon could easily have swept the British expeditionary forces into the sea, but instead chose to take his best troops to join the army of six hundred thousand men invading Russia. Most of them came from the southern climes of Europe, where the severity of a Russian winter was unimaginable and they were never seen again. Wellington pressed home his advantage and invaded France.

The Regent himself, though the proud owner of many splendid uniforms, remained as far from the actual fighting as possible. He claimed to have been in action, even at Waterloo, but it is still not known whether he was fooling his listeners or himself. Despite his

ARTHUR WELLESLEY, 1ST DUKE OF WELLINGTON, AT THE TIME OF WATERLOO

championing of Admiral Nelson and claims to have fought the French, he remained a Francophile in many respects, as did most of the upper classes. But, as the savage cartoonists of his day liked to point out, the Regent was not really English. His parents were both German – his mother barely spoke English. His father tried to speak it so well that he was caricatured for his self-consciously precise pronunciation.

The Regent's unpopularity soared as he paraded his finery and went begging for more money to fuel his extravagant lifestyle while Parliament was imposing crushing taxes to pay for the war. Many Conservatives were actually afraid lest the Regent's degeneracy, selfishness and callous disregard for the plight of his subjects might spark off a wave of social unrest, just as the extravagance of Marie

BANKRUPT MERCHANT JOHN BELLINGHAM SHOOTS SPENCER
PERCEVAL IN THE LOBBY OF THE HOUSE OF COMMONS

Antoinette and Louis XVI had inspired the Revolution in France.

However, there was no mechanism by which Parliament could suspend granting him full powers, which he was duly given in 1812. He promptly attempted to slip some of his old Whig cronies into the Cabinet by persuading the Prime Minister, Spencer Perceval, to form a coalition. Unsurprisingly, Perceval was unwilling to help his rivals; but discussions came to an abrupt end with an extraordinary, and thankfully unique, event in the history of Britain. On 11 May 1812, the Prime Minister was assassinated in the lobby of the House of Commons. The man who shot him, Bellingham, had a grudge against the British government for failing to help him when he had been imprisoned in Russia. After endless dithering, the Regent eventually appointed the High Tory Lord Liverpool to take Perceval's place.

Liverpool's government was dominated by Lord Castlereagh, first as Foreign Secretary and later as Leader of the House. No other Regency politician has been credited with exerting a stronger, wider or worse influence on politics or the country as a whole. Castlereagh was an unfeeling, narrow-minded and dogmatic man who was widely detested by everybody outside the Tory establishment. He hated Napoleon and lobbied hard to continue the war against him, not in the name of liberty but in order to restore the corrupt regime that the Revolution had overthrown. Castlereagh committed suicide in 1822 but not before he had brought in legislation of a brutal and suppressive nature that created in large part the unrest that marked Britain in the later years of the Regency. 'I met a murderer on the way,' wrote the poet Shelley, 'He had a mask like Castlereagh.'

Murder and death were the subjects of conversation around the Kentchurch dinner table that evening in the company of their guest, Mr Newman, in whose honour they had prepared a Gothic banquet. The diners were garbed in their own interpretation of Gothic costumes. Captain Glover had a stake through his heart;

Lady Devonport wore a black veil; Mr Gorell Barnes had a spider's web painted on his cheek; and several of the ladies had the frighteningly pale complexions of the near-dead. On the table were suckling pig and snails accompanied by a magnificent blancmange with Gothic arches, decorated with ivy. Not unnaturally, given Mr Newman's expertise, conversation turned to vampirism. Before the Regency, vampires had been briefly mentioned in poetry and German folkloric stories, but they were more like our modern-day zombies – disgusting, mindless, peasant-class oddballs. It was a book by Lord Byron's physician Dr Polidori, *The Vampyre,* published in 1819, that started the image of the dark, sinister nobleman who was a snappy dresser and preyed on innocent young women. Only when Bram Stoker wrote *Dracula* in 1897 was the vampire genre fully established, but most cinematic versions of the evil blood-sucker still owe more to Dr Polidori's meticulous nobleman than to Stoker's boorish and ill-mannered anti-hero.

The vampire in Dr Polidori's book was not a figure of his imagination but a thinly veiled portrait of Lord Byron, the Romantic hero. *The Vampyre* was written with Byron's tacit permission and was in fact based on a plot outline of his. The great poet appeared flattered by the attention and unperturbed by the connection. The Romantics were not immune to the appeal of the Gothic imagination; they enjoyed it, in much the same way that intellectuals today may love Westerns or other forms of popular entertainment. But the crude horrors of the Gothic novel made it undeniably inferior, in their eyes, to the great sweeping works of human emotion (and conscious artistry) which their own works displayed. (It is of course just possible that their condescending attitude may also have been related to the fact that their Gothic rivals were far more commercially successful than they were.)

REGENCY CONTRACEPTION

A length of sheep's gut, tied at both ends with ribbon, was used by some men to prevent venereal infection. It was hopeless for preventing pregnancy, however. Contraception was virtually unheard of although prostitutes were known to resort to sponges soaked in vinegar – to little effect.

'The horror genre, throughout the ages, uses the neuroses of the time to titillate and frighten its audience. There have always been neuroses around death, of course, and sex – they are probably universal – and the vampire is the Regency way of expressing those. It is hardly surprising that sex and death were very closely linked in people's minds when one in three women at the time died in child-birth,' related Mr Newman, cheerfully.

All this talk of vampires gave Mrs Hammond an idea. For the past few days she had been closeted in her room writing sketches for the guests to perform. Initially this was to take the form of a play, since amateur theatricals were very popular at Regency house parties. Some great houses were so well known for their productions that famous actors from London were hired to bolster the performances of the guests. The Priory, country seat of the Abercorn family, was particularly famous for its recreations of contemporary plays like *The Wedding Day* and *Who's the Dupe?*. During one visit, described by Lady Caroline Lamb in a letter to her grandmother, she and the other guests were involved in a full-scale production. The services of the famous painter Sir Thomas Lawrence had been called upon for set decoration, and Mrs John Kemble was brought in to direct the actors. The plays were followed, as was the tradition in the West End, with a farce, which in this instance was specially written by George Lamb, brother of the future Prime Minister and brother-in-law to the infamous Caroline. At Kentchurch, Mrs Hammond had decided to proceed directly to farce without the unnecessary complication of a play to introduce it. After meeting Mr Newman, she and Mr Everett (seizing the opportunity to display his set-design skills) decided upon a Gothic theme – *Mrs Hammond's House of Horror*. The guests set to work designing and painting flats and props, making costumes and learning their lines. Lady Devonport lent a hand with some of the sketches and the two ladies could be seen doubled up with laughter as they invented witty or scandalous ways to expose the foibles and eccentricities of their fellow guests that had emerged during the Regency experience.

Meanwhile, the men were continuing their sabre practice in preparation for the display that would take place at the end of the house party. Their skills had developed to such an extent that they were capable of riding with one hand clutching the reins and the other a sabre, and (in theory at any rate) slicing the tops off melons on sticks as they galloped along.

After one particularly strenuous session they returned to the house to be greeted by man called a 'surgeon'. This was Steve Bacon, a 'medical re-enactor'. He handed his card to Mr Gorell Barnes and asked whether his services might be

MR BACON, THE VISITING SURGEON, CHECKS A LEECH IS GETTING ITS FILL OF MR FOXSMITH

MR BACON DISPLAYS HIS THIRSTY LEECHES

of use to the men of the house. His fees, he claimed, were very moderate. While he explained the various cures and procedures he had on offer, he unravelled the tool roll he was carrying, to reveal a terrifying selection of knives, lancets (for letting blood), directors (to make sure the incision was shallow), cauterising irons (to close an incision), retractors (for holding a wound open) and leeches (to suck blood). He could bleed, purge, vomit or cup his clients, or perform an enema. He explained that a bleeding might be beneficial to the men after such exertion and to reduce any bruising they might have sustained. Mark Foxsmith was the only man who felt that a bleeding might be an interesting experience and his love of animals gave him the courage to face an intimate encounter with the leeches, which were at the time swimming in a glass vial on the surgeon's table. He sat in the drawing room, with the ladies attending to his every whim, and a small but thirsty leech was placed on his arm.

It was the fashion in the Regency for men and women to be bled in the spring. After a hard winter it was seen to be an aid to health, to rebalance the 'humours' (bodily fluids) and calm or stimulate the nervous system, depending on what was required. A surgeon could perform this task, as could a blacksmith or a 'bone setter', who was like a modern-day osteopath in that he would manipulate the whole body as well as setting limbs. A surgeon had a status similar to a blacksmith's – although he was often less skilled. His training might consist of no more than an apprenticeship to another surgeon (who might himself be unskilled) or nothing at all, since there was no official register for surgeons. In the absence of anaesthetics or antibiotics, no deep incisions could be made into the body and a surgeon could treat only those things on or near the surface, such as skin tumours (the Regent had one removed from the top of his head in 1821).

Not surprisingly, surgeons were not the first port of call in the event of illness. Most medical emergencies would be sent first to the kitchen, where the cook would undoubtedly have a copy of Eliza Smith's *The Compleat Housewife*. This contained a large array of 'receipts' for herbal preparations with medicinal benefits, based on thousands of years of knowledge of plant use. These home remedies were often effective for minor ailments, and only if they failed, or in the event of a broken bone or chronic illness, would a surgeon be called.

The ancient idea of one's health being governed by the four 'humours' of the body still held sway in the Regency. The four bodily humours were blood, black bile, yellow bile or choler, and phlegm or mucus. One of these humours was generally considered to be dominant in each person and would influence their constitution and character. For example, those with excess yellow bile were easily angered, while those with dominant black bile were melancholic. To appreciate fully the precariousness of health in the Regency it was important for the guests at Kentchurch to realise that a simple cut could kill them, a fractured limb could result in death or permanent disability, and a cold could develop into lethal pneumonia. For all the genuine threats to one's health at this time, hypochondria was especially fashionable among the aristocracy (who were, after all, the only people who could indulge in it). Jane Austen's mother infuriated her daughter by making a point of being ill much of the time – lest anyone forget that her father had a title.

The leech spent ninety minutes

THE TOOLS OF THE SURGEON'S TRADE ENCOURAGE THE HOUSE-GUESTS TO CONSIDER HERBAL REMEDIES

feasting on Mr Foxsmith before dropping off, satiated. Asked whether he felt the experience had promoted a sense of well-being and rude health, Mr Foxsmith paused and thought carefully. 'No,' he said calmly, and settled back in his chair.

GLASS ARMONICA

The musical highlight for the guests at Kentchurch came with the arrival of Alistair Malloy, the country's only virtuoso of the 'armonica' and one of fewer than ten people in the world who play this instrument. Invented by the American philosopher and statesman Benjamin Franklin in the 1780s, a series of crystal balls rotate, one inside another, to create a clear and haunting sound. Mr Malloy first gave the guests a Masterclass with 'musical glasses' – drinking glasses filled with different levels of liquid, set in a wooden frame. Later, they listened spellbound to his demonstration of the armonica and then joined in with the glasses.

Unanimously, the guests declared the extraordinary musical entertainment one of their best experiences in the house. 'To hear live music, particularly the armonica, because it's very emotive, was fantastic,' enthused Captain Glover. 'In 2003 we listen to music all the time, there's music wherever we go, and here that has suddenly disappeared. It was such an unusual sound, like a cross between a flute and a violin that can play chords. I never knew this existed. And to have someone so unique as Mr Malloy to come in and share that passion with us I think was very special.'

If Mr Foxsmith now looked as pale as a ghost, this was nothing compared to the phantoms the guests were about to see. Mrs Rogers had earlier received a gentleman's card on which was written: MR MERVYN HEARD, LANTERNIST. Somewhat perplexed, she received Mr Heard, who explained that he was an itinerant entertainer with a show called *Cupid's Magic Lantern*. In his luggage he carried two Regency magic lanterns, an assortment of original sound effects, and a unique collection of early-nineteenth-century lantern slides. After dinner that night a mysterious monk appeared to usher the party into the darkened drawing room. Before them hung a draped sheet of waxed muslin. A voice began moaning and chattering and a spooky image appeared on the screen. Gradually the guests could discern a human skull with glowing eyes that suddenly began to move and a jawbone that clattered up and down in time to a disembodied voice. A whole skeleton then appeared, seated on a chair and wearing a military hat. This was Napoleon, 'Boney', who was promptly carted off the screen by an image of George III, dressed as Neptune. What the guests were experiencing was a phantasmagoria, the closest the Regency ever got to cinema. And when they felt their shoulders being draped with seaweed and water splashed on them from behind, it became apparent that 'feelaround' cinema was far from being a twentieth-century invention.

The phantasmagoria evolved in France during the Revolution. It involved spooks, apparitions, skele-

MISS BRAUND AND CAPTAIN GLOVER SERENADE
EACH OTHER WITH WATER MUSIC

tons and all things Gothic and was used initially by con-men to trick spectators into believing that they were seeing real ghosts. In the 1780s, a German called Paul Philidor decided to expose these charlatans by revealing how the so-called 'ghosts' were created. He designed his own magic-lantern show, called it *The Phantasmagoria*, and embarked on a tour of the capitals of Europe. Philidor arrived in Paris as the Terror was at its height and made the tactical mistake of sending up Robespierre in his show. He was thrown into prison and was minutes from the guillotine when his great friend Madame Tussaud intervened on his behalf. His show

OLDER, MARRIED WOMEN WERE OFTEN FAR MORE INTERESTING TO REGENCY GENTLEMEN
AS THEY HAD MORE TO SAY – AND THE FREEDOM TO SAY IT!

caught on and was copied, often using disused convents for a setting and employing old monks as ushers. The supernatural remained the common theme of the shows, and they were accompanied by piano music, 'surround sound' effects (created by actors who would shriek, scream or rattle chains) and some form of commentary. Most wealthy Regency households had soon bought their own lanterns and ghostly slides, or were hiring itinerant lanternists to put on shows to amaze and frighten the guests. Our modern guests, used to the special effects of *Star Wars* or *Scream III*, were underwhelmed by the phantasmagoria itself but as pleased as their Regency forebears at the opportunity to sidle up in the darkness and enjoy greater proximity to members of the opposite sex than any other occasion allowed.

The following day the young people were allowed to walk to the picturesque Grossmont Castle, a Gothic ruin which they could admire, paint and sketch. As Mrs Rogers suffered from sore feet, she chose to remain behind and invited the other chaperones to join her to gossip, sew and finish the Regency revue. Giddy at the prospect of a sortie without their chaperones, the young people set out in high spirits, followed by footmen carrying their art materials and a picnic lunch.

An appreciation of landscape was, of course, a must for all young Regency hopefuls and was particularly important if the Gothic imagination was to be fully indulged. Emily, the heroine of *Udolpho*, spends at least half the two-volume novel in raptures about the scenery she passes through. And, depending where she is, she takes care to classify it correctly: as sublime, picturesque, romantic or classically undulating.

'I love it here,' said Miss Conick. 'It's so beautiful I wouldn't want to be anywhere else, but I'm not sure romance will flourish, despite the setting, because nobody wants to look like a fool. We all want to meet a partner and no one wants to be portrayed as just chasing anything that moves.' Captain Glover agreed: 'You know, it's hard to pursue romance when your every move is on camera or being listened to through these radio mikes,' he said. True love, however, conquers all, and it seemed that a few of the guests were developing genuine, if largely secret, attachments. Mr Everett was still holding a torch for Miss Hopkins, whose feelings towards him were confused by her loyalty to Miss Braund (who was herself smitten by Mr Everett). And the countess? She was the quietest of all the guests, but her interest in a certain gentleman had also been noted . . . Would the revue planned by Mrs Hammond give her an opportunity to faint into the arms of her Mr Darcy? As Miss Crawford says boldly before choosing her part in the amateur theatricals at Mansfield Park: 'Which gentleman among you am I to have the pleasure of making love to?'

Regency amateur dramatics were a perfect opportunity to further romantic liaisons (or at least to indulge in licentious behaviour). In *Mansfield Park*, the theatricals provide the core of the book. The play, *Lovers' Vows*, allows the guests to muscle their way into the roles that will bring them into close proximity to the men or women they desire. Under the umbrella of 'theatrical performance', they can then indulge in all-out flirting without the risk of censure.

But did this elaborate role-play, both on stage and in their lives at Kentchurch, allow the participants to discover and express their real selves, desires and personalities? Or was Jane Austen right when she suggested in *Mansfield Park* that role-playing runs the risk of destroying a person's sense of their real self and leads only to confusion, dissatisfaction, a loss of dignity and a weakening of moral standards? Were the guests at Kentchurch 'acting' or being their normal selves? Were the romantic feelings emerging between some guests the result of escaping from their 'real' lives, like a holiday romance? Was Lady Devonport's passion for Mr Foxsmith genuine or partly inspired by the freedom her titled position gave her in Regency society?

The Gothic revue, while encouraging humour, did not fuel *amour* and brought the guests little closer to answering these questions. Although Mrs Hammond made sure her charge, Miss Braund, had a chance to show off her pretty singing voice, all the songs and poems were performed solo, so romantic opportunities were few and far between. The only duet involved Mr Gorell Barnes, who acted out a marriage of convenience – to night-watchman Mr Dean.

The finale of the show went to Mrs Enright, the 'oracle' of Kentchurch whose powers of prophecy were called into question as she remained oblivious throughout the recitation to a vampiric hovering near her throat, that of the Countess Dracula:

> *I'm the Oracle of Kentchurch;*
> *It's a very dull position.*
> *My biggest fault, if any,*
> *Is of prophecy omission.*
> *I'm famous for my wisdom*
> *And my third eye – this is true,*
> *And statesmen call with questions*
> *And I tell them what to do.*
> *Will Turkey ever win the war?*
> *Should hair be short or long?*
> *My answer, dear, is crystal clear*
> *And very often wrong.*

AMATEUR THEATRICALS WERE A SOURCE OF SCANDAL AND INTRIGUE IN JANE AUSTEN'S TIME

SERVING HERSELF UP FOR STARTERS, THE COUNTESS KNOCKS THE GUESTS OUT WITH HER ICING-SUGAR LOOK

CHAPTER SEVEN

THE AGE OF ROMANCE
ROMANTICISM, SEX AND SCANDAL

Then wherefore should we sigh and whine,

With groundless jealousy repine;

With silly whims, and fancies frantic,

Merely to make our love romantic?

LORD BYRON

ONE EVENING, the guests walked in to dinner to find an unusual table decoration. They were constantly surprised by the chef's ability to create gorgeous centre-

pieces, but an entire naked woman decorated with fresh flowers, fruit and icing sugar? 'Oh my God, it's breathing!' gasped Miss Francesca as she led the gaggle of guests towards the table. 'Who is it?' Her face obscured by a mask of peacock feathers, the lady's identity was well hidden, even if her charms were well exposed.

The idea of serving oneself up naked, while courageous, was not original. Lady Caroline Lamb, desperately in love with Lord Byron and prepared to catch his attention in any way poss- ible, was said to have been brought to him on a large silver serving dish carried by two footmen. The lid was removed and there she lay in tri- umphant nudity. However startled the famous poet might have been at a lover appearing as an

CAPTAIN GLOVER GETS IN THE 'ROMANTIC' MOOD
BY HELPING HIMSELF TO OYSTERS

appetiser, he could not have been more amazed than the guests at Kentchurch when they realised that the table decoration was, in fact, the last person they would have expected to do such a thing: the countess.

What had driven the quietest, most reserved and most impeccably behaved guest to such a rash act? Who was her Lord Byron? And would the affair end as tragically for the countess as it had for Lady Caroline Lamb?

The episode had begun earlier that week with a story in the daily newspaper:

'It has been discovered that a certain lady of the highest rank is not all she seems.' There was only one possible suspect. The countess blushed and professed with emotion that one could not believe anything one read in the papers. Her companions, however, began to return some of the aloof behaviour she had been displaying towards them since her arrival at the house.

'We guessed it was about the countess immediately,' said Miss Braund. 'We thought her title must be bogus and for a while it was difficult to talk to her as we felt she had been assuming airs and graces that were unfounded. In fact, I think she is just someone who likes to be alone a lot.'

At the start of the Regency house experiment, the countess had concocted a good story to hide her poverty: 'I decided to pretend to have had a racy past and to have gambled away large sums in Paris,' she explained. 'For this reason, my father had severely limited my allowance during my stay in England.' So successful was this tactic that her fellow house-guests were sure the newspaper story related to her title rather than her fortune. She spent a few uncomfortable days more alone than usual, although she appeared to find great comfort in the presence of Mr Gorell Barnes, whose attentions towards her seemed unaffected by the gossip.

Scandal-mongering was a salient feature of the Regency, which saw the birth of the gutter press, whose scurrilous and often libellous broadsides were frequently aimed at the upper echelons of society, in particular the Regent himself. If a country gets the press it deserves, this was certainly true during

THE EXHIBITION STARE CASE, AN EXUBERANT AND SAUCY ENGRAVING BY THOMAS ROWLANDSON

the Regency. A certain section of the *haut ton* behaved with such amazing vulgarity, ostentatious excess and sexual infidelity that newspapers did not have to look far for salacious scandal to spice up their pages, and to some extent the British press was less restricted than publications on the Continent. However, there was also a political reason for the emergence of these publications. By 1815 there were about 250 newspapers in Britain, the majority of which were local. In the absence of television, radio and telephones, it is easy to see why newspapers were devoured with avidity. However, in 1815 the Tory government under Lord Liverpool decided to increase stamp duty on papers to fourpence a copy, raising the price of those publications that paid the duty to sevenpence. The aim of this increase in duty was to ensure that papers were affordable only to the wealthy, who were on the whole more likely to be sympathetic to Tory policies and papers. Those papers whose editorial line was hostile to the government, in other words those that demanded reform and showed support for the radicals, would now be beyond the means of their readership, i.e., the poor. The net effect of forcing up the price of papers and cutting off the mass of readers was the creation of a disreputable 'black-market' press that was nearly always radical and anti-establishment in outlook. These papers were cheap and frequently employed virulent language. As a Victorian chronicler of the Regency newspapers noted: 'Much appeared in the journalism of those times which no lady of delicate mind would read aloud, and which no gentleman, however gay he might be, would dare to read in the hearing of a lady.' So much of this material was grossly libellous that many prison sentences were imposed on writers and editors, with the result that lowly and often undistinguished hacks became martyrs to the cause of free speech.

Brilliant but vicious cartoonists added their talents to those of the writers in ripping through the hypocrisy of the time. Gillray, Rowlandson and Cruikshank were the triumvirate of leading Regency caricaturists. James Gillray's cartoons were so popular that there were often queues outside the print shop where he worked. He died in 1815 while still in his fifties, although he had stopped working four years earlier, a victim of hard drinking and overwork. Thomas Rowlandson came from a comfortable middle-class background and in his early career spent time in Paris and at the Royal Academy School, painting serious subjects. He had inherited quite a substantial fortune but gambled it all away so recklessly that he

spent much of his life in debt and had to work his way out of it by turning to car-
icature, satirical cartoons and book illustrations. In marked contrast to the other
two, George Cruikshank was an aggressive teetotaller, successful when still only in
his early twenties. His cartoons were effective and popular in the later years of the
Regency and into the Victorian era.

Along with the rise of the gutter press came that other ephemeral creation, the
'celebrity'. There had, of course, been famous people before 1810 but it was during
the Regency that the press (and large sections of the population) discovered the joy
of idolising an individual and then destroying their reputation. Arguably the first
such celebrity to undergo this process was Lord Byron. He was headline news in
the paper that raised suspicions about the countess, and the guests decided to find
out more about him since several of the men laid claim to 'Byronic' qualities, and
it was in everybody's interest that the men learn what was required of a Romantic
hero. To this end, Mrs Rogers announced that they would have a dinner in honour
of Lord Byron later in the week, after which the men were to recite poems that they
themselves had composed. Almost without exception the men quailed at the
prospect. Accomplishment number one for the Romantic hero – the ability to write
poetry – was clearly not one to which they would take easily. Mrs Rogers also
announced that there would be a dance at Kentchurch this same week, a double-
whammy for the men – poetry *and* dancing. Being a Regency Don Juan was proving to be hard work.

The young Byron lived in poor surroundings in Aberdeen until he was ten,
when he inherited the title from his great-uncle. He was then educated at Dulwich,
Harrow and Cambridge, where he led a fairly dissipated life. His first collection of
poems was badly reviewed, so he set out with a friend on a lengthy Grand Tour. As
the usual destinations for the tour lay within the French Empire, with which
Britain was at war, they went instead to Spain, Portugal, Greece and Turkey. Byron
spent two years away, for the most part in the 'exotic' eastern reaches of the
Mediterranean, the Ottoman Empire. Byron was impressed by what he saw and
became deeply attached to Greece. On his return in 1812, the first two cantos of
Childe Harold's Pilgrimage were published and, as he so famously said, 'I awoke to
find myself famous.'

With the success of *Childe Harold*, the author was invited into society – an

George Gordon Byron, 6th Baron Byron by Thomas Phillips

MR GORELL BARNES GETS ADVICE FROM HIS FELLOW
GUESTS ON HOW TO PEN A POEM

astonishingly handsome, chestnut-locked young lord with a well-developed attitude of world-weary disdain. The Duchess of Devonshire wrote, 'the subject of conversation, of curiosity, of enthusiasm almost, one might say, of the moment, is not Spain or Portugal, Warriors or Patriots, but Lord Byron. His book is on every table, and himself courted, visited, flattered, and praised wherever he appears – the men are jealous of him, the women of each other.' His public life was a performance and women fell for it in droves.

The 'Byronic hero' was the ultimate Romantic figure and enjoyed an extraordinary vogue both during Byron's lifetime and for some years afterwards in Britain, Europe and America. Although the male narrators of his poems each had subtly different characteristics, they provided a basic list of key ingredients for any aspirant hero. A composite Byronic hero needed to be proud, ideally aristocratic, moody, cynical, defiant, miserable in his heart yet seeking sensation (often in sexual liaisons), a noble outlaw, scornful of mankind, implacable in revenge yet capable of deep and strong affection. Piracy or poetry would be his ideal career options.

> She rose, and pausing one chaste moment, threw
> Herself upon his breast, and there she grew.
>
> This was an awkward test, as Juan found,
> But he was steeled by sorrow, wrath, and pride:
> With gentle force her white arms he unwound,
> And looking coldly in her face, he cried,
> . . . Love is for free!
>
> BYRON, *DON JUAN*

Since much of Byron's writing was based on his own experiences, and the poems' 'narrators' seemed to be reflections of the author, Byron himself became the ultimate Byronic hero. As he said of the difficulties any future biographer would have:

> What I think of myself is, that I am so changeable, being every thing by turns and nothing long, – I am such a strange melange of good and evil, that it would be difficult to describe me. There are but two sentiments to which I am constant, – a strong love of liberty, and a detestation of cant, and neither is calculated to win me friends. I am of a wayward, uncertain disposition, more disposed to display the defects than the redeeming points in my nature; this, at least, proves that I understand mankind, for there is no crime of which I could accuse myself, for which they would not give me implicit credit.

Young women sought to save him by the purity of their love – and popular sentimental Regency fiction gave them all the attitudes and adjectives they needed to declare this intention in their letters to him. Older society women, on the other hand, were intrigued by the smouldering passion so well described in his verse and so apparent in his manner. He was invited everywhere and soon lived up to all expectations by beginning an affair with an eccentric young woman who was an equally reckless romantic – Lady Caroline Lamb.

'Mad, bad and dangerous to know' was her verdict on their first meeting, and this proved more than true for her. Caroline had a reputation as a delightful but impulsive eccentric from an early age. In 1805, only just twenty, she married William Lamb, later to be prime minister as Lord Melbourne. The match did not last long and both went their own way without a public separation. She continued to behave like a tomboy and in 1811, at the age of twenty-six, was still attracting attention by such public antics as 'jumping over a couch at some assembly'. She kept her hair short and curly and could disguise herself as a pageboy when she sought to escape attention. Her upbringing did not teach her to steer clear of illicit sexual liaisons: her mother, Lady Bessborough, had a long and notorious affair with Granville Leveson-Gower and had two children by him. Her aunt was the famous Georgiana, Duchess of Devonshire, who had an affair with Charles Grey and finally lived in a *ménage à trois* with her husband's mistress

A WISTFUL LADY CAROLINE LAMB BY SOCIETY
PAINTER SIR THOMAS LAWRENCE

(who also happened to be her best friend).

When first introduced to Byron at a ball, Caroline Lamb stared hard at him for a moment and then turned away without speaking. Surrounded as he was by fluttering females, this tactic was highly effective and a madly passionate affair soon began, conducted as much in public as it was in private. They exchanged romantic letters and verses and after late parties she would always be seen leaving in Byron's carriage.

At Kentchurch Court, the countess appeared to be inspired by what she had learned about Lady Caroline. Indeed, despite the two centuries which separated them, there were startling similarities between the two women in both looks and behaviour. The countess too had sought to 'catch' her man (Mr Gorell Barnes had soon emerged as the front runner for her admiration) by behaving with cool reserve and feigned lack of interest. Like Lady Caroline, the countess's status allowed her the freedom to flout social convention, behave badly and indulge her every whim. So, when she decided she needed a new dress to wear to the dance at Kentchurch she ignored her own poverty, ordered a dress for £20 (approximately £1000 in today's money) and gaily asked the host to pay for it. Her gamble paid off, for not only did he take care of the expense, he also asked her if she needed anything else. In Regency terms this would be tantamount to an engagement, since a woman was not supposed to accept a gift from a man unless he had first asked for her hand. After hearing about Lady Caroline's ploy to serve herself up naked to Byron, the countess had decided to do the same. With the gossip promoted by the newspaper article now surrounding her, she perhaps had less to lose than before.

'I felt it was time to take more challenges, be more outrageous and shock people. I know I was seen to be the least likely woman in the house to appear naked on the table,' said the countess. It was less clear whether the countess knew how the nine-month affair between Lady Caroline and Byron ended. 'As to yourself, Lady Caroline,' wrote Byron, 'correct your vanity which has become ridiculous – exert your caprices on others, enjoy the excellent flow of spirits which make you so delightful in the eyes of others, and leave me in peace.' Byron was already involved with others, including a certain Mrs Webster – an affair which threatened to lead to a duel with her jealous husband. Byron took humorous consolation in the thought that his death in such circumstances 'would be so *dramatic* a conclusion; all the sex would be enamoured of my memory, all the wits would have their jests, and the moralists their sermon. Caroline Lamb would go wild with *grief* that *it did not happen about her*.'

Mr Gorell Barnes, himself possessing some Byronic qualities (an air of world-weary boredom in particular), was distracted from the naked countess, the travails

of writing poetry and the complications of Regency dancing by a strange letter he received from an anonymous member of the Kentchurch Society of Dilettanti. The letter informed him of the presence of a secret society that used to hold meetings in the cellars of the house. 'It is approaching fifty years to this day that our erudite principal Sir John Scudamore revived the notorious Hell-Fire Club in the bowels of the house. We have considered the possibility of combining this commemoration with a celebration to the glories of our great hero, Lord Byron, and we hope that you will take up this mantle in our absence.'

The letter finished with the Old French words '*Fay ce que voudras*' – 'Do what you will'. Somewhat perplexed, Mr Gorell Barnes found out that a

THE COUNTESS SEEMED THE LEAST LIKELY CANDIDATE TO BEHAVE OUTRAGEOUSLY

secret clubroom existed below the Terrace Room for the exclusive use of male members of the household. His steward gave him the key and, accompanied by Captain Glover, he descended the steps at the east end of the house and found himself in an underground cavern. The men were astonished to see the walls covered in the sculpted naked bodies of classical nymphs and satyrs, intertwined in amorous embraces or freely exhibiting their genitalia. Several interconnected rooms were thus decorated, and in the furthest from the door was a shelf containing erotic books such as John Cleland's *Fanny Hill*, Thomas Rowlandson's *Erotic Cartoons*, the Marquis de Sade's *120 Days of Sodom* and Ovid's *Love Poems*.

The Hell-Fire tradition, if such a limited movement can be called a tradition, began in the sixteenth century with the French author François Rabelais, who published his unconventional views on creating the 'perfect community', whose sole tenet would be 'Do what you will.' This idea became a focus for a variety of different groups or individual writers, who dreamed up their own 'ideal community' or went as far as forming clubs to promote it. The only club known to be called 'the Hell-Fire Club' was suppressed by an order of Parliament in 1721 for acts of 'immorality and profaneness'. It consisted of about forty 'persons of quality' of (almost uniquely) both sexes. The reason for the club's suppression was not that it held orgies (seemingly plenty of persons of quality held orgies) but because of its pursuit of blasphemy. The Hell-Fire Club members arrived for meetings dressed as Biblical figures or saints and then played their roles for laughs. They staged mock-rituals making fun of Christian dogmas, drank large quantities of 'Hell-Fire punch' and ate dishes such as Holy Ghost Pie. This was an era when the Church was widely discredited as corrupt and com-

DANCE TRIBUTES TO BACCHUS IN THE HELL-FIRE CLUB

promised, a mere organ of the government. The repression of the Hell-Fire Club was an attempt to quash anti-clerical feeling. Although details are murky, the club's leading light seems to have been Philip, Duke of Wharton, a clever and rebellious young man connected to the highest aristocracy in the land but vehement in denouncing its wrongs. The best-known club based on Hell-Fire principles was begun in 1753 by Sir Francis Dashwood, and members included Lord Sandwich (inventor of . . .) and, briefly, Benjamin Franklin. Membership was all-male but women were shipped in to meetings held at an old Franciscan monastery, where elaborate and possibly quasi-satanic rituals

THE BRILLIANCE OF THE KENTCHURCH DESIGN TEAM SEEN IN ALL ITS GLORY IN THE HELL-FIRE CLUB

were enacted. Dashwood's club largely died out in the 1770s and the fading embers of the Hell-Fire spirit were finally extinguished before the end of the century.

Regency society had its own scandalous private clubs and Byron belonged to many of them. He was a perfect Hell-Fire hero – proud, anti-establishment, aristocratic, sexually experimental and rebellious. The men agreed that an evening celebrating the lewder aspects of Byron's life was far more tempting than reciting poetry to girls. However, Mr Gorell Barnes and Captain Glover were worried about what the women would say if, after the dinner Mrs Rogers had arranged in Byron's memory, the men slipped off to this den of iniquity. The two men kept their discovery secret and joined in the dance that evening as if they had no inkling that beneath the dance floor were rooms full of writhing bodies and books of Regency pornography.

'There are but three great men in the nineteenth century – Brummell, Napoleon and myself,' said Byron.

The time had now come for the Kentchurch men, in their quest to master the role of the Romantic hero, to discover dandyism. Byron himself had been a dandy in his youth and his looks were very important to him. He was born with a club foot, for which his mother had heartlessly taunted him. He felt this handicap to be a bitter humiliation and excelled in sports, perhaps to compensate. He played cricket for his school and was frequently to be found at Gentleman Jackson's studio, receiving boxing lessons from the champion. He rode, fenced, shot (not birds, since he preferred inanimate targets) and was a superb swimmer. He cared greatly about his 'image' and was fashionably dressed, if not to the extent that Beau Brummell might have liked. Of the dandies, Byron said, 'They were always very civil to *me*, though in general they disliked literary people.' King of the dandies and unofficial monarch of London society before his fall from grace was, of course, George Bryan 'Beau' Brummell.

The day after the dance, Mrs Rogers received a calling card from Mr Nick Foulkes, journalist, author and 'modern-day dandy'. He arrived wearing purple trousers and a brightly patterned waistcoat and soon charmed the hostess into an invitation to join the house party for a few days.

During his stay, Mr Foulkes taught the men how to perform their 'toilette' in a manner that would elevate them into high society. A dandy was to be urbane, elegant, yet totally masculine. The dandies set the tone of Regency society in the early years as the élite arbiters of fashion. The man who led them, however, was the grandson of a valet. Thanks to Brummell, the highly ornamental and bejewelled fashions of the eighteenth century were replaced by absolute simplicity. All the implements in his dressing room, such as brushes and spitting dishes, were made of silver since, in Brummell's own words, 'it is impossible to spit in clay'. His ablutions alone took two hours and when asked the name of his hairdresser Brummell replied: 'I have three. The first is responsible for my temples, the second for the front and the third for the occiput.' His room was always brimming with fashionable admirers and imitators, including the Prince Regent and the Dukes of Bedford, Beaufort and Rutland, hoping to see how he managed to tie his enormous neck-cloths. In the daytime, Brummell wore a perfectly fitting dark blue coat with brass buttons, leather breeches, top-boots and a stiff white cravat. Coats and breeches often fitted so closely that both valet and wearer struggled to get them on, and it could be impossible to sit down. The high, starched cravat further restricted movement and the Kentchurch men found that their clothes were scarcely more comfortable than the women's.

'This jacket is killing me. I am so hot I think I will expire and it is so tight, and the sleeves so long, that I can't move with it on,' moaned Mr Everett. 'We must never take our jackets off in the company of ladies or in any place where we might come across a lady. The men's clothes do look very good, I think, but evening dress is damned uncomfortable.'

How Brummell came to wield such influence, even over the Prince of Wales, is unclear. The lift of an eyebrow could plummet a social aspirant into despair; his quizzing glasses were a lethal weapon; and he once reduced the prince to tears when he criticised the cut of his new coat. He had charisma and charm but his superior attitude began to wear a little thin with his royal friend. At a ball in 1814, the prince arrived in the company of the eccentric dandy Lord Alvanley, and studiously ignored Brummell. Furious at being cut in public, Brummell shouted out the fatal words: 'Alvanley, who is your fat friend?' The prince never spoke to Brummell again. Driven to ruin by his huge debts, Brummell fled into exile in France to avoid prison (only peers were exempt from prison for debt). He refused to publish his memoirs even though he had been offered large sums for them, and lived in genteel poverty, eventually dying in Caen's lunatic asylum.

The career of the third of Byron's 'great men of the nineteenth century', Napoleon, had also come crashing to the ground during these years. Napoleon was often depicted as a Romantic hero and he was admired by Byron and other liberal-minded members of society. Byron was born in revolutionary times and was inspired by the spirit of the French Revolution and the American Declaration of Independence: 'We hold these truths to be self-evident, that all men are created equal, that they are endowed by their Creator with certain inalienable Rights, that among these are Life, Liberty and the pursuit of Happiness.' And yet Byron lived in a country where fewer than one in forty of the population could vote. For nearly the whole of his life the repressive Tories were in power, and thus Byron's 'strong love of liberty' put him on Napoleon's side against the absolutist monarchs of Europe. In his journal entry for 18 February 1814 he wrote, 'Napoleon! – this week will decide his fate. All seems against him but I believe and hope he will win. What right have we to prescribe sovereigns to France. Oh for a Republic!'

After twenty years of war with France, the final act of the drama was fast approaching. In 1813 the Prussians, Russians and Austrians won the Battle of Nations against Napoleon at Leipzig, while Wellington was trouncing the French in the south, capturing King Joseph's sword and Marshal Jourdan's baton, both of which he sent back to the Regent as gifts. In early 1814 the Allies reached Paris, forcing Napoleon to abdicate, and Wellington won a hard battle at Toulouse, for which he was made a duke. The Comte de Provence returned to France to become

Louis XVIII and Napoleon was exiled to the Isle of Elba.

Byron too was forced into exile, although his departure was voluntary. After extracting himself from the complicated romance with Lady Caroline Lamb, he indulged in several affairs with older, married women, including his half-sister, Augusta Leigh. She was all that was left of his family and he clearly loved her. Byron even suggested they flee to the Continent together, but they were afraid that their relationship would become public knowledge. Byron convinced himself that marriage might save him from this scandalous liaison and was guided by Lady Melbourne (who once said, 'Anyone who braves the opinion of the world sooner or later feels the consequences of it') towards her niece, Annabella Milbanke, heiress to a great fortune. As they made their way to the wedding his friend remarked, 'Never was a lover less in haste', and it was an unsuitable match from the start. Annabella appeared to have married him in the hope of 'reforming' him with her strongly Christian views – a hopeless task, even had his attitude to marriage been more positive:

GEORGE BRYAN 'BEAU' BRUMMELL
AT THE HEIGHT OF HIS POWERS

> 'Tis melancholy, and a fearful sign
> Of human frailty, folly, also crime,
> That love and marriage rarely can combine,
> Although they both are born in the same clime;
> Marriage from love, like vinegar from wine –

A sad, sour, sober beverage – by time

Is sharpen'd from its high celestial flavour

Down to a very homely household savour.

Byron felt marriage to be a humiliating state for a man. 'All my coupled contemporaries,' he had scoffed only a few months before proposing for a second time
to Annabella, 'are bald and discontented.' His behaviour while married was so
extreme, marked by wild rages, black moods, drinking bouts and nights spent with
dancing girls, that Annabella and Augusta worried that he was going mad. A year
after their marriage, only a month after the birth of their daughter, Annabella left
him. Their divorce proceedings created a roar of outrage against Byron, augmented by the scandalous hints of incest that emerged. On 16 April 1816 Byron
finally decided to flee public vitriol (and his debts) and sailed to the Continent. He
died in Greece at the age of thirty-six, while helping to organise the Greek war of
independence.

The dinner in honour of Byron was graced by the presence of Mr Foulkes,
the poet Simon Armitage and a new guest at Kentchurch – Mr James Carrington.
Mr Carrington's pocketbook informed him that *'You are an itinerant musician with
the benefit of being particularly well connected.'*

Mr Carrington is the modern equivalent of a poet. He is a rock star (in waiting), affable and handsome – slightly Byronesque even, with his curly chestnut hair,
pale face and the romantic associations of his vocation. His first night in the house
was to prove highly exciting!

Mr Gorell Barnes informed his new guest and the other men that they would
not retire to the drawing room after dinner that evening but would descend instead
to the Hell-Fire Club. The host himself, however, was in two minds as to whether
he would join them. He realised it would be a gross dereliction of duty to abandon
the ladies after a celebratory dinner, particularly since they had guests. In the event,
the ladies retired in the company of Beau Foulkes, while Mr Gorell Barnes conve-
niently forgot his qualms and led his guests downstairs to their Rabelaisian antics.
A footman guarded the door to the club, myriad candles illuminated the rooms,
hookah pipes were primed and a small band played oriental music in honour of
Byron's love of the eastern Mediterranean. Suddenly, the music grew louder and
three dancing girls, clad only in diaphanous short tunics, began a sensuous ritual

THE GENTLEMEN ENJOYED THE RELAXED PLEASURES OF HELL-FIRE SOCIETY

on stage. They were maenads, female followers of Bacchus, and their dancing ended with them splashing red wine over themselves with wild abandon. The men drank, caroused and followed their own Bacchanalian rituals, heedless of the scandal they were creating. 'It was amazing,' said Mr Everett. 'The girls were very beautiful and the dance was certainly erotic. We all ended up drinking a vast amount and dancing too.'

Upstairs, the women were wondering what had happened to the men. Several of the younger ones went looking for them outside and soon came across the door of the club, from which issued strange music and a strong smell of tobacco smoke. On being refused entry by the guard, the girls rushed back to their fellows and devised a plan: they would dress up as men and talk their way in. If that failed, Mr Foulkes would tell the footman he had brought some friends of his to the club and request entry as an honoured house-guest. Only the countess refused to be involved in the scheme. The chaperones were livid at being kept in the dark about

THE WOMEN PREPARE TO PENETRATE THE FORBIDDEN SANCTUM OF THE HELL-FIRE CLUB

the men's plans for the evening and shocked that such nefarious practices should be going on under the same roof as them. They therefore chose to turn a blind eye to the girls' plans. Captain Glover's room provided all the male attire necessary and soon the girls were at the door, demanding to be allowed entrance. Mr Gorell Barnes was fetched. Amused by the girls' prank, he went back inside to tell the men that a group of locals was outside, trying to gate-crash. As the men rushed out to defend their honour the women caught a brief glimpse of the dancing girls inside. Shocked and deflated, they retired to bed.

'The Hell-Fire club was fantastic, great fun,' confessed Mr Everett the following day. 'We had these beautiful girls dancing a "salutation to the wine" and we were smoking bongs, and there was good food and a lot of booze. The place looked breathtaking. It was a fascinating insight into that side of Regency life, being so formal most of the time and then suddenly going to a club, ripping off your clothes, boozing and having sex . . . not that there was any of the latter going on with us. I'm just gutted to have made such a slip-up afterwards, in my drunken state.'

Mr Everett's 'slip-up' had been to shout up to Miss Hopkins, who was sitting at her bedroom window, that the dancing girls were a lot prettier than any of the house-guests (though in somewhat cruder terms than this). She was not the only woman offended by the antics of the previous night. The chaperones held a conference at breakfast to decide whether they should leave the house, taking their charges with them. No Regency woman worth her salt would have ignored an insult of this magnitude. Mr Gorell Barnes eventually placated the chaperones and Victoria's mood was improved by her interest in the new house-guest – Mr Carrington. He had in fact stepped into Mr Everett's place the previous evening and serenaded her in some style.

Since Captain Robinson's departure, there had been fewer men than women at the house. Of the four remaining eligible men, Mr Foxsmith was so devoted in his attentions to Lady Devonport that the couple were entirely absorbed in each other every evening after dinner. The host, either out of a desire not to cause offence or out of general insouciance, claimed not to be romantically interested in any of the female guests – although his attentions to the countess somewhat belied this. Captain Glover was in hot pursuit of Miss Braund, and Miss Francesca was now frequently seen delivering eggs to the hermit, which left Miss Conick and Miss Hopkins twiddling their thumbs. Mr Everett was still sighing over Miss Hopkins (whom he had been pursuing avidly since their arrival) but his recent outburst seemed to have reinforced her lack of interest. They had stolen a kiss on a previous evening, but Miss Braund had confided in Miss Hopkins that she also held a torch for Mr Everett, and had done so since her arrival. Unsure of her own feelings, Miss Hopkins thought she had better stop encouraging Mr Everett and instead direct his attentions towards her friend. Her noble efforts came to nought and it was clear that Mr Everett was still smitten by the independent and gregarious Miss Hopkins. She, however, was clearly taken with Mr Carrington, and he, it seemed, with her.

MRS ENRIGHT PAINTING THE SCREEN FOR THE NEW ARRIVAL'S ROOM

CHAPTER EIGHT

Sugar and Blood

The Regency passion for fighting and pudding

Miss Lambe was about seventeen, half mulatto, chilly and tender,
had a maid of her own, was to have the best room in the lodgings,
and was always of the first consequence in every plan of Mrs Griffiths.

Jane Austen, *Sanditon*, unfinished last novel

'I'M NOT SURE WHY, but my nose has really been put out of joint by the idea of a new arrival,' admitted Mrs Enright. At breakfast that morning Mrs Rogers had received a letter from a Miss Tanya Samuel, the 'wealthy and well-bred daughter of a family from Africa and the West Indies'. The female guests were thrown into a flurry of activity by this announcement. In keeping with Regency custom, a room needed to be found for her, gifts purchased or made, and a special dinner and entertainment organised in her honour.

'I'm not sure why it has affected me so much,' continued Mrs Enright. 'Partly I think it is because my charge is already considered the lowest in the pecking order and this new girl might render her chances of an engagement even more remote. And then, there are far too many women here already; we don't need another.' The handsome Mr Carrington had returned to London to attend to business, so once again the

Miss Samuel takes pity on the lady's
companion and dresses her for a ball

number of eligible men had dropped to four and more than one of the women was sighing forlornly. The hostess had already written to him with an invitation to return. 'He has a face like a sunrise,' said Mrs Enright wistfully. 'I hope I'm not feeling sexual jealousy about this new girl; at my age, I thought I would sail through this whole experience with serenity. I am used to closed communities, having worked in the army, and was quite prepared for what I would find here.

But I admit to being surprisingly troubled by this latest announcement.'

'We think the new guest is black because she is from the West Indies, although of course she could be white,' said Miss Conick, who was nervous about how a black woman might be received in the house. 'I had one very interesting conversation where I objected to the slave figurines that are in the drawing room: I find them really offensive; they are symbols of a terrible, dark period in human history. But I've heard people saying, "Don't be so stupid, they're beautiful," and it makes my flesh crawl.'

Apart from being one of the most politically aware and engaged members of the household, Miss Conick is especially attuned to the issue of race since her paternal grandfather is black. Only she and Captain Glover had expressed much interest in the wider political situation in the Regency at this point, the others being apparently more absorbed in the politics unfolding within the house. 'If I were describing Kentchurch in Regency terms,' said Miss Conick, 'I would have to say it is probably a Tory rather than Whig establishment. But even saying that is overstating the situation as most people here seem nervous to express any sort of political opinion or simply don't seem to have them. They are truly apathetic.'

Given the size of her fortune, Miss Samuel would be the second-highest-ranking young woman in the house, and a good-sized bedroom was needed to accommodate her and her extensive luggage, which arrived ahead of her. Perched precariously on top of the hand-barrow carrying Miss Samuel's trunks was an ornate cage containing two lovebirds and a letter from the heiress asking Mrs Rogers to take care of them until her arrival. This was clearly not a woman who would be prepared to share a bed or live in a tent. In the end the hostess

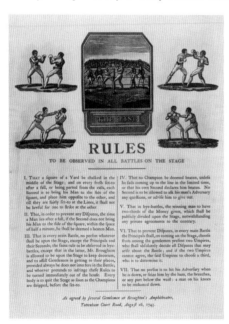

BROUGHTON'S RULES REMAINED IN FORCE UNTIL THEY WERE SWEPT AWAY BY THE MARQUESS OF QUEENSBERRY'S RULES IN 1867

agreed to move into her boudoir and bequeath her exquisite bedroom to the new arrival.

The men took little part in the arrangements for the new guest, since they were devoting their time to organising their own, secret, men-only event. The professor, Peter Radford, had discussed with the host the possibility of organising a meeting of 'the Fancy' on the Kentchurch Estate. The Fancy was the name given to a notorious and powerful group of men of all ages and classes that emerged around 1800 to finance, organise and bet on sport. As

'SCRATCH IS MARKED OUT IN PAINT

the popularity of sport grew during the first twenty years of the nineteenth century, so did the allure of the Fancy. These men thrived on the thrill of taking risks with their money, their health and sometimes even their lives. The Fancy had no formal membership or structure, but its 'members' had well-known meeting places, their own way of dressing, a favourite tipple (gin) and a private language. They exuded an aura of excitement and risk, which drew in fresh adherents whenever a major new event was staged. Their inspiration was Gentleman Jackson, the Regency sporting superstar.

The Fancy was involved in every sport, but above all with pugilism, or prize-fighting. There were organised prize-fights, usually arranged by two gentlemen of the Fancy, who put up a 'purse' (often substantial sums of money) for which the fighters would compete. Several side-bets would then also be placed – on how long the fight would last, who would be first to be knocked down or draw blood, lose teeth or need stitches, etc. These bare-knuckle matches were a cross between wrestling and boxing, a combination of blows and throws which would continue until one of the contestants could no longer stand up. The rules of engagement were published in 1743 by Jack Broughton, and separate 'Articles of Agreement' were also drawn up for all major fights, to define and regulate those points that could lead to a dispute between the principal parties.

Gentlemen did not take part in prize-fights, but were almost always in attendance to support and finance the fighters – despite its being illegal. Fights had been
banned because the large and unruly crowds that gathered to watch were seen as a
potential threat to public order. As a consequence, all prize-fights were arranged in
semi-secrecy with only a few people being entrusted with the time and venue until
the last moment – very like a modern rave. Despite these precautions, many thousands of spectators would turn up to watch the fight, often joined by the local
Justice of the Peace (incognito, of course). Those JPs and county magistrates who
were less pugilistically inclined, however, would arrest the fighters and sometimes
the fight organisers as well, if they found out about a forthcoming bout.

Mr Gorell Barnes was very excited at the prospect of hosting the Fancy, and
he and the professor immediately went on a scouting expedition to find the right
venue. Although gentlemen would not themselves participate, knowledge of how to
fight and spar was considered an essential skill. Pugilism was the very height of
fashion, and thousands of men threw themselves earnestly into training and practice. The uncertainty provoked by the Napoleonic Wars may have played its part in
advancing the cause of pugilism, as did the Fancy's campaign to stamp out effemi-
nacy. Fighting was a demonstration of 'manliness' – a quality that could potentially
save the country from foreign threat – and was therefore deemed patriotic.

Early the following morning the men clad themselves in loose white breeches
and flowing white shirts, and practised their moves on the back lawn of the house.
Their breeches were held up with colourful handkerchiefs, as was the fashion of the
time, and they wore black pumps on their feet. Regency 'sports' shoes were thin-
soled, with no traction, cushioning or support.

Inside the house, meanwhile, the women were preparing for the new guest's
arrival. Mrs Enright, laying aside her initial misgivings, had painted her a screen,
depicting a beautiful exotic bird being attacked by a snake. As the trainee pugilists
were enjoying a well-earned draught of ale at the end of their practice, a carriage
arrived in the courtyard. Maids and footmen rushed out to attend and the eyes of
all the men were fixed on the carriage door.

Miss Tanya Samuel finally emerged – six foot tall, dignified and beautiful.
Two maids strewed red rose petals on the ground before her feet and Mrs Rogers

MISS SAMUEL IS THROWN INTO THE DEEP END OF THE REGENCY EXPERIENCE arrived at the door to greet her. Tanya's pocketbook informed her that

> As part of an affluent family, you are the toast of London society, which is
> enamoured of your refined ways and your creative abilities. You have been
> heralded as being at the fashion vanguard but you have also shown your
> sensibility to the suffering of your fellow man by taking up the cause of
> abolition.

'I knew I was going to be a high-ranking woman and I am coming in here to
stir things up a bit!' said Tanya. 'When I told people I was going to the Regency
House Party, living the life of a black heiress who's come from the colonies, they'd
drink everything in and then about five minutes later they'd say, "So you're in the
house as a maid?"! You have to laugh because we're not really given information
about the black experience in Britain. I got people arguing with me – "No, it can't
possibly be right" – and I'm saying, "Yes, it can possibly be right."'

Although the majority of Britain's black population (perhaps around twenty
thousand) belonged to the 'lower orders', there were several examples of black
people being accepted into British high society, provided of course that they had
fortune or status. Queen Charlotte herself, mother of the Regent, was of mixed
race, being directly descended from Margarita de Castro y Sousa, who was a part
of the black branch of the Portuguese royal house. Her favourite portraitist, Sir
Allan Ramsay, clearly celebrated her mixed heritage in his paintings. Ramsay himself was a vociferous opponent of slavery and married the niece of Lord Mansfield,
the English judge whose 1772 ruling was the first in a series of judicial edicts that
finally ended slavery in the British Empire.

Mrs Hester Piozzi, in a letter to a friend in 1802, noted 'a black lady covered
in finery, in the Pit at the Opera, and tawny children playing in the gardens of the
Squares with their nurses'. She observed that 'men of colour in the rank of gentlemen' were a sign of social change. This change was not welcomed by all: a disapproving American visitor noted in 1805 that a black man, dressed fashionably and
arm-in-arm with a well-dressed white woman, could walk along Oxford Street
unmolested and largely unremarked.

On the evening of Miss Samuel's arrival, a magnificent banquet in her honour
was presented by the ever-inventive chef, who chose to emphasise the exotic and
sweet dishes that so pleased the Regency palate. The table was decorated with an

enormous sugar sculpture portraying a benign vision of plantation life, complete with smiling slaves. 'The dinner, oh my God, was actually a really full-on meal,' said Miss Samuel. 'I've not eaten so much ever, in one sitting at least. Absolutely gorgeous, excellent food. It was very sugary, based on a Caribbean theme.'

'There was this very provocative centrepiece of sugar,' noted Miss Francesca. 'I know Miss Samuel has come here in the role of an abolitionist and I think she was expected to comment, but I felt she wasn't going to be drawn on it until she really wanted to be. She will tackle those issues in her own time: very Regency, in a way, to do it in a civilised fashion.' The following morning, however, the weekly newspaper held a front-page article that pulled many of the guests up short:

> Slavery yet exists. The wealth derived from the horrid traffic has created an influence that secures its continuance; unless the people at large shall refuse to receive the produce of robbery and murder, namely sugar and tobacco. With us it rests either to consume these commodities and be partners in the crime, or to exonerate ourselves from guilt, by spurning from us the temptation. So necessarily connected are our consumption of the commodity and the misery resulting from it, that in every pound of sugar or two ounces of tobacco used, we may be considered as consuming two ounces of human flesh. We also perpetrate the destruction of an alarming number of seamen by the slave trade and spread inconceivable anguish, terror and dismay, through an immense continent, by the burning of their villages, tearing parents from children; breaking every bond of society, and destroying every source of human happiness.

Although the slave trade was abolished in Britain in 1807, Britain's sugar colonies in the West Indies continued to depend on slave labour. Abolition was the hottest political topic of the Regency, and the boycott on sugar and tobacco was supported by many eminent people.

How should the house-guests respond to this news? Should they boycott sugar and tobacco, as the newspaper recommended? Captain Glover and Miss Samuel argued effectively for the boycott, adding to the case against slavery contained in the newspaper article. Several guests chose to maintain their silence and others, particularly the chaperones, seemed unconvinced by the arguments. The debate was causing a rift within the house party, just as it had across the country

TO BE SOLD on board the Ship *Bance-Island*, on tuesday the 6th of *May* next, at *Ashley-Ferry*, a choice cargo of about 250 fine healthy

NEGROES,

juft arrived from the Windward & Rice Coaft. —The utmoft care has already been taken, and fhall be continued, to keep them free from the leaft danger of being infected with the SMALL-POX, no boat having been on board, and all other communication with people from *Charles-Town* prevented.

Auftin, Laurens, & Appleby.

N. B. Full one Half of the above Negroes have had the SMALL-POX in their own Country.

during the Regency. The guests eventually decided to boycott sugar and tobacco for twenty-four hours, starting from four in the afternoon that day.

'I felt rather awkward,' admitted Miss Samuel later. 'I was rather thrown in at the deep end during that debate. I am the latest arrival at the house so it's hard to start throwing your weight around, and that's not my tactic in daily life anyway.' Mrs Hammond was vehement in her opposition. 'I am absolutely completely against being ordered not to smoke,' she said. 'We're supposed to be showing that we're against oppression, and we've been oppressed in order to show that. I'm feeling oppressed. I'm in slavery.' Mr Everett was sceptical of the usefulness of the ban, whereas Mr Foxsmith was all for it. 'The only good thing people say about sugar is that it tastes nice,' he said. 'Pathetic! And it's even worse to know that in order to get sugar they had to enslave people.' For Miss Francesca, it was useful to draw a comparison with modern life. 'I would hope that if I'd lived in 1816 I would have eaten less sugar and I hope that I would have joined a protest against slavery but, as a massive lover of sugar, I can see that it's very difficult and you've got to be a strong person to give up things. In 2003 it's all very well saying slavery was awful *then*, but I think there are an awful lot of things that we probably let happen today because we can't face up to depriving ourselves of tiny things.'

For most of the eighteenth century, Britain had been supplying an average of over twenty-three thousand slaves a year to the West Indies, and by the 1790s that figure had risen to forty-five thousand. Britain's slave trade was a major contributor to its economy, buttressing its maritime trade, supplying essential labour for its colonies and providing vital capital for industrialisation. Bristol, Glasgow and Liverpool all became major ports and splendid cities as a direct result of their part in the slave trade. However, the British also gleaned deep national pride from being 'free' – 'Britons never, never, never shall be slaves'. Liberty and independence for the individual was *the* political ideology of the eighteenth century.

A highly vocal anti-slavery campaign arose, led initially by British Quakers and spearheaded eventually by the Christian evangelist William Wilberforce. 'The unwearied, unostentatious, and inglorious crusade of England against slavery may probably be regarded as among the three or four perfectly virtuous acts recorded in the history of nations,' announced one nineteenth-century historian. The Lord Chancellor in 1807 said that ending the trade was 'our duty to God, and to our country which was the morning star that enlightened Europe, and whose boast and glory was to grant liberty and life, and administer humanity and justice to all'.

The first petitions for the abolition of slavery were gathered in 1788, when one hundred of them were sent to Parliament, and popular support for the proposal did not diminish during the Regency. In 1814, at the Congress of Vienna that followed Napoleon's defeat, a proposal was made to renew the rights of French slave merchants. This suggestion roused the English to fury, and within a month 806 petitions, bearing the signatures of one and a half million protesters, were sent to Parliament.

That night, the guests at Kentchurch ate a dinner entirely devoid of sugar. It appeared that everyone managed to abide by the smoking ban as well, though the topic of slavery (and for that matter the issue of race in modern Britain) was not actually discussed. Miss Conick was disappointed by her fellow guests' attitude. 'It was amazing how many people just wanted to brush the politics under the table,' she observed. ' "Have another drink and enjoy yourself" was Mr Everett's motto, and most of the other guests were happy to abide by it. It seemed as though they were terrified of expressing an opinion for fear of provoking an argument.' Miss Hopkins agreed: 'I think it's very sad that people are frightened of discussing a topic openly because they are worried about how they will be perceived. Surely if you really believe in something you'll stand up and voice it. I do. It is so ironic. We're sat here enjoying this fantastic opulence. Yeah, and how did we get the money to do it?'

Miss Hopkins and the other house-guests were diverted from the boycott the following morning by

MENU FOR THE SUGAR
BANQUET

Callaloo soup
Salt pork and crab
Sweet-pickled John Dory
Sugar-baked ham
Roast sweet potatoes
Guineafowl and pheasant
Sweet chicken pie
Turnips and swede
Sweet parsnip tart
Sweet spinach tart
Baked pineapple with rum and
peppercorns
West Indian pudding with ginger
Coffee ice cream
Lemon and muscovado ice (sorbet)

DISCUSSIONS ON POLITICS ARE RARE AT KENTCHURCH COURT

the appearance of an illustrious musician and dandy, Austin Howard. Intrigued no doubt by reports of his dazzling charms, the young women rushed to greet him. Mr Howard's pocketbook informed him that

> *You are back in England after a stint in Europe. Your reputation precedes*
> *you as you have been seldom out of the scandal sheets. Your attention to style*
> *has been noted — so much so that you are considered something of a dandy.*

Ladies have been said to throw themselves at the foot of your carriage. Such a stir did you cause amongst them with your performance at the Munich Opera House that you were forced to remain in your dressing room lest a fracas ensue. While parents should be warned to be watchful of their daughters in your company, your musical performance and charm deservedly delight all.

Austin Howard is an entertainer, performer and composer, known for his provocative but amusing musical exhibitions. He has worked at the Young and Old Vics and now runs a website company. He had written to the host the previous week, explaining that he was in the area and was prepared to perform with his quartet at Kentchurch. To lighten the mood of the house, his offer was accepted.

Mr Howard had created his repertoire for the Kentchurch soirée with care, choosing a range of music from the Regency era that included classical pieces, ballads, dances and popular songs. Two pieces were of particular interest. One was Beethoven's 'Kreutzer' Sonata, written originally for the renowned Regency violinist George Bridgtower. The second was a ballad by Bridgtower himself, a lover's lament entitled 'Henry'. George Polgreen Bridgtower was a fascinating Regency character. A musical prodigy, he was born to a Barbadian father and an Austro-German mother and raised in the summer palace of Prince Esterhazy, in Eisenstadt, where his father was the prince's valet. Haydn also lived at the palace for many years and took the young George under his wing. George was only nine when he made his professional début in Paris in 1789 and within a few months was playing for the King and Queen of England. A courtier noted, 'The young performer played to perfection, with a clear, good tone, spirit, pathos and good taste.'

After many concerts across the country, the boy was taken under the wing of the Prince of Wales. For fourteen years, Bridgtower held the post of first violinist in the Prince of Wales's private band, which moved between Carlton House and Brighton Pavilion. He also played at Covent Garden, Drury Lane and the Haymarket as soloist or principal violinist. He met Beethoven in 1802 on a visit to Vienna and was described by the great composer as 'a very able virtuoso and an absolute master of his instrument'. Bridgtower gave the first performance of the 'Kreutzer' Sonata in Vienna in 1803, with Beethoven at the piano. As there had been insufficient time to make proper copies of the sonata, Bridgtower had to read

Beethoven's scrawled notes and, at one point, was forced to improvise. The composer leaped up and hugged him, shouting, 'Once more, my good fellow!' The two men later argued over a woman, and Beethoven changed the name of the sonata from 'Bridgtower' to 'Kreutzer', the name of another violinist whom he had never even met.

Mr Howard threw himself into his role at Kentchurch and flirted outrageously with all the women, considering this to be appropriate behaviour for any self-respecting dandy. It is fortunate that Beau Brummell was not present with his quizzing glasses, since he certainly would have been taken aback by Mr Howard's interpretation of dandyism. Mrs Enright was charmed. 'Mr Austin Howard is black. There's no other way of saying that. Very handsomely black and with very charming manners and a most alluring personality. I look forward to talking to him quite a lot and of course I mustn't hog him from the girls. I'm sure they won't allow me to because I have noticed with what extreme grace and precision he divides his time equally between the ladies.' The younger women, having fallen for him on his arrival, were less impressed by his flirting and their ardour soon dimmed. He redeemed himself in their eyes, however, with the musical soirée, which took the guests by storm. After the classical pieces, he launched into a medley of Regency songs to a rock'n'roll beat. Within minutes all the guests, including the usually sedate Mrs Rogers, were up and boogying – a modern move, perhaps, but entirely in the Regency spirit.

'We had the most fantastic evening of Regency music with Mr Howard and his brilliant quartet,' said Mr Everett. 'The two children who played in the quartet were simply superb, and it was so nice to have some real music, and very beautiful music. Howard had a wonderful voice, the band played exquisitely and it was one of those very happy evenings. I think the highlight was when he suddenly broke into a bit of rock'n'roll and sang the "Byron Bygone Dandy Man" song. I haven't laughed so much in weeks and weeks.'

And 'if music be the food of love', Bridgtower's ballad to a broken-hearted lover certainly seemed to ignite strong emotions in some of the guests. With the chaperones distracted, Mr Everett seized the moment to ask Miss Hopkins to take a turn around the garden, now in darkness. She obliged, and was treated to an earnest proclamation of his undying devotion. Unbeknown to either of them, however, Miss Braund had also taken advantage of the cool of the evening and was sitting on the grass just a few feet away. Frozen with embarrassment, and unsure whether it was better to announce herself immediately or stay hidden in the darkness until they had gone, she overheard the entire conversation. Miss Hopkins, with compassion and generosity, declined Mr Everett's advances. She explained that she liked him very much, but since he was also the object of Miss Braund's affections, it would be unkind of them to start a romance under her very nose – little realising the accuracy of her remark. Her concern for Miss Braund's feelings was complicated by her own doubts. She found Mr Everett kind and thoughtful and capable of beautifully romantic gestures such as making love tokens for her. She had once mentioned to him that lavender helped her sleep and had recently found an acorn encircled by a stem of lavender on her pillow. Her mildly tender feelings for him, however, had been eclipsed by the much stronger emotions aroused in her by the dashing Mr Carrington, despite the brevity of his stay. Mr Everett, full of plans for the beautiful things he and Miss Hopkins could do together in the romantic world of Regency Kentchurch, was thwarted.

Mr Everett had little chance to mope the following day, however, for he was to be an umpire for the Fancy, who were congregating in the meadow by the gatehouse. The site had been well chosen: the meadow was large enough to hold the many thousands of spectators that were expected over the course of the morning; trees provided shade, under which the ale stalls and spit-roast were being set up; and near by the river dividing Herefordshire from Wales wended its lazy path westwards.

While the ring (a turfed area enclosed by a rope and with posts at each corner) was being erected, the professor arrived early to draw up the articles of agreement for the fight and to supervise the final payments to the 'purse'. Captain Glover and Mr Gorell Barnes both put up a hundred guineas for the boxers to fight for. Mr Everett threw down another two hundred guineas, making a handsome purse that would have attracted the country's best boxers in the Regency. The gentlemen were divided into two teams. One team would support the 'home' fighter, Mr Tim Dean, the chief night-watchman at Kentchurch, while the other would support the 'guest' fighter, whose identity was still unknown.

Mr Dean is, in reality, a bodyguard who runs his own security company,

protecting individuals and film sets and advising on health and safety. He has the
stature and physique of Gentleman Jackson (although taller and heavier at six foot
two and eighteen stone), and his strength and gentlemanly manners made it hard
to see how anyone could stand up to him, male or female. He was an excellent boxer
in his youth and is well informed on the history of the sport. His close acquaintance with Broughton's rules and the reality of bare-knuckle fighting, combined
with the on-hand expertise of the professor, ensured that the Kentchurch meeting
of the Fancy was historically accurate to the last detail.

Due to its illegality, none of the men had told the women in the house about the fight. Two of the younger women however had discovered (by means unknown) that something unusual was afoot on the estate and were keen to know more. Miss Braund and Miss Hopkins, realising that the secrecy surrounding the event signalled that their presence would be unwelcome, procured men's clothes for themselves and escaped the watchful eyes of their chaperones by feigning illness. Dressed as young village men, they crept out of the grounds and followed the smell of the pig-roast until they found the crowds gathering around the ring.

Before the start of the fight, Mr Dean's patron, Captain Glover, and his supporters took him off for a 'scientific' breakfast of eggs. A high-protein diet was popular at the time among fighters or those gentlemen developing their fighting physiques. At two o'clock Gentleman Dean was led to the ringside by his second and his 'bottle holder' – the man responsible for providing the fighter with water, brandy and oils. His opponent, however, had still not arrived. This could have been because he wished to put him off, or to dramatise his own importance, or perhaps because he had been arrested by the local magistrate.

Suddenly a chorus of jeers and boos arose from the crowd near the trees. A group of men was approaching the Kentchurch boundary from the other side of the river – in other words, from across the border. Dean's opponent had arrived. He was hoisted on to the shoulders of his second and his bottle holder, and the group waded across the river. It was none other than Matt Skelton, seven-times world kick-boxing champion, and now ranked fifth in the British Heavyweight Championship (and tipped to win the title), despite having taken up boxing only a year ago. This was to be a fight to remember.

Captain Glover gave Mr Dean his hat, which he threw into the ring, thus issuing the challenge to fight. Mr Gorell Barnes replied by handing his own hat to Mr Skelton, who threw it in by way of reply. Then came the 'pose down'. The two fighters removed their shirts and stood in their stockings and breeches, flexing their muscles for the expectant crowd beside two small statues of classical athletes that had been placed in the ring. The professor shouted out happy comparisons between the athletes of antiquity and the gods standing before them, proclaiming the size and strength of both men, their previous wins, the closeness of the match and so on, thereby inciting the crowd to a fever pitch of excitement. Bets started flooding in, alcohol flowed, the fighters began to taunt each other and the crowd

MEETINGS OF THE FANCY DREW LARGE CROWDS
FROM EVERY SOCIAL BACKGROUND

became more and more raucous. Miss Hopkins and Miss Braund stood near the ale stall, hiding behind huge tankards and under caps. Not one of the gentlemen had recognised them, even though Mr Gorell Barnes had walked past Miss Braund five times and even bumped into her once.

'It was incredible to spy on the men without them knowing we were there,' said Miss Braund. 'They were completely different to how they are in the house. To see Everett yelling and yelling, and Captain Glover getting so worked up.'

'It was definitely one of the best moments of the whole house party,' agreed Miss Hopkins. 'It was fun to be exposed to something so male. Not for the faint-hearted, admittedly, but I'm lucky in the sense that I've been to kick-boxing fights and I grew up in Yorkshire so I've seen one or two fights. Sat there with a big pork pie in one hand and a tankard of ale in the other, it was really fantastic!'

At last, each man took to his corner. Beside each fighter stood his umpire, whose job was to call out if he saw the opponent commit a foul (but keep quiet if his own fighter did). A referee, standing outside the ring, would decide on the merits of the call. Umpire for Mr Dean was Mr Everett, and umpire for Mr Skelton was Mr Foxsmith. The referee was the professor. Chalk lines or 'scratches' were drawn three feet apart, and the gentlemen came up to stand behind them. This practice gave rise to the term 'coming up to scratch'. The rounds were not of fixed duration but ended when one fighter hit the floor, and the fight as a whole ended when one man was unable to come up to scratch.

A cry of 'Time!' from the referee started the fight. Within seconds a tremendous roaring and yelling arose as the crowd began to bay their support for their man. The first round ended after only nine seconds when Mr Skelton surprised his opponent by charging him at full speed and knocking him down. Mr Dean remained on the floor until his second and his bottle holder came to carry him back

MATT SKELTON SLIPS EFFORTLESSLY INTO THE ROLE OF REGENCY PUGILIST

to the corner, as was the procedure in the Regency. Each fighter had thirty seconds in his corner before the referee once again shouted, 'Time!' to indicate the start of the next round. They were then carried back to 'scratch' by their seconds.

Boxing was one of the few ways that black men could become successful and accepted in Regency society. The first black boxer in Britain of whom any record has been preserved was Joe Leashley, a fourteen-stone African who is said to have shown 'great activity, skill, and game [pluck]; pourtraying a knowledge of the art, superior to most amateurs'. Later came Bill Richmond. The son of Georgia-born slaves, Richmond came to Britain in 1777 at the age of fourteen as a servant to the future Duke of Northumberland. He learned to box in the course of a series of

fights with soldiers and anyone else who insulted him. He was also a remarkable athlete and cricketer. He moved to London and became a bodyguard to Lord Camelford, an important and wealthy member of the Fancy. Through this association Richmond soon became famous for his sporting prowess, his ability to teach fighters and his great conviviality. The public house he ran, the Horse and Dolphin, at the bottom of Leicester Square, became one of the most popular haunts in London, much frequented by the Fancy. Next door to the pub he ran a boxing academy, where he gave more formal lessons to hundreds of pupils.

Richmond's protégé and fellow American Tom Molineaux, became even more famous than his teacher and might well have won the heavyweight championship of England had he not been tricked out of it. He was born in 1784 in Virginia and became slave to a rich playboy, who staked $100,000 that the young man would beat another slave in a boxing match. Tom was promised $500 and his freedom if he won. He did, and worked his passage to England as a deckhand in 1809. 'An entire stranger, destitute of friends or money', he was welcomed by Richmond, who went on to give him further training. Molineaux faced the notorious Tom Cribb in a fight that went thirty-nine rounds; the men's faces were so battered by the end that they were unrecognisable. When Cribb went down, two hundred spectators rushed into the ring, racist taunts were shouted and Molineaux's finger was broken in the scuffle. Just when it seemed as though Molineaux had won, Cribb's second shouted out that Molineaux was hiding bullets in his fist. By the time the charge had been proved false, Cribb had managed to rise to his feet. Molineaux eventually retired but challenged Cribb to a return match in a letter which ended: 'I cannot omit the opportunity of expressing a confident hope, that the circumstances of my being a different colour to that of a people amongst whom I have sought protection will not in any way operate to my prejudice.'

THE HERMIT SELLS 'T-SHIRTS' – 'I WAS AT THE FANCY' AND 'SAY NO TO BARE-KNUCKLE BOXING'

The return match was held at the border of the counties of Leicestershire, Lincolnshire and Rutland to a record crowd of up to twenty-five thousand spectators, a quarter of them nobility and gentry. It was one of the great sporting events of the nineteenth century. Molineaux was knocked out in the eleventh round, but he went on to win several prize-fights and also travelled to Ireland to give exhibition fights.

The Kentchurch fight continued for twenty-six rounds and until the final few rounds it was impossible to tell who would emerge the victor. 'It was one of those moments when I was truly there,' said Mr Everett, 'when suddenly it came to life and I was back two hundred years.

THE GENTLEMEN OF THE FANCY ENJOY A TANKARD OR TWO

I'm leaning on the edge of the ring with my tankard of ale and swigging it down, looking around the crowd, jeering faces, people shouting, people really getting into it, it was *fantastic*. I will walk away from this project not only a better man, not only a changed man, but more a man than I've ever felt before. An actual man. And that's a wonderful feeling to have inside.'

The Fancy and the training they had received from the professor had been equally revealing for Captain Glover. 'Here I am at forty-one, finding that I'm quite good at certain things, like boxing and fencing and riding, and thinking, Damn! I wish I'd learned this when I was twenty. Being able to embrace life and saying, "Try this" or "Try that". It's what this whole Regency experience has been about: to appreciate life and understand ourselves and our full potential – no one's forced us to do it; we've enjoyed it.'

Suddenly the crowd's hollering increased in volume. After eighty minutes of close-fought struggle, Mr Dean was unable to come up to scratch. Matt Skelton had won the fight. Although they were keen to stay and cheer on the victor and cheer up the loser, the two girls decided they had better return to the house to avoid detection. Downing a final pint of ale, they staggered back to the corseted world of chaperoned propriety.

FAMOUS ANATOMIST PROFESSOR GUNTHER VON HAGENS AND A PLASTINATED CORPSE

CHAPTER NINE

LIFE, DEATH AND ANATOMY

REGENCY REVOLUTIONS IN SCIENCE

It was on a dreary night of November that I beheld the accomplishment of my toils. With an anxiety that almost amounted to agony, I collected the instruments of life around me, that I might infuse a spark of being into the lifeless thing that lay at my feet. It was already one in the morning; the rain pattered dismally against the panes, and my candle was nearly burnt out, then, by the glimmer of the half-extinguished light, I saw the dull yellow eye of the creature open; it breathed hard, and a convulsive motion agitated its limbs . . . His eyes fixed on me. His jaws opened, and he muttered some inarticulate sound, while a grin wrinkled his cheeks. He might have spoken, but I did not hear; one hand was stretched out, seemingly to detain me, but I escaped and rushed downstairs

MARY SHELLEY, *FRANKENSTEIN: OR, THE MODERN PROMETHEUS*, 1818

THE HERMIT RUMINATES ON DEATH
IN HIS RURAL RETREAT

LADY DEVONPORT'S soft voice conveyed all the tension and horror of the scene in which Dr Frankenstein brings his creature to life, as she sat on a low wooden stool in the ancient stable block, reading to Mr Foxsmith. They had both heard stories from the grooms and stablehands about strange occurrences in there. This is the oldest part of the house and consists of a small downstairs room with a fireplace in one corner and a narrow wooden spiral staircase leading up to two large rooms above. Several people had claimed to have heard footsteps in the upstairs rooms when there was no one up there. The principal groom, well known for his sanguine temperament, had eventually refused to sleep in the

downstairs room after twice waking up and seeing a figure standing on the staircase and watching him. Lady Devonport and Mr Foxsmith, whose passion for each
other had only grown over the weeks at Kentchurch, decided to spend their first
full night together in the romantic, if eerie setting of the stables – ghost-watching.

The idea for *Frankenstein* came to Mary Shelley in a nightmare. In 1816 she
went on holiday to Switzerland with her husband Percy Bysshe Shelley, Lord
Byron and Dr Polidori. On being cooped up for several days by bad weather, they
passed the time by challenging each other to write ghost stories. As she explained
in her preface to the 1831 edition of the book, 'Many and long were the conversations between Lord Byron and Shelley, to which I was a devout but nearly silent
listener . . . Perhaps a corpse would be reanimated; galvanism had given token of
such things: perhaps the component parts of a creature might be manufactured,
brought together, and endued with vital warmth.' Later, she saw in her turbulent
dreams 'the pale student of unhallowed arts kneeling beside the thing he had put
together . . . the hideous phantasm of a man stretched out, and then, on the work-

THIS PAINTING BY JOSEPH WRIGHT OF DERBY REVEALS THE AMBIVALENCE OF MANY SPECTATORS
OF SCIENTIFIC EXPERIMENTS. THE RARE COCKATOO IS AN EMBLEM OF LOVE, AND ITS SUFFERING IN
THE PUMP ALLUDES TO THE ARROGANCE AND POTENTIAL CRUELTY OF THE EXPERIMENT.

LADY DEVONPORT AND MR FOXSMITH ARE INSEPARABLE

ing of some powerful engine, show signs of life, and stir with an uneasy, half vital motion . . . '

Frankenstein was published anonymously in March 1818. Reviewers wrote extensively about it and treated the powerful tale seriously, convinced that its author must be a man. The story's central theme, that of a man destroyed by the huge, unlovable, lonely creature he has created, highlighted the perils of irresponsible science and raised questions about the potential dangers of man's scientific and technological power outstripping his wisdom. The tale is all too relevant for us today, immersed as we are in debates about genetic modification and cloning.

The idea that a man of science could create a new life artificially was not simply the wild fantasy of a fiction writer. In 1791, the Italian Luigi Galvani was studying the reactions of muscles to electricity and noted that a dead frog's muscles became animated when simultaneously placed in contact with brass and iron. He thought the muscles of the frog created an electrical current when in contact with these metals, which caused spasm and movement. Although electricity appeared to 'give life' to muscles, there was no real understanding of how this happened, and for this reason Mary Shelley was rather vague about the mechanics that infused 'a spark of being' into Frankenstein's monster.

The force of electricity was only beginning to be understood, but it clearly possessed almost magical properties. Perhaps men of science were uncovering the secret of life? Might electrical forces be the spark needed to bring the dead back to life, or to create life in constructed beings? This was not an entirely new idea even in the Regency. The Ancient Greeks had expressed a similar notion in the Prometheus myths, and it was from these that Shelley took the subtitle for her novel. Prometheus was a rebellious but proud god who stole fire from heaven to give to man in an attempt to overthrow the tyrant god Zeus. In another version of the myth, Prometheus is known as Plasticator, a demi-god who modelled figures out of clay and animated them by placing them in the rays of the sun. For this he was punished, being chained to a rock by the god of fire and later being thrown into the regions of hell.

Revolutionary thinking was an integral part of Mary's life, just as it was for her husband, the radical poet Shelley. He was working on his epic poem *Prometheus Unbound* at the same time that Mary was writing her novel. Shelley had been fascinated by science as a youth, experimenting with electricity and chemicals and later reading the latest scientific works, particularly those of Sir Humphry Davy and Erasmus Darwin. He explored the potential for science to free the individual, and his work is peppered with images of space travel, flight and leisure-creating devices. He was expelled from University College, Oxford, for publishing a pamphlet 'On the Necessity of Atheism' and ostracised from his wealthy, established family. He was an enthusiastic reader of the work of the radical philosopher William Godwin, who was married to the eminent writer and pioneer of women's rights Mary Wollstonecraft. Godwin argued for the 'perfectibility' of man, 'being continually made better' by the forces of reason and benevolence. Like a true Romantic, Shelley substituted 'imagination' and 'love' for 'reason'. He eloped with Harriet Westbrook when only nineteen and they had a child. In 1813 they moved to London, where Shelley became almost a part of Godwin's family circle and where he met Godwin's sixteen-year-old daughter, Mary. They fell in love, but Godwin forbade the union and told Shelley to keep away. In the early morning of 27 July 1814, Shelley (aged twenty-one) left his wife and child and eloped with Mary, accompanied at Shelley's invitation by Jane 'Claire' Clairmont, who was fifteen (and who later had a child by Byron). A triangular relationship developed which endured until Shelley's premature death. The three lived abroad, mainly in Switzerland and Italy. Mary had two daughters before she and Shelley married in 1816, after hearing of Harriet's suicide.

This was probably the happiest period in Mary's life, which was otherwise overshadowed by tragedy. Shelley was drowned in a boating accident in the Bay of Spezia near Livorno in 1822 at the age of twenty-nine; two of their three children died in infancy.

Mr Foxsmith and Lady Devonport did not finish the tale of *Frankenstein* the night of their ghost-watching. In their hours of wakefulness, however, they devised a plan to mount a 'Science Week', during which every person would study some aspect of Regency science. They would also host a special 'Science Night' to which guests would contribute demonstrations, talks or experiments on a scientific theme to further their collective understanding of the subject. The idea was accepted with interest by most, a lack of interest by a few and positive revulsion by Mrs Hammond. 'I hate science! I'm going to write a poem about how much I hate it!' she exclaimed. Mr Foxsmith felt sufficiently encouraged to write to Dr Frank

James of the Royal Institution, inviting him to come and demonstrate some experiments of the Regency.

Dr James, Reader in the History of Science, arrived a few days later with several large trunks of apparatus. After a splendid dinner the guests removed to the library, where Dr James and Mr Foxsmith had spent the afternoon setting up his instruments, including an 'electrical machine' to demonstrate to the guests the process of 'galvanism'. He could not recreate Galvani's actual experiment with a frog since the RSPCA forbade it, so he replaced the frog with a less sensitive victim – a light bulb. While constructing a battery to fire up the bulb, Dr James explained briefly the developments in the understanding of electricity that led to the invention of the battery, of which Mary Shelley must have had some knowledge. By the middle of the eighteenth century a machine had been developed that, using friction, could generate electric shocks (often for the amusement of the public). A mile-long chain of Carthusian monks were all shocked at once by a single machine. The public interest in electricity aroused by such stunts led to arguments about the propriety of demonstrating these 'marvellous' effects in public. Was electricity a material or a divine emanation? A political controversy arose along party lines in Parliament, with the Whigs championing the scientific demonstrators and the High Tories claiming that it was blasphemy to expose God's secrets before an ignorant populace.

SCIENTIFIC RESEARCHES! NEW DISCOVERIES IN PNEUMATICS! OR AN EXPERIMENTAL LECTURE ON THE POWERS OF AIR.
CARTOON BY HAROLD KNIGHT

Despite, or perhaps because of, the controversies surrounding electricity, 'electrifying' machines became hugely popular and eventually cheap enough to find their way into the homes of the gentry, such as the one shown in Diana Sperling's painting in which her brother-in-law is 'electrifying' his family. By the end of the eighteenth century electric-shock therapy was being tried out in medicine and was claimed to help relieve symptoms of ague, blindness, palsy, dropsy, deafness

MAY 25TH. HENRY VAN ELECTRIFYING. FAMILY ENTERTAINMENT REGENCY STYLE

and hysteria. Many remained sceptical, however, and when a friend of Jane Austen's asked his physician if he should try electrical treatment, she wrote: 'I fancy we are all unanimous in expecting no advantage from it.'

As the above painting shows, scientific experimentation was one of the few areas of Regency life in which women could participate on something approaching an equal footing with men. When the Royal Institution was founded in 1799, women were able not only to attend lectures but also to become members. Women took full advantage of this opportunity and often formed at least half the audience at popular public lectures – although this did prompt some criticism of the institution on the grounds that allowing women to participate suggested a 'lack of seriousness'. Although women were rarely encouraged to pursue their own research, they were allowed to assist and write up results and were consequently able to popularise science for a wider audience of both adults and children. Maria Edgeworth's book *Harry and Lucy*, published in 1801, introduced young readers 'to the first principles of many sciences or rather the facts upon which those principles are founded'. Ada Lovelace, Lord Byron's daughter, combined the life of a socialite with that of a mathematician and writer. She studied geometry, astronomy and mathematics and became a friend of the computer pioneer Charles Babbage, disseminating his work through her writing.

The first and possibly best public expositor of science in London, who also visited many great country houses discussing his experiments and discoveries, was Humphry Davy. His findings, especially on the relationship between chemistry and electricity, made a great contribution to nineteenth-century science and technology. One of his early discoveries (for which many of us owe him thanks) was the ability to purify nitrous oxide gas, which eventually provided the world with the first non-life-threatening anaesthetic. In his youth he displayed great brilliance, experimenting with chemicals all day and writing verse at night. The poets Coleridge and Southey met him in Bristol and became close friends. He was appointed Assistant Lecturer in Chemistry at the newly founded Royal Institution at the age of twenty-two and quickly promoted to professor and director of its laboratory. His public lectures were a huge success and he threw himself into the many commissions that he received from industry, agriculture, shipbuilding and war. He is possibly best known for inventing the miners' safety lamp, which prevented the lethal explosions caused by a naked flame. He was knighted in 1812.

It was the far-sighted Davy who employed the twenty-two-year-old Michael Faraday, the poor bookbinder's apprentice who became Davy's assistant at the Royal Institution in 1813 and went on to make some of the greatest discoveries in science. Faraday was born into a family too poor to give him a classical education and taught himself from the books available. He spent the Regency experimenting with electricity and published his work on electrical motors in 1821, and the first part of his major work, *Experimental Researches on Electricity*, a decade later. By understanding the relationship between electricity and magnetism, and looking for practical applications of this relationship, Faraday led the way to the massive leaps in technology of the later nineteenth century such as electric lighting, the telegraph and electrical motors and appliances.

THE GUESTS ENJOY THE VELOCIPEDE RECONSTRUCTED BY
MR FOXSMITH FROM REGENCY DIAGRAMS

However, Faraday's brilliant discoveries were founded on the work of Galvani and his contemporaries. Dr James illustrated this point by putting sheets of blotting paper soaked in sulphuric acid between metal plates made of copper and zinc. He explained that when Alessandro Volta heard of Galvani's experiment with the frog, he realised that the current was not created by the frog's muscles but between the two lumps of metal. He was then able to produce, for the first time in history, a steady source of electricity with an invention he called a 'Voltaic pile' – now known as a battery. When Dr James had built a pile of about twelve plates of metal and pieces of blotting paper, he connected it to the light bulb – which lit up!

DAY 16

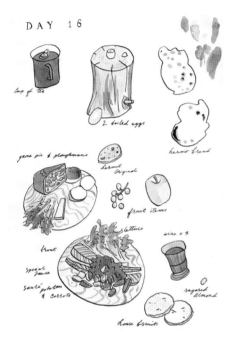

tea of tea
2 boiled eggs
game pie & ploughmans
hermit Original
hermit bread
fruit items
lettuce
wine x 3
trout
special sauce
sauté potatoes & carrots
sugared almond
house biscuits

ZEBEDEE HELM LOST OVER TWO STONE
AND DREW EVERY MORSEL OF FOOD THAT
PASSED HIS LIPS AT KENTCHURCH COURT

As well as witnessing great leaps in the understanding of hitherto mysterious phenomena, this was also an era of speculation about the origins of life on Earth. There were various theories in circulation concerning the 'evolution' of the planet and the creatures that lived upon it, among them that posited by Erasmus Darwin (Charles Darwin's grandfather). E. Darwin was as talented as he was fat (a semicircle had to be cut in his dining table in order to accommodate his stomach) and he epitomised the happy union of science and art: he was an inventor, a designer, a poet and an entrepreneur. After studying fossils preserved in the Castleton caves near his home, he came increasingly to believe that all living organisms had descended from a single ancestor. This was the first step on the path to the modern notion of evolution.

One of his many enthusiasms was for botany, and his poem about the sex life of plants, 'The Botanic Garden' (1791), became the favourite reading of one particular couple at Kentchurch, encompassing as it did both science and passion. For example, of the orchid, Darwin wrote:

Hence on the green leaves the sexual pleasures dwell,

And Loves and Beauties craw'd the blossom's bell;

O'er the pleas'd stigma bows his head;

With meeting lips, and mingling smiles, they sup

Ambrosial dew-drops from the nectar's cup;

Or buoy'd in air the plumy Lover springs,

And seeks his painting bride on Hymen-wings.

Gaily did Lady Devonport read out the poem to Mr Foxsmith as they researched ideas for their Science Night. Their relationship progressed along its evolutionary path during the many hours they spent secluded in the library or about the grounds. They had abandoned all pretence that their relationship was simply a meeting of minds and had found a new description to account for their constant public displays of affection – it was a 'passionate friendship'. 'Lady D', as Mr Foxsmith affectionately called her, 'and I have just spent ten minutes staring into a patch of white flowers without talking. It was utterly sublime. The terror and beauty of nature hit me and I have never had such a heightened sense of awareness before.'

However, so unrelenting was the couple's mutual joy that Mr Gorell Barnes was forced to have a quiet word with them to suggest more tact and discretion in their deportment. Lady Devonport's behaviour was scandalous in Regency terms and her neglect of her charge, Miss Hopkins, was also to have serious consequences.

The couple were not alone in their pursuit of passion. Miss Francesca spent many hours, even whole days, in the hermit's shack. Her initial excuse was that she was delivering him food and rescuing him from imminent starvation. However, as the days passed and his diet improved, she cited 'experiments making toffee apples with the hermit' as the reason for her absence. This boldness, coupled with the neglect of her duties, did not go unnoticed and she too suffered the ignominy of receiving a lecture on the proper behaviour of a lady of dependent and inferior status from her guardian.

While the Regency was noteworthy for many leaps forward in scientific knowledge, not all the latest 'discoveries' could boast much in the way of scientific credibility.

An unusual parcel was delivered to Mr Foxsmith as he worked hard on preparations for the Science Night: a head, accompanied by a note from Mr Carrington explaining that he was returning to the house but thought 'Foxy' might like this head in advance. Intrigued, Mr Foxsmith examined the contents further. It turned out to be a 'phrenological' head, complete with instructions on how to read a person's character traits by feeling the bumps on their skull. Phrenology became a craze

MISS FRANCESCA GETS HER TEETH INTO THE
HERMIT'S CULINARY CREATIONS

TOFFEE   APPLE

in the Regency, allowing men and women to rub their hands over a part of each other other's anatomy (albeit not a part known for its erogenous qualities). And, temporarily at least, it achieved a certain scientific and intellectual credibility.

Mr Carrington himself was expected the following day. 'I like him a lot,' confided Miss Hopkins, 'and I am looking forward to him coming back so that I can have an opportunity to get to know him better. I am not saying that I prefer him to Mr Everett, I'm just saying that I like him and I find his company a lot easier than Mr Everett's. Whether it is friendship or attraction between us I don't know yet, but there are genuine emotions at play and that scares me.' Miss Hopkins had made Mr Carrington a tambourine with FOLLOW THE BEAT OF YOUR HEART stencilled on to it and placed it on his pillow to await his return. The ladies were grouped on the 'chapel landing' to greet him when he arrived, and as he approached they moved apart to reveal a grand piano that had been ordered by Mrs Hammond.

'It was so nice of them to think of me like that. The piano is wonderful and Miss Hopkins' tambourine blew me away,' said Mr Carrington, somewhat incredulous at Miss Hopkins' overt display of affection for him. 'It was a really sweet thing to do, though I'm not sure I would ever have the courage to make my feelings so plain.'

With a rock'n'roll reputation to maintain, Mr Carrington had decided he would stir things up in the house, and he had ample opportunity to do so on the first night of his return, when Mr Foxsmith decided to hold a Phrenological Evening and make use of the head Mr Carrington had sent. For once the guests were allowed to touch each other without contravening the rules of etiquette (although the lack of shampoo made this a less pleasurable experience for some).

PHILOPROGENITIVENESS

2 *Small:* Decided aversion to children; want of parental feeling.

4 *Moderate:* Indifference to children and pets, no anxiety for them.

6 *Full:* A due regard for children, but not blind partiality.

8 *Large:* Strong degree of parental affection and tenderness.

10 *Extra large:* Excessive fondness for children; too indulgent.

ADHESIVENESS

2 *Small:* Destitute of affection; always desirous of change.

4 *Moderate:* Changeable in love of affection; very fond of variety.

6 *Full:* Constancy, pure affection, platonic and sincere attachments.

8 *Large:* Unalterable affection; enduring all things for love.

10 *Extra large:* Passionate and devoted in attachment to friends.

The countess discovered that Mr Gorell Barnes' head displayed a love of 'sex, defiance and wonder'. Regardless of its poor scientific credentials, he seemed pleased with this assessment. Miss Francesca found the hermit to have 'congeniality and an aptitude for marriage, solicitude and sex'. Again, the subject did not demur. Captain Glover agreed heartily with the assessment of him as someone with a love of children, selfishness, stability, firmness, spirituality and application. 'That's very accurate,' he said. 'I'm impressed by this guy,' he added, pointing to the head. Mr Everett's cranium, examined by Miss

*CALVES HEADS AND BRAINS OR A PHRENOLOGICAL LECTURE.
AN ENGRAVING BY L. BUMP (SIC)*

Conick, was said to reveal a love of 'sex and marriage, solicitude and geniality'. While others thought this a fairly accurate assessment, Mr Everett did not. In fact, the entire exercise appeared to try him greatly and his mood was silent and angry, though this may have been related to the fact that Miss Hopkins had chosen to feel the skull of his rival, Mr Carrington. In contrast to Mr Everett, Mr Carrington considered Miss Hopkins' reading of his head to have been reasonably accurate. 'Gregarious, intuitive, domestic, slightly defensive,' she had concluded. 'That's fifty per cent right,' he declared. 'I am gregarious and intuitive – I can sum people up pretty quickly. But not the rest.' If Miss Hopkins retained any notions of enjoying familial bliss with Mr Carrington, this might have been a good moment to reconsider.

All this bodily manipulation had aroused in Mr Carrington and Miss Hopkins a clearer idea of whether their association was to be of a friendly or a romantic nature. While the other house-guests were busy discussing the merits or otherwise of their phrenological readings, Mr Carrington led Miss Hopkins out of the Terrace Room. This assignation was halted when Miss Hopkins recovered her senses and fled back indoors. 'Yes, Mr Carrington and I ended up in a clinch but I scurried off to bed before anything else could happen,' said Miss Hopkins. But

MR CARRINGTON'S AFFECTION FOR MISS HOPKINS WAVERED,
BUT HIS CHARM WAS HARD FOR HER TO RESIST

where was Lady Devonport? How could she have allowed such a transgression to occur?

After Miss Hopkins' flight, Mr Carrington swaggered back to the Billiard Room and proclaimed to the men gathered there that he had just 'got off' with her. A hush descended and Mr Everett turned a ghostly white. Mr Gorell Barnes tried to tease Mr Everett into a better mood but his plan backfired. Mr Everett unleashed his wrath and resentment at Miss Hopkins' treatment of him on his poor host. An almighty row ensued, which was heard by the women in their upstairs corridor, and the men parted for the night on very bad terms.

'My bad mood of yesterday evening,' said Mr Everett the following morning, 'pertains to Miss Hopkins, because she's just given me the cold shoulder. It's a bit harsh because at the beginning it seemed there was a closeness and an attraction

THE HERMIT FINDS SO MANY ANIMAL SKELETONS ON HIS RAMBLES THAT HE FORMS THEM
INTO A SCULPTURE TOPPED BY THIS SIGN

between us and I still feel very attracted to her despite being given the old heave-ho. But I was talking to Oliver, my valet, this morning, and he said, "Sir, I wish I could come up with a nice answer. But all I can say is . . . " and I knew what he was going to say. Absolutely simultaneously we both just went, "Women!" Fickle, confusing creatures, can't live with them, can't live without them.'

A certain amount of apologising and patching-up healed most of the rifts between the men, and at Mr Foxsmith's suggestion all the guests were brought together to make some kites. Mr Foxsmith wanted to repeat a famous experiment by Benjamin Franklin, who had been interested in electricity and was well known for his work on lightning and 'pointed conductors'. He attempted to draw down lightning by flying kites in storms. Fortunately, the experiment failed, and unlike several others he avoided being killed by electric shock. Undeterred, he went on to suggest that lightning conductors be placed on the roofs of tall buildings to prevent the devastating fire often caused by lightning strikes. In May 1752, in the small French village of Marly, a metal rod placed on a church roof safely carried the force of a lightning strike to the ground, proving Franklin's theory. Within a few years churches from Portugal to Poland had sprouted conductors.

It was a glorious summer's evening when the house-guests began climbing Garway Hill with their home-made kites. It seemed that this brief respite from the confines of the house was exactly what was needed. The magnificent view from the top of the hill put Kentchurch and their Regency experiments into a wider context and the social fabric began to mend – although some broken hearts did not. Mr Everett remained withdrawn and Mr Carrington, in a somewhat heartless (though Byronic) manner, told Miss Hopkins that the previous evening had been a mistake. During the walk Miss Hopkins said, 'It has become plain that another romance is doomed in the house. Carrington's certainly not given me any indication that my feelings are reciprocated, so we've got this bizarre situation where Lisa likes Everett and he doesn't like her, Everett likes me and I don't like him and I like Mr Carrington and he doesn't like me. It's all a bit unfortunate.'

The following evening Mr Foxsmith opened the Science Night spectacular by arranging the guests into a human 'orrery'. This was a recreation of the Regency view of the solar system, for which the house-guests had made models of planets

which they wore on their heads as they walked in circles around Miss Conick, who took the role of the Sun. An orrery was a clockwork model of the solar system, the first one of which had been made for Charles Boyle, fourth Earl of Orrery, at the start of the eighteenth century. Many of the house-guests had more than a passing interest in astronomy and Mr Foxsmith and Mr Everett were passionate about it.

The astronomers of the eighteenth and early nineteenth centuries discovered that there must be many as yet unidentified planets and asteroids, and they put forward the hypothesis that the planets might have been formed by explosions, collisions or even from a rotating cloud of gas. Mr Foxsmith had a particular interest in the astronomer William Herschel. In 1781 Herschel and his sister Caroline observed a greenish object in the constellation of Gemini which did not look like a star. It proved to be a new planet, the seventh and most distant in the solar system as it was then understood. They named it Georgium Sidus (the 'Georgian star', later renamed Uranus) and its discovery caused a sensation, since its presence doubled the known size of the solar system. Herschel was appointed Royal Astronomer to George III and was knighted in 1816. His sister, who acted as his 'assistant', discovered eight comets in as many years through her own observations and later published a catalogue of 2500 nebulae and star clusters.

'What's that?' called the countess from her bedroom window to Mr Gorell Barnes. She had been watching the evening sky from her window seat and saw an orange-coloured object appear above the horizon. Mr Gorell Barnes fetched the telescope from the library and pointed it at the strange appearance. He then went and fetched Mr Everett to show him how to use it.

'That's Mars,' said Mr Everett. 'You can see it more clearly this month than at any other time in the last sixty thousand years,' he explained.

'It was beautiful,' said the countess later. 'It was like having your own personal planetarium. It was so immediate. It was like the science at the time, where experiments happened before your eyes. You are feeling it, you can smell it, and it has an immediacy that we're not used to.'

Although most 'scientists' in the late eighteenth and early nineteenth centuries were able to conduct their research while still believing in the over-arching presence of God ('I do not go up to the first cause,' said Erasmus Darwin), a few did not. When Pierre-Simon Laplace (the 'French Newton') presented the first part of his work *Traité de Mécanique Céleste* to Napoleon in 1799, the story goes that the latter asked, 'What function do you assign to God in your book?', whereupon Laplace replied, 'I was not in need of that hypothesis.' The idea of an entirely mechanistic world and the implication that God was now surplus to requirements threatened to undermine the essentially theocratic world-view to which most people adhered. The finiteness of human life, the significance of death, the idea of there being no afterlife were, for many, destabilising.

However, the fragility of life could hardly be ignored, especially for women. Childbirth remained the commonest cause of death among women aged twenty-five to thirty-five. In 1817, an event occurred which reminded the nation that the hand of death that snatched away women in childbirth could visit any home, from the poorest to the richest. Princess Charlotte, the next heir to the throne and the Regent's only child, had been an object of national affection, particularly among women, since her birth in 1796. She was as much loved as her father was despised. As a plump and wayward adolescent she had a strained relationship with her warring parents and insisted on marrying Prince Leopold of Saxe-Coburg for love, having earlier rejected the suitor her father had chosen for her. It was a happy marriage and soon the pair were expecting their first child. Her labour began on 3 November 1817 and continued for two days. She gave birth to a stillborn son and died at 2.30 in the morning of the 6th. She was only twenty-one and her death was appalling news. 'No description,' wrote a journalist of the time, 'can exaggerate the public sympathy and the public sorrow . . . The

THE EVENTS OF SCIENCE WEEK ALLOWED THE YOUNG MEN
AND WOMEN TO SPEND MORE TIME TOGETHER

nation would have resigned all the rest of her family to have saved her.' Her famous obstetrician, Sir Richard Croft, racked by guilt, committed suicide three months later, (although he has since been exonerated by modern medical researchers).

A subscription to build a monument in her memory, initially open only to women and with no donation to exceed a guinea, collected over £12,000. The marble statue that was built by Matthew Wyatt with the proceeds was placed in St George's Chapel at Windsor. The dead princess was shown prostrate beneath her shroud, with just one limp hand protruding. Above the corpse, an immortal image of her accompanied by her baby, folded in the arms of an angel, soared towards heaven.

The women at Kentchurch were moved to tears on hearing this story. As Miss Hopkins said, with meaning:

> We were all in our nighties talking in Miss Samuel's room and we had a really lovely chat about how horrible men are! We felt we could talk to each other openly about things that are obviously painful and that we've had trouble getting over. But oh my God, men! Men are at the root of it all! The more I learn about men the more I just think, I can't be both-ered with you. I know it's not all men but it seems to be all the ones I end up going out with. Why does anyone ever get married? Goodness knows why they did in the Regency because they had a one-in-three chance of dying in childbirth. Honestly, it just feels like marriage was hell. Is being a governess really that bad? It might have been boring but at least you weren't being subjected to men who have affairs, and dying in childbirth.

The final guest that week at Kentchurch did little to distract the guests from their meditations on life and death. An anatomist by training, Professor Gunther von Hagens describes himself as a modern-day Prometheus, or Dr Frankenstein, in that he gives new life to dead bodies. He has invented a process in which the fluid content of corpses (about 70 per cent) is replaced by plastic, thus making the specimens durable, odourless and non-perishable. After preserving the cadavers he is able to stand them up without support and arrange them in various poses. Some of these poses are (unconsciously, apparently) modelled on famous paintings or sculptures, such as *The Thinker* or *Man Holding His Skin*. He is not the first to have done this. The French artist Fragonard had injected corpses of humans and animals with metals in the second half of the eighteenth century and created his extraordinary horse and rider in this way. Von Hagens' 'plastinates' have caused controversy for several reasons. Do they preserve the dignity of the human being? Do they infringe the human right to respectful treatment after death? Are they truly 'educational', as he claims, or are they merely being used to express his own artistic concerns and promote his own interests? When he came to the house, sev-eral of the guests were reluctant to meet him.

A MODERN-DAY 'FRANKENSTEIN' AND HIS ASSISTANT, FELICITY RUPERTI

'I am like Frankenstein,' he said to the guests who were ranged on the hall-way steps, looking down upon a fully dissected, fifty-year-old female corpse lying on the table in front of him. 'Only I don't need electricity to bring my corpses to life but instead put them into lifelike poses. This way, we can forget this is a corpse. The dead can in this way help the living.' Anatomy, like other developing sciences in the eighteenth and nineteenth centuries, provoked as much fear among lay people as it did enlightenment among scientists. The need for dead bodies for dis-section sparked a new 'niche' career, that of grave robber, or 'resurrection man'. Although Henry VIII had decreed that hanged criminals could be given to anatomists for dissection, and although the penal code in Regency Britain was harsh, the supply from the gallows could never satisfy the demands of the anatomists. Anatomies had been performed since the Renaissance, but they had always provoked disquiet among the populace. If man was made in God's image, was it right to desecrate his body after death? What happened to a person's soul if his dead body was dissected? Did this form of public display take away our last ves-tige of dignity?

Before dinner, each guest was invited to enter the Billiard Room, where a plas-tinated corpse of a female was laid out on a table. They could spend time with the body alone before being faced with a more extensive exhibition of specimens after dinner. Miss Samuel was enlightened by the experience. 'I thought the plastinates were exciting, fascinating. I was pleased to have the opportunity to see so clearly into a human body.'

'They looked like models in a creepy toy shop,' said the hermit. 'Like dolls, not like real people. I've skinned enough rabbits to know that it's really difficult to get the skin off something and these models showed that; they were quite hacked about.' Zebedee had spent a great deal of time contemplating death during his stay in the hermitage. 'There are bones of dead animals all over the place here and I'm making a sculpture out of them. Seeing so much death has made me appreciate the beauty of dead things.' At the entrance to his dwelling he carved a stone with the opening line of Shelley's *Queen Mab*: 'How wonderful is death'. 'But I don't think plastination is a dignified thing to do to a corpse,' he concluded, 'and I wouldn't sign up for it.'

Miss Braund's attitudes, on the contrary, were entirely turned around. 'I was so anti it, didn't want to see any of it before he came,' she said. 'But I was absolutely fascinated and I learned more in twenty minutes than all my Biology lessons put together.'

The chef, with his usual flair, created a dinner rich in humour to honour the professor's visit. Von Hagens was presented with a large ox heart to dissect and serve to his fellow diners, accompanied by quails in coffins and eels in aspic. 'He did an interesting comparison between Gorell Barnes's and Captain Glover's hands,' said Mr

'QUAILS IN COFFINS' ARE SERVED
TO THE FAMOUS ANATOMIST TO
DISSECT FOR HIS DINNER

Foxsmith, 'telling them about the type of muscles that they had, which both of them were absolutely mesmerised by.

> There is a human behind the notorious anatomist he has anxieties before the first incision into a body, he has nightmares of being put on trial by his own plasticated bodies saying that he didn't represent them well enough, and him saying, 'I'm sorry, I'm just doing the best I can.' When he looked at me he almost looked straight into me, like he could see the size of my heart and my lungs and my kidneys and the blood flowing around. That must be a very uncanny skill to have. I didn't find this unsettling, I just found this very intense.'

It seemed that the anatomist had an unusually piercing gaze, as most of the guests reported that he had 'sized them up' for dissection!

Von Hagens discussed his next project, called 'The Superhuman', in which he is creating a 'perfect' human from the body parts of different dead people. Some of the guests around the table wondered how closely this 'modern-day Frankenstein' might tread in the footsteps of his benighted predecessor. 'I will not lead you on, unguarded and ardent as I then was, to your destruction and infallible misery. Learn from me, if not by my precepts, at least by my example, how dangerous is the acquirement of knowledge' – Mary Shelley, *Frankenstein*.

A Regency romance?

CHAPTER TEN

WATERLOO AND PETERLOO

WAR AND POLITICS ARRIVE AT KENTCHURCH

On with the dance! Let joy be unconfined;

No sleep till morn, when Youth and Pleasure meet

To chase the glowing Hours with flying feet –

But hark! – that heavy sound breaks in once more,

As if the clouds its echo would repeat;

And nearer, clearer, deadlier than before!

Arm! Arm! It is – it is – the cannon's opening roar!

BYRON, *CHILDE HAROLD'S PILGRIMAGE*, 1816

LADY CAROLINE LAMB and her brother, Frederick Ponsonby, were both guests at the Duchess of Richmond's ball the night before the Battle of Waterloo. Lady Caroline wrote to her mother-in-law, Lady Melbourne: 'That fatal ball has been much censured; there never was such a Ball – so fine and so sad – all the young men who appeared there shot dead a few hours after.' Wellington's army was based in Brussels and, since there seemed to be plenty of time before Napoleon could move, the city was filled with officers' wives and fashionable London visitors who treated the campaign rather as if it were an event on the social calendar. On 15 June the most important members of society in Brussels

'AM I NOT THE VERY MODEL OF A MODERN NAVAL GENTLEMAN?' ENQUIRES CAPTAIN GLOVER OF HIS AUDIENCE

attended a ball given by the Duchess of Richmond for over two hundred guests. One guest described the scene:

> The ball was at its height when the Duke of Wellington received *positive* intelligence that Napoleon had crossed the Sambre with his army and taken possession of Charleroi. The excitement which ensued, on the company being made acquainted with Napoleon's advance, was most extraordinary. The countenances which a moment before, were lighted

up with pleasure and gaiety, now wore a most solemn aspect. The guests little imagined that the music which accompanied the gay and lively dance at her Grace's ball, would so shortly after play martial airs on the battlefield, or that some of the officers present at the fête would be seen fighting in their ball dresses, and, in that costume, found amongst the slain . . .

The Allies lost thirty thousand men; and almost all Wellington's aides-de-camp, most of them members of the English nobility, were killed or wounded. Caroline's brother lay on the battlefield bleeding and without water for eighteen hours – yet he survived. His famous account of the preparations is memorable:

[Wellington] had every reason to expect that the whole of Bonaparte's army would immediately fall upon him, before he could collect his army on the position of Waterloo. I was with him, the Duke, just in front of the line of cavalry, when we were all observing the preparations and movements of the immense mass of troops before us. He was occupied in reading the newspapers and looking through his glass when anything was observed, and then making observations and laughing at the fashionable news from London . . .

THE BATTLE OF WATERLOO, 18 JUNE 1815

To bring the dreadful realities of the Battle of Waterloo home to the guests at Kentchurch, the historian Andrew Roberts was invited to talk to them over a dinner commemorating the Duchess of Richmond's ball. Mr Roberts arrived with various relics from the battle, including the teeth of dead soldiers, which were worn by women as dentures and considered to be the height of fashion. He talked the guests through the events of 19 June 1815, and the battle that ended twenty-two years of war. He explained that Wellington, who had not taken a single day off in the

THE GENTLEMEN DRILL WITH THE LOCAL MILITIA FOR A POSSIBLE FRENCH INVASION

previous six years of the Peninsular War, had studied Napoleon's tactics. Napoleon however, regardless of the fact that Wellington had beaten six of his generals, had never studied Wellington's form. And so, despite his heavy losses, Wellington emerged victorious.

Roberts enumerated the appalling casualties, vividly recounting that blood ran six inches deep in places. The many amputations needed after the battle were occasioned by the bone-crushing lead bullets used by the musketry on both sides. The only item of clothing used specifically for protection was the 'stock', a leather collar worn around the neck. (When soldiers stood to attention, they were 'standing stock still'.) As foot-soldiers fled from the enemy, chasing cavalry would slash at them with their sabres in a downwards motion, cutting the chest and stomach, then flick up the curved blade, inflicting terrible wounds to the head and neck. Face wounds were not usually fatal but neck wounds were – hence the stock. Andrew Roberts vividly described the physical crush of battle, the smells and sounds, the ground knee-deep in bodies and the looting of the corpses in the days that followed.

> I was wounded in both arms, my horse sprang forward and carried me to the rising ground on the right of the French position, where I was knocked off my horse by a blow to the head . . . I attempted to get up but a Lancer who saw me plunged his lance into my back. My mouth filled with blood and my breathing became very difficult as the lance had penetrated my lungs, but I did not lose my senses . . . A squadron of Prussian cavalry passed over me. I was a good deal hurt by the horses – in general horses will avoid trampling upon men but the field was so covered, that they had no spare space for their feet – Frederick Ponsonby.

'Andrew Roberts brought along a whole lot of fascinating artefacts from the Battle of Waterloo,' enthused Miss Braund. 'A sabre, a bullet ball with gunpowder, and this *vicious* thing for deserters that would have been punched into their cheek or their breast and then smothered in gunpowder so that they would have had it for the rest of their lives. It was really odd to hold something found on the battlefield that was actually used. A sabre's not just used for fun. It's actually something that would have been used to kill people. It just makes everything so real.'

'The human cost of Waterloo was very desperate and awful to hear about,' said Lady Devonport after Mr Roberts' talk. 'I can't believe human beings weren't as desperately unhappy at the loss of someone they love; it doesn't matter whether it's 1815 or 2068, I don't think that ever changes.'

Napoleon surrendered one month after the Battle of Waterloo and was exiled to St Helena. 'His only remark to Wellington was "*Quelle affaire!*" ("What a business!"),' related Mr Roberts. 'I think that is the punchline of the nineteenth century.' The Bourbons were reinstated in France and the people of Europe found themselves once again ruled by the emperors and kings of Russia, Prussia, Austria and Britain. Britain, at last at peace with the world, could now go to war with itself. The economic situation was disastrous: more than £100 million had been raised for the war effort out of income taxes, a disproportionate amount of which had been paid by the poor. A slump in world trade, combined with the problems created by the return of thousands of soldiers, led to high levels of unemployment. A series of harvests failed, that of 1816 being the worst in living memory due to the eruption of Tambora, a volcano in present-day Indonesia, that led to a 'year of no summer', as Byron described it. The Corn Laws, passed in 1815, which excluded the import of foreign wheat until the local price had reached eighty shillings a bushel, meant a significant (and deeply resented) rise in the price of bread.

By protecting the price of British wheat and imposing heavy taxes on imports, the government benefited the landowners and larger farmers at the expense of the smallholders and labourers. The wages of a rural labourer dropped from around fifteen shillings a week to six shillings – if he was fortunate enough to find a job, that is. Unemployed men searching for work outside their parish could be arrested as 'vagabonds'; illnesses arising from malnutrition were the main cause of death among the working class; and there were thousands of half-starved unemployed families on Poor Relief. In 1816 the first of a series of riots that erupted all over the country occurred at Brandon, near Bury. Fifteen hundred rioters, armed with spiked sticks and carrying a flag inscribed BREAD OR BLOOD, demanded a fixed maximum price for bread and meat. They set the barns and hayricks of their landlords on fire but ceased when their demands were met a few days later. The price of flour was reduced and wages were increased, but only for a fortnight. In the following weeks further riots broke out across the country, leading to pitched battles with the militia. Two rioters were killed and seventy-five arrested, of whom five were hanged, five transported abroad for life and many others transported for between seven and fourteen years. The sentences were widely regarded as horrific.

Although incidents of unrest soared after 1815, they were not unknown before then. Indeed, while the prince was celebrating the start of his regency in fine style, a protest by the framework knitters of Nottingham against the production of inferior stockings by unskilled labourers using wide frames took place, and the inferior machines were smashed. Under the leadership of the mythical 'General Ludd', protests soon spread.

The pace of change that had seen almost half the population leave the country for the city in just fifty years was bound to create tensions. The Industrial Revolution had created a new form of worker, one whose life was defined by time-and-motion economics, repetitive actions, strict and exhausting shifts, dirty towns and slum dwellings. The 'dark satanic mills' sucked in poorly paid women and children and introduced the practice of competition as a means of securing employment and driving down wages. The Luddite movement is usually ascribed to the workers' fear of losing their livelihoods to machines and a desire for a minimum wage, but it may equally well have arisen from people's fears of being turned into nothing more than a machine themselves – or at least of being treated like one by their new employers. William Blake used the mill as a symbol of dehumanisation.

The Luddites, small groups of locally organised agitators, were not a revolutionary network, and the government's response to their smashing of machines seemed excessive, even at the time. A bill was introduced in Parliament to establish hanging as the official punishment for the crime of breaking a machine. Byron, whose own estate near Nottingham was close to a centre for Luddite activity, tried to halt it.

> Suppose it is passed. Suppose one of these men, as I have seen them –
> meagre with famine, sullen with despair, careless of a life which your
> lordships are perhaps about to value at something less than the price of
> a stocking-frame – suppose this man (and there are a thousand such from
> whom you may select your victims) [is] dragged into court to be tried for
> this new offence by this new law, still there are two things wanting to
> convict and condemn him; and these are, in my opinion, twelve butchers
> for a jury and a Jeffrys for a judge . . .

Nevertheless, the Act was passed and in 1813 seventeen Luddites were executed in York. This caused most of the protesters to turn instead to the newly formed political groups campaigning for universal male suffrage, the Hampden Clubs. The last significant Luddite attack took place at a Loughborough lace factory in February 1817.

The imposition of the death penalty for machine-breaking simply added one more crime to the list of 160 offences that were punishable by hanging. The penal code was extraordinarily harsh, with public floggings carried out for such crimes as stealing some oats or candles. In 1817 Brixton Prison introduced the treadmill, on which a prisoner was forced to climb the 'everlasting stairs' for hours on end. Public executions were held across the country and multiple hangings often attracted crowds of up to thirty thousand. Children as young as seven were deemed

LIVING OFF THE LAND (BUT AVOIDING GAME-KEEPERS) WAS THE LOT OF POOR FAMILIES

legally responsible for their actions; a boy of six was said to have cried 'pitiably' for his mother on the scaffold, and an eight-year-old was hanged for stealing two handkerchiefs. The handkerchiefs were of ordinary linen and cost a tiny fraction of the money spent by the Regent on '3 Rich Gold and Spotted Muslin Hand-kerchiefs', the bill for which came to nearly £2000 in today's money.

When the Regent opened Parliament in January 1817, a large crowd jeered him and threw stones at his carriage. Windows were broken and the prince claimed to feel a stone or bullet pass his face. A small hole was certainly found in the window afterwards. Captain Gronow wrote of 1816–17: 'A most dangerous period. The spirit of the people in England, exasperated by taxation, the high price of bread, and many iniquitous laws and restrictions was of the worst possible nature. In the riots and meetings of those troublous times the mob really meant mischief; and had they been accustomed to the use of arms, and well drilled, they might have committed as great excesses as the ruffians of 1793 in France.'

The prince, always highly fearful that the mob violence witnessed during the French Revolution might one day overwhelm Britain, was greatly disturbed. His prime minister and government reacted as if the *sans-culottes* were at the gates, and suspended Habeas Corpus, which meant that anybody under suspicion could be thrown into gaol and kept there. An ancient Act of Parliament dating back to Edward III was reintroduced, allowing magistrates across the country to imprison any person they felt was liable to commit an act prejudicial to public order – in other words, anybody whose face they didn't care for was in danger of being thrown into gaol. Magistrates in 1817 were not recruited from the 'lower orders' and were not, on the whole, inclined well towards them. An Act prohibiting meet-ings of more than fifty people within a mile of Westminster was in force, as were strong measures against 'seditious libel' – a usefully vague phrase that covered whatever the government did not like. Lord Sidmouth, the Home Secretary, sent a circular to all local magistrates encouraging them to suppress 'seditious publica-tions', which usually meant anything that urged reform.

Stones were not the only weapon to be used against the Regent; his household accounts proved far more effective. The extreme Whig George Tierney, a magnif-icent debater and authority on finance, pointed out that in under three years at Carlton House the furniture alone had cost the country £260,000, the upholstery a further £49,000, and plate and jewels £23,000. The Regent's debts were £339,000.

To understand the stomach-churning excess of the Regent's spending, one should remember that in the entire United Kingdom there were only about 250,000 people with an income over £700 a year. The half-million shopkeepers were pleased if they made £150 a year. A million farmers, minor clergy and a few schoolmasters received around £120. Artisans earned around £55 a year; miners, who worked long hours in appalling conditions, received about £30; and agricultural labourers around £15. Even if fifty labourers saved up for their entire working lives and spent nothing on themselves, their combined wages would not have paid for a single piece of ormolu for which the Regent paid £29,000.

The appalling situation for the working class in Britain during the Regency was described to the young women at Kentchurch by a surprise visitor, MP Clare Short. The meeting took place in secret in the stable block, since it was considered deeply unattractive for unmarried women to hold political opinions, let alone express them. Ms Short's vivid depiction of the lot of the working classes in Britain during the Regency fired the young women with indignation and a desire to do something in the house to express this. But what? Women were not allowed to vote, regardless of their wealth or title, although there was no specific Act forbidding them. It was not until the 1832 Reform Act that women were specifically prohibited from voting – possibly because larger numbers of them sought to do so. The massive disruptions of the eighteenth and early nineteenth centuries – defeat in America, the revolution in France, unprecedented economic and social change at home – provoked a restatement of the differences between the sexes and of the need for female subordination.

'It's very un-Regency for ladies to talk politics at the table,' said Miss Hopkins, 'but how frustrating it must have been if the gentlemen were waffling on, being pompous and talking about current affairs, politics, finance and science, and for women not to be allowed to have an opinion. If a gentleman made a comment that was factually incorrect, she would not have been able to contradict him. I really don't know how they coped with it, having that level of education and not being allowed to use it. I don't envy that at all. I feel proud that I can sit round a dinner table and be able to have an opinion that is listened to by others.'

The author of *The Laws Respecting Women* summed up the position of women in 1777 (a position which had not changed by the Regency): 'By marriage the very being or legal existence of a woman is suspended. Every wife except a queen regnant is under the legal authority of her husband. She can't let, set, sell, give away, or alienate any thing without her husband's consent. Her very necessary apparel, by law, is not her own property.'

Stripped of her individual identity by marriage, a woman could not be a citizen, or ever hope to possess political rights. Clare Short explained that even those women who enjoyed wealth and property were excluded from the political sphere on the grounds that they were deemed not to possess similar faculties to men. The differences between the sexes were carefully explained by Jean-Jacques Rousseau's *Emile*, which was published in 1762 and went through five English-language editions before 1770. Woman, Rousseau claimed, was born to obey. Physically weaker and less clever than a man, a woman was dependent on her menfolk more than they on her. A woman's contribution was vital but different, and should be confined to the home, where she could exercise a gentle and improving sway over her husband and forge the next generation. 'Even if she possesses genuine talents,' Rousseau argued, 'any pretension on her part would degrade them. Her dignity depends on remaining unknown; her glory lies in her husband's esteem, her greatest pleasure in the happiness of her family.' Rousseau's sexual politics proved immensely influential in Britain, both among conservative moralists like Hannah More and Jane Austen, and even on the feminist Mary Wollstonecraft. 'Man must necessarily fulfil the duties of a citizen, or be despised . . . while he was employed in any of the departments of civil life, his wife, also an active citizen, should be equally intent to manage her family, educate her children, and assist her neighbours,' she wrote in *Vindication of the Rights of Woman* in 1792. She encouraged women to influence the political sphere through their influence in the domestic sphere.

Despite the pressure on women to repress any political urge they may have felt, change was afoot in the Regency. Working-class women began to form their own reform societies or attend public meetings. Many of them took to wearing white, as a token of their virtue and to justify their unorthodox behaviour. Women could call it their 'duty' to become involved in movements like Chartism, the Anti-Corn Law League, anti-slavery and universal male suffrage. They did not, they claimed, seek the vote for themselves but rather wanted to support their menfolk.

Certainly many Regency women did assume roles of political significance. Elizabeth Fry, a Quaker, became one of the era's most prominent political reformers. In 1810 she became a preacher in the Society of Friends and, after seeing the terrible conditions for women in Newgate Prison, she devoted her life to prison reform at home and abroad. She founded hostels for the homeless and several charitable societies. In the upper echelons of society, the great Whig hostesses had no fear of expressing political views at their house

ELIZABETH FRY ADDRESSING INMATES
AT NEWGATE PRISON

parties nor of being condemned as 'blue-stockings'. The term 'blue-stocking' arose from parties held by Mrs Montagu (a society hostess of the end of the eighteenth century) for her well-read and educated women friends. She did not allow cards or dancing at these events, the joy of conversation being the only entertainment. A few men of sufficient intellectual calibre were sometimes invited. Although being a blue-stocking was enough to leave a girl on the shelf for ever among certain sections of society, others were only too delighted to find themselves in the company of intelligent and opinionated women. That many educated women were passionate about politics can be seen from their letters, and more than a few even dared discuss the state of the nation over dinner – not always to the pleasure of the listener. As Prince Puckler-Muskau observed: 'English ladies are best reached through politics. Lately one has heard nothing at table, at the opera, even at the ball, but Canning and Wellington from every lovely mouth; indeed Lord Ellenborough complained that his wife plagued him with politics even at night. She had terrified him by crying out suddenly, in her sleep: "Will the Prime Minister stand or fall?" '

The countess was deeply affected by meeting Ms Short. 'I don't think I had a real political conscience or any interest in talking about politics before, but this talk has really made me think about the world around me and how women have fought for me to be able to do that. I feel I have changed. It really has changed and politicised me.'

The ladies decided they would mount a play – a perfectly acceptable occupation – but make the subject the débâcle of Peterloo, since women were famously involved in the event. Saying nothing to the men, Miss Conick set to work on it with the help of the other women, in particular the countess, while Lady Devonport composed a poem in homage to the woman whose portrait was mounted on her bedroom wall and for whose predicament she had been feeling more and more sympathy.

The unrest that characterised the latter half of the Regency was reflected at the house party in the hostilities that broke out between Mrs Enright and her hostess, Mrs Rogers. There were few issues on which the two women saw eye to eye, and when Mrs Rogers denied Mrs Enright the pleasure of going riding, on account of her 'lowly status', the tension between them erupted in spectacular fashion! Mrs Enright became so exasperated by her hostess that she hurled a plate into the fireplace and stormed out of nuncheon. The atmosphere in the house turned frosty; a few took sides, and those that didn't kept their heads down.

While the younger women prepared for their play, Mr Gorell Barnes decided that, in true Regency tradition, he would hold a fair for the servants and workers of his estate to show his appreciation. All the staff would be given the day off to enjoy themselves; food and drink would be provided and games organised; and the highest social classes would mingle with their inferiors for a few hours. The female staff would have the chance to win a smock (to be embroidered by Miss Braund) and the men a flitch of bacon.

Meanwhile, Captain Glover was informed of a prize he had won: not a small item of clothing or some bacon, but a baronetcy. He had been

POEM

Poor caged lady, stroll or stride
Mask the clever mind that you must hide.
Poor caged lady, stroll and walk
To take you from the fatuous talk.
Poor caged lady, stroll and ride
To escape the rules you can't abide.
Poor caged lady, stroll and wince
In your clothes that bind and shoes that pinch.
Poor caged lady, stroll and play,
Waste away another day.
Poor caged lady, stroll in defiance
With your head full of poetry, maths and science.
Poor caged lady, stroll and dance
As to the future you advance.
No more caged ladies will there be;
Your unborn sisters will set us free.
Lady Devonport

awarded a large sum in prize money, following his capture of a French vessel during the war. A part of this money he had wisely used to earn himself a political favour at court, which had resulted in his being honoured with a title. From now on, Captain Glover was to be addressed as Sir Jeremy. At dinner that evening Sir Jeremy sat beside Lord Temple-Morris, whose knowledge of the political history of this period proved fascinating for all the guests. Lord Temple-Morris spent twenty-seven years in the House of Commons, mainly as a Conservative MP but crossing the floor to New Labour in his last four years. He was raised to the peerage in the Dissolution Honours List and 'sent upstairs'.

'Sir Jeremy was very switched on to the history,' said Lord Temple-Morris, 'and we talked about his new title. There was no Tory Party as such that he could have made a donation to in return for an honour, but he could have been financially "kind" to the Regent, who was always short of cash, and in return something would have been "found" for him.' His knighthood would have been hereditary – he could have passed it to his son – but he would still have been a 'commoner'. To be a peer, you needed to hold one of the five noble ranks – from baron on the lowest rung, rising through viscount, earl, marquess and duke. In a situation very similar to that in Jane Austen's *Persuasion*, Sir Jeremy had achieved rapid advancement in the navy. 'Captain Wentworth, with five-and-twenty thousand pounds, and as high in his profession as merit and activity could place him, was no longer a nobody.'

Sir Jeremy thought not only of himself when considering how to spend his new-found wealth. He asked Miss Braund if he might buy her a dress, something he had been requesting since his first few days in the house. She politely refused. Despite so little encouragement, Sir Jeremy had been consistent in his attentions towards her, even writing 'B HAPPY' in straw and flowers on the lawn beneath her window one night. Now that Sir Jeremy was the gentleman of second highest status in the house, Mrs Hammond wasted no time in encouraging her charge, Miss Braund, to reconsider her rejection of his suit. Sir Jeremy had behaved with utmost propriety towards her, and was now almost beyond her reach as a wealthy baronet. Miss Braund herself was beginning to question her refusal of him and her attraction to Mr Everett, who had after all never returned her favours and was apparently blind to all except Miss Hopkins. Was she being foolish in turning her back on such an advantageous match and such a generous friend? Certainly there was more sparkle in her eye when discussing Sir Jeremy with her friends than had been observed there before. 'Glover's so courteous to the people sitting next to him at dinner,' she said, 'making sure we have everything we want, much more so than any of the other men. He's always been fighting my corner, which is just lovely, and that's what you want in a partner, someone who's going to back you to the hilt and be there for you, no matter what.'

As Lord Temple-Morris explained to the guests in the Terrace Room after dinner, the political system in Britain was hardly equitable during the Regency. Three hundred and fifty-five seats in the House of Commons were controlled by 87 peers, and a further 213 by 90 of the richest commoners, all by their possession of rotten boroughs. These were bought and sold for an average £6000 plus an annual fee of £1500 to £1800. (They could, however, cost a great deal more. Castlereagh's first seat was said to have cost his father, Lord Londonderry, £60,000 – paying the price no doubt for his son's unpopularity. Lord Egremont bought Midhurst for £40,000 but it was a prime borough since the patron owned all the 'burgage' [tenancy] rights and it contained only one man entitled to vote.) Seats were even offered for sale in newspapers:

To Gentlemen of Fortune

Any two gentlemen, who would wish to secure seats at the next Parliament, may be accommodated at the borough of Launceston. There are but 15 votes, majority 3. All letters directed for A.B. to be left at the Exeter post-office, will be duly attended to. 29 January 1819.

The early nineteenth century was the high point of aristocratic influence over the House of Commons. One in four MPs was married to the daughter of another MP. Many others married the daughters of peers, or were themselves related to the peerage (connection to a noble family was the usual path to being elected to Parliament). Their Lordships not only filled the Upper House but also influenced the election and conduct of members of the Lower House. The cry for reform of this iniquitous system came not only from the poor but also from the new industrial barons in the Midlands and the North, who were demanding better representation and more political influence. Less than 5 per cent of the population were able to vote, and the majority of those came from the aristocratic and landowning families who already held political power and influence.

AN ESTATE WORKER BOBS FOR APPLES DURING THE KENTCHURCH COURT FAIR

FEMALE ESTATE WORKERS AND HOUSEHOLD STAFF COMPETE FOR A SMOCK – A GAME TODAY,
BUT A SERIOUS RACE FOR IMPOVERISHED REGENCY SERVANTS

The day of the staff fair dawned bright and hot. While the guests dressed and took
breakfast without the help of servants, up on the plateau above the house stalls for
food and drink, games, a cricket pitch, a lamb roast and other entertainments were
being set up. The early nineteenth century saw a revival of the upper-class tradition of entertaining the lower orders. Although the organisers may have intended
these events to improve relations between themselves and their workers, they
tended instead to emphasise feudality. The blue-stocking Elizabeth Montagu had
been a pioneer at reinventing this kind of entertainment. Apart from a famous
annual dinner for chimney-sweeps at her London house, she gave regular servants'

balls, harvest dinners and dances for her farm labourers, and dinners for Sunday-school pupils and their teachers at her country house in Berkshire.

The Dukes and the Marquesses of Buckingham were perhaps the most lavish in their staff entertainments. At their three houses of Stowe, Wotton and Avington, they laid on separate feasts for the tenantry, the servants, the local corporation or townspeople, and the yeomanry. Even ordinary birthdays within the family were excuses for further communal feasting. Lady Buckingham's birthday dance was described by a house-guest with honesty: 'We all danced with the tenants . . . I laughed a great deal to see the different mixture of people. We could hardly breathe it was so hot and the smell was beyond anything.'

CLIMBING THE GREASY POLE FOR A FLITCH
OF BACON THAT MIGHT HAVE KEPT
A FAMILY FROM STARVATION

For some of the guests at Kentchurch, the fair proved to be a highlight of their visit. 'After being at the fair for about five minutes,' said Mr Everett, 'I just couldn't quite believe what I was seeing, I welled up. It was one of the most remarkable and moving experiences of my life; I just felt like I had gone back in time. This is what it would have been like. Everyone really chilled out. I mean, I'm sure that I probably drank too much but I was enjoying myself.'

For others, the enjoyable day had a darker resonance. 'We have all bought into this idea of having "presence" that belonging to high society entitled you to,' observed Miss Conick:

It's easy to see how people thought themselves a cut above footmen and maids because you could see it happening at the fête. And although the day was amazing, I found some aspects really sad – particularly the footmen climbing the greasy pole. When this happened two hundred years ago it was a bit of sport with a token prize for the entertainment of the

THE FAIR PROVES TO BE A HIGHLIGHT FOR THOSE GUESTS WHO SOMETIMES
FEEL CLAUSTROPHOBIC WITHIN THE CONFINES OF THE HOUSE

aristocracy. But the workers clambering up that pole would have really
wanted the bacon. There was such a huge discrepancy between the lives
of the guests who sat around the table every night and the people who
served them. And it's sad and scary how easily you slip into it.'

The annual attentions of landowners towards their workers were not sufficient to quell the calls for reform, and neither was the murderous suppression of
discontent. The night after the fair, braziers were taken into the laurel walk to the
east of the house, and here the guests congregated after dinner, as darkness was
falling, to watch the young ladies' play about the Peterloo massacre. The chaperones, in their silks and turbans, shawls and lace, sat in chairs brought to them by
footmen while the men stood behind them, clutching glasses of port. The flames
of the braziers cast frenetic shadows over a painting of the massacre which formed

A MAID RESTS HER WEARY FEET AT THE END OF THE FAIR

the backdrop to the event. One by one, the women came forward, relating events of the day, interspersed with eye-witness accounts from the time.

In March 1819, three leading radicals in Manchester decided to hold the largest political meeting in the nation's history in order to protest against the Corn Laws and to appeal for parliamentary reform. Leading radicals and the popular speaker Henry 'Orator' Hunt agreed to speak. The local magistrates were concerned that such a substantial gathering of reformers might end in a riot, and arranged for a large number of soldiers to be in attendance. Four squadrons of cavalry of the 15th Hussars (six hundred men), several hundred infantrymen, the Cheshire Yeomanry Cavalry (four hundred men), a detachment of the Royal Horse Artillery and two six-pounder guns, the Manchester and Salford Yeomanry (120 men) and all Manchester's special constables (four hundred men) were called in. As one eye-witness related:

THE PETERLOO MASSACRE BY GEORGE CRUIKSHANK, 1819.
THE LADY IN WHITE ON THE PLATFORM IS THOUGHT TO BE MARY FILDES

A little before noon on the 16th of August, the first body of reformers began to arrive on the scene of action, which was a piece of ground called St. Peter's Field, adjoining a church of that name in the town of Manchester. These persons bore two banners, surmounted with caps of liberty, and bearing the inscriptions: 'No Corn Laws', 'Annual Parliaments', 'Universal Suffrage', 'Vote By Ballot'. Numerous large bodies of reformers continued to arrive from the towns in the neighbourhood of Manchester till about one o'clock, all preceded by flags, and many of them in regular marching order, five deep. Two clubs of female reformers advanced, one of them numbering more than 150 members, and bearing a white silk banner. A band of special constables assumed a position on the field without resistance. The congregated multitude now amounted to a number roundly computed at 80,000, and the arrival of the hero of the day was impatiently expected.

The growing crowds were well marshalled by stewards, who had been trained by the radicals for just such occasions. It seems likely that the authorities mistook this responsible approach to maintaining order for a form of organised para-militarism. Estimates of the numbers gathered vary from 30,000 to 153,000, but William Hulton, Chief Magistrate, concluded there were at least 50,000 people gathered by midday.

At length Mr. Hunt made his appearance, and after a rapturous greeting, was invited to preside; he signified his assent, and mounting a scaffolding, began to harangue his admirers. He had not proceeded far, when the appearance of the yeomanry cavalry advancing toward the area in a brisk trot, excited a panic in the outskirts of the meeting. They entered the enclosure, and after pausing a moment to recover their disordered ranks, and breathe their horses, they drew their swords, and brandished them fiercely in the air. The multitude, by the direction of their leaders, gave three cheers, to show that they were undaunted by this intrusion, and the orator had just resumed his speech to assure the people that this was only a trick to disturb the meeting, and to exhort them to stand firm, when the cavalry dashed into the crowd, making for the cart on which the speakers were placed.

One of the radicals on the platform was Mary Fildes. A passionate proponent of reform (and birth control), she was a founding member of the Manchester Female Reform Group, created in the months prior to the Peterloo meeting. Several reports claimed that the Manchester and Salford Yeomanry attempted to murder Fildes while they were arresting the leaders of the demonstration. One eye-witness described how 'Mrs. Fildes, hanging suspended by a nail which had caught her white dress, was slashed across her exposed body by one of the brave cavalry'. Although badly wounded, Mary Fildes survived.

The people began running in all directions; and from this moment the yeomanry lost all command of temper: numbers were trampled under the feet of men and horses; many, both men and women, were cut down by sabres; several, and a peace officer and a female in the number, slain on the spot. Mr. Hunt was led to prison, not without incurring considerable danger, and some injury on his way from the swords of the yeomanry and the bludgeons of police officers; the broken staves of two of his banners were carried in mock procession before him.

Local eye-witnesses claimed that most of the sixty yeomanry who went to arrest the speakers were drunk (others had earlier reported them drinking in pubs), although their commander insisted that the troops' erratic behaviour was caused by the horses being afraid of the crowd. The yeomanry were a self-funded volunteer corps who were utilised though not controlled by government. Landowners or industrialists, farmers, shopkeepers and professional men often created their own yeomanry groups who, under the banner of 'peace-keeping', could also take repressive measures against anyone in the locality who showed radical or even independent views.

Less than forty minutes after the start of the meeting, eleven people had been killed and about four hundred wounded. Three of the dead and at least a quarter of the injured were women. One of those was Mary Fildes' daughter, who was walking towards the meeting with her four-year-old son William, when the yeomanry knocked her down and trampled her child to death. Orator Hunt was badly beaten by the special constables who arrested him and again by General Clay, who received him at the magistrates' house. Even clerical magistrates showed no pity: 'I believe you are a downright blackguard reformer,' *The Times* quoted one of them as saying to him. 'Some of you reformers ought to be hanged, and some of you are sure to be hanged – the rope is already around your necks.'

The Kentchurch guests were shocked. 'The hairs on the back of my neck stood up as Miss Conick read out

Thomas Ashworth	Manchester	Sabred and trampled
John Ashton	Oldham	Sabred and trampled
Thomas Buckley	Chadderton	Sabred and trampled
James Crompton	Barton	Trampled
William Fildes	Manchester	Trampled
Mary Heys	Manchester	Trampled
Sarah Jones	Manchester	Not recorded
John Lees	Oldham	Sabred
Arthur O'Neill	Manchester	Trampled
Martha Partington	Manchester	Trampled
John Rhodes	Hopwood	Not recorded
Joseph Ashworth	Manchester	Shot
William Bradshaw	Bury	Not recorded
William Dawson	Saddleworth	Sabred and trampled
Edmund Dawson	Saddleworth	Sabred

their names and causes of death. It made the event extremely real,' said Sir Jeremy, whose new title belied his radical tendencies.

From the accounts gathered at the time it emerged that the local yeomanry, rather than the regular soldiers, were largely to blame for the loss of life and high numbers of casualties. The officers and troops of these volunteer bands, poorly disciplined and ill-trained to cope with large crowds, panicked when they found themselves amid a throng of many thousands, linking arms against them or pushing their feet out of their stirrups. More recent theories also suggest that the unprovoked savagery meted out by the yeomanry was inspired by their hatred of the working-class reformers (some of whom they probably knew by sight) who were demanding rights that would threaten their privileged status. Eye-witness accounts bear out this theory:

> One of the cavalry called out to another, 'There's Saxton, damn him run him through.' The other said, 'I'd rather not, I'll leave that for you to do.' When I got to the end of Watson-street, I saw ten or twelve of the Yeomanry Cavalry, and two of the Hussars cutting at the people, who were wedged close together, when an officer of Hussars rode up to his own men, and knocking up their swords said, 'Damn you what do you mean by this work?' He then called out to the Yeomanry, 'For shame gentlemen; what are you about? The people cannot get away.' They desisted for a time but no sooner had the officer rode to another part of the field, than they fell to work again.

Although the authorities attempted to quash or censor all reports of the massacre, news spread quickly and the overwhelming response was horror that the government was now prepared to use the same tactics against British people that it had employed against Napoleon. The deaths of women drew particular condemnation, for there was an unwritten understanding that, while men might have power over women, they were also responsible for protecting them. Far from being ashamed, the Home Secretary, Viscount Sidmouth, sent a letter of congratulation to the Manchester magistrates for the action they had taken. Parliament also passed the notorious Six Acts, which forbade any group from arming themselves, drilling, organising 'seditious meetings' or publishing inflammatory political journals. The Regent also sent his thanks to the military and magistrates for their 'decisive and efficient measures for the preservation of peace' – thereby losing for himself the massive popularity he might have won had he demanded to know why so many of his innocent subjects had been mown down without provocation.

'Talking about the Industrial Revolution, the revolts and the strikes, Peterloo and the Luddite movement, gave me a stressed feeling inside,' admitted Miss Hopkins. 'My father is an industrialist and so I would have been inadvertently responsible for the harsh treatment of these workers and I felt overwhelmingly guilty about it. I settled myself by thinking that I don't agree with exploitation in my modern life, and I hope the people that work for my company don't feel exploited, although they may have a different opinion on that.'

'We emphasised the role that women played at Peterloo,' explained Miss Conick, 'because we felt very politicised by the events of this week at the house. Although three women died at Peterloo, it took another hundred and fifty years for us to get the vote.'

To end their performance, the young women of the house came forward, one by one, and joined their voices together in a slow crescendo of protest as they recited the last few verses of 'To Walk in the Visions of Poesy', Shelley's response to Peterloo.

> And that slaughter to the Nation
> Shall steam up like inspiration
> Eloquent, oracular;
> A volcano heard afar.
>
> And these words shall then become
> Like Oppression's thundered doom
> Ringing through each heart and brain,
> Heard again – again – again –
>
> Rise like Lions after slumber
> In unvanquishable number –
> Shake your chains to earth like dew
> Which in sleep had fallen on you –
> Ye are many – they are few!

MR GORELL BARNES RECEIVES INFORMATION CONCERNING UNREST WITHIN THE COUNTY

A DEJECTED MR FOXSMITH PONDERS THE IMPOSSIBILITY OF HIS LOVE

CHAPTER ELEVEN

THE FINAL ACT
OUT WITH A BANG, NOT A WHIMPER!

When you are of an age to think of settling, let your affections be placed
on a steady, sober, religious man, who will be tender and careful of you
at all times . . . Do not marry a very young man, you know not how he
might turn out; it is a lottery at best but it is a very just remark that
'It is better to be an old man's darling than a young man's scorn.'

A MOTHER'S ADVICE TO HER DAUGHTER, 1801

THE LAST WEEK of the Regency House Party at Kentchurch Court began with a
bugle call from the stable yard. The guests hurried
down to the breakfast room, to find a lottery crier
who prevailed upon them to apply for tickets.
Lottery madness was rife during the Regency
among all levels of society. Despite being illegal,
many private lotteries were held each year, with
ticket sellers 'puffing up' their own scheme by
wearing ornate gold and red clothes and carrying
huge, decorated placards. The only official lottery
was held annually by Order of Parliament. In
1811, the first year of the Regency, the tickets cost
£10 and the total prize money offered was
£600,000. A bidding war would then begin: tickets
would usually be sold at around £17 to brokers,
who then sold them on to lottery agents for £20,
who would then put another layer of profit on the

THE COUNTESS IS EXPOSED

ticket before selling it eventually to members of the public. Lotteries were a very
good source of revenue for the government and were continued despite the parliamentary debate of 1808 that roundly condemned them: 'The foundation of the lottery system is so radically vicious, that your Committee feel convinced that under
no system of regulations which can be devised will it be possible for Parliament to
adopt it as an efficacious source of revenue, and, at the same time, divest it of all
the evils of which it has, hitherto, proved so baneful a source.'

As well as buying tickets, people could also 'insure' a number for a shilling, and be given a pound, for example, if it won. This form of gambling on the lottery was most popular among maids and footmen, and it was estimated that they spent on average twenty-five shillings a year – a huge sum for someone earning only a few pounds. Insurances were often sold by 'morocco men', so-named because they carried large, red morocco-leather-bound books in which to note down their business. Although the books gave them entry to every level of society, from the mistress of a house to the maidservants, the morocco men were not popular. They had the reputation of being expert diddlers, persuading people to part with their money and promising huge rewards for small amounts invested. The parliamentary committee examining the case for and against lotteries heard many depositions from lawyers representing families ruined by gambling. Stories abounded of industrious, successful fathers turning into vicious and drunken addicts, and wives reduced to stealing from their husbands, and children from their parents, to buy tickets. Suicides were frequent and many ended their days living on charity, in the poorhouse or in gaol. However, the rare big wins were widely publicised by the lottery agents, particularly if they themselves had sold winning tickets. Nothing has changed.

The guests at Kentchurch, now habituated to gambling after seven weeks at the house, all wrote off for tickets carrying their lucky numbers. 'An extraordinary woman arrived this morning blowing a trumpet,' reported Mrs Enright with some incredulity. 'The prize was a vast amount of money and even the lesser prizes were exceedingly attractive. The tickets were five

A LOTTERY SELLER TRUMPETS HER WARES
IN THE STABLE YARD

pounds but I beat the woman down to one pound. I feel I did rather well, which I won't have done at all, of course, if I lose.'

In the Regency, the winning tickets were drawn by a blindfolded orphan boy at the Guildhall in London. Huge crowds would assemble on the day of the draw. The state lottery of 1815, for example, was drawn on 7 June and £624,400 was given away in prize money. The top prize was £40,000 but the Treasury still made the tremendous profit of £224,311. This continued for many years until the voices raised against the immorality of the state lottery were sufficient to lead to its prohibition in 1826.

While the house-guests waited impatiently for the results, another lottery was to begin – that of choosing a partner.

Each young man and woman had the last week to decide who they wanted to accompany them as they left the house party on the last day – a symbolic gesture designed to force them to choose whom they might have married had they really been living in the Regency. They had to consider not only who had displayed the qualities they sought in a partner in terms of mutual compatibility and attraction, but also their 'suitability'

LOVE AND RICHES.

Oh! charming Miss May
If you'll only be mine,
Every pleasure that Wealth
Can procure shall be thine.

Away! you old fool
I am not such an elf,
To barter my bliss
For your ill-gotten pelf.

Good bye, my gay lass,
But you shall remember
The slight you now pass
Upon Mr. December.

Good bye, my old Dad
But don't be in a rage.
I'm griev'd you're so sad
And I pity your age.

Your true lover, June
Begs to offer his hand,
Whose heart and whose love
You may ever command

I acknowledge your worth,
But we're both of us poor
And love cannot keep
The wolf from the door

But Fortune you'll own can grant all your wishes
And make you both happy in Lottery riches.

Farewell, then, to care, and to church haste away,
The gay Mr. June shall be married to May.

IN THE REGENCY, MONEY COULD BUY YOU LOVE

in Regency terms. Although the choice of partners at Kentchurch was limited, this was an accurate reflection of the Regency marriage mart. Circles of acquaintance were necessarily small, limited by the difficulty and expense of travel, the importance of kith and kin and the exclusion of anyone not in one's social milieu. Many young men and women would have had to choose from only a handful of available partners. As Mr Darcy observed to Elizabeth Bennet: 'In a country neighbourhood you move in a very confined and unvarying society.' 'But people themselves', replied Elizabeth Bennet, 'alter so much, that there is something to be observed in them forever.'

The house-guests at Kentchurch had certainly 'altered so much' over the past nine weeks, each affected by the 'Regency roller-coaster', as they called it, of living and loving as people had done two hundred years earlier. Now that it was time for them to make a decision on who they wanted for a partner, the chaperones were called upon to discover from their charges which man they admired most. They were, of course, free to influence that decision as they saw fit. The chaperones would form a panel and interview all the young men in turn and would then debate among themselves who was to be paired with whom, though the men had the final veto.

Of course, some preferences had already been made very clear during the preceding weeks – such as Mr Everett's for Miss Hopkins and Sir Jeremy's for Miss Braund – yet the women themselves were secretive or confused about their own choices. Miss Hopkins vacillated almost hourly between the dependable Mr Everett and the exciting Mr Carrington, while Miss Braund had set tongues wagging by flirting outrageously with Sir Jeremy (who bestowed a kiss upon her) although they both claimed to be 'just friends'. Were they playing a clever game, keeping everyone guessing about the exact nature of their relationship? Would Sir Jeremy's real feelings be revealed during his interview with the chaperones? Miss Braund's chaperone was certainly backing the match. 'I will be robustly arguing for it to the point of busting a gut,' she said. 'I am going to be a good chaperone and will promote Sir Jeremy to the hilt. I won't take no for an answer and it's no good any of the other chaperones now deciding that he's marvellous for their girls, no good at all.'

This dithering was the female prerogative in the Regency and possibly the only time in a woman's life when she could hold centre stage. Women were assumed to have the upper hand during courtship and were expected to sit in calm judgement as they made their choice. In the words of one Regency chaperone to her young charge:'When a

SIR JEREMY AND MISS BRAUND STRAY FROM
REGENCY IDEAS OF DECORUM AND MODESTY

lady is courting, she is to keep herself at a genteel distance, lest the conquest afterwards might be reckon'd cheap. You must be wary of Easy Compliances that may distinguish the Desire of Marriage.'

Wooing and courtship, while often the result of genuine emotion, were quite ritualised. Catching the object of one's affection was planned with military precision by men and the vagaries of the chase enjoyed. Setbacks were welcomed for the expression of 'delicious melancholy' that they allowed. It was perfectly acceptable for men to weep profusely in public or bespatter their love-letters with their tears. It became so fashionable for men to cry (led by the frequently tearful Regent) that some women suspected the ink of their lovers' missives to have been 'cried upon' with the artful shake of a sponge.

Once a suitor's campaign had succeeded and been accepted by both families, long and tedious negotiations were entered into concerning the marriage settlement. This was usually done by the couple's legal guardians, which at least allowed the lovers to blame all mercenary considerations on their relatives, freeing them to claim theirs as a 'love match'. 'Where does discretion end and avarice begin?' says Elizabeth Bennet in *Pride and Prejudice*. When Elizabeth and Charlotte discuss Charlotte's decision to marry the unctuous Mr Collins (a clear case of sense winning out over sensibility), Charlotte admits that she is 'not romantic' and asks only for 'a comfortable home'. Mr Collins's company is 'irksome' but, in her eyes, the state of marriage as a 'preservative from want' is more important than the personal qualities of the marriage partner. Jane Austen makes it clear that the economic realities of her society all but force Charlotte to marry Collins. Regency women were utterly dependent on men for money, and even those who had money placed in trust for them before marriage would have seen it administered by the men in their families, either a spouse or father. The majority signed away all their wealth and property to their husbands on marriage. Women motivated purely by passion, however, like Elizabeth's sister Lydia, are seen as succumbing to 'pure folly' and acting in selfish and damaging ways – her elopement with Wickham puts all the Bennet girls' prospects of marriage at risk, since no decent man would now want a 'connection' with their family. Mr Darcy struggles with his own pride for several chapters before straddling the huge social gap he perceives to exist between himself and Elizabeth and asking for her hand.

It is not surprising that Regency women hoped to find men of means *and* merits. However, as life expectancy for Regency men was lower than that for women, the resultant disparity in numbers (the first ever census in England and Wales, taken in 1801, put the population at 8,893,000 with over 400,000 more women than men) meant that competition for the best husbands was intense. The average age of women who did marry was twenty-seven, unless you happened to be an heiress (and fewer than 10 per cent of heirs were female), in which case it was twenty-four. Male heirs felt no need to rush such an important decision and generally tied the knot in their late twenties or early thirties, while over a quarter of them remained bachelors for life.

Once marriage negotiations were finally settled to both families' satisfaction, it was in the bride's interest to marry with the utmost haste, as any engagement that did not end in marriage was detrimental to a young lady's reputation. Marriages often occurred within ten days of settlement.

Just as today, there were happy and miserable marriages. Some couples managed to create a partnership of some equality, despite women's dependency in law. Others give us nightmarish visions of the tortures many women endured at the hands of vicious but all-powerful husbands. As the blue-stocking Elisabeth Robinson noted: 'Wedding puts an end to wooing . . . Men get up off their knees and, metaphorically at least, women get down on them.' Men had the right to drag home any wife who ran away – even if she had fled from drunken physical abuse or the threat of death. A man could legally rape and beat his wife and, no matter how dreadful her suffering, any woman who left her marital home was subject to social ostracism thereafter.

There was no going back once married. Lady Devonport had written to her own lawyer at the start of the Regency house project to find out about the possibility of getting a divorce in 1811. 'There were only four in 1811!' she exclaimed in horror. 'It was almost impossible to get one! The only grounds were that you had married a close relation without realising it or that you had married under the age of twenty-one without your father's consent.' It was chilling for the chaperones to know that, had they been living two hundred years ago, divorce would not have been an option. Instead, they would have been trapped in an unhappy marriage until released by their own or their husband's death. As one observant spinster noted: 'Really, there is so much Care in a Married State and fiddle faddle in most Men's Tempers that I Esteem myself vastly happier in having nothing to do with 'em . . .'

'This Regency marriage business is such a cattle market!' burst out Lady Devonport, whose behaviour during the past nine weeks had revealed some unconventional attitudes.

> It is really like buying and selling horses. People of my generation have said that when daughters of theirs have got married their fiancés have come and asked for 'permission for their hand'. In my hippyish way that makes me sick. I don't like the idea of giving people away – women aren't 'property' to be traded around. My daughter wasn't given away, she walked into the church by herself. So I am playing the game quite happily but I still think it stinks. And if I'd lived in the Regency I just wouldn't have done it, I'm quite positive about that.

More than one of Kentchurch's young maidens was considering opting out of the 'cattle market' altogether rather than accept its indignities, the inequalities of the married state or the unhappiness of a loveless or even violent match. 'Mr Gorell Barnes has just told me that men were allowed to beat their wives as long as the stick was no thicker than their wrist!' said a horrified Miss Conick. 'I know he was just winding me up, but it isn't a very appealing thought.' Miss Conick was starting to consider alternatives to matrimony, such as becoming a famous courtesan and starting her own literary and political salon. Although Regency courtesans were more famous for publishing their memoirs than encouraging literary talent ('Publish and be damned,' said Wellington to his one-time mistress, the infamous Harriette Wilson, whose scandalous reminiscences were so popular they were reprinted thirty-five times in the first year), Miss Conick's idea was not impossible as long as she was very successful (financially as well as fashionably) at her chosen profession. Or was the plan simply a ruse to cover up the fact that she had not given up all hope of attracting the attention of Mr Gorell Barnes? If she remained independent she needed to remember that the lot of widows, old maids (unmarried women over thirty) and dependent daughters was precarious. The 'genteel poverty' in which they lived was usually severe financial hardship. Since it was unseemly for a gentlewoman to work, particularly in the few fields open to women (such as

A passionate friendship blossoms outside the 'horse trading'

domestic service and teaching), she had no way of alleviating the misery of her situation. Unmarried daughters and their widowed mothers were usually forced out of their homes on the death of their father or husband, with the arrival of the new heir. Jane Austen's *Sense and Sensibility* begins with Mrs Dashwood, and her three daughters, being forced, on the death of her husband, to leave her home and make way for her stepson and ghastly daughter-in-law (Mrs John Dashwood) who have now inherited Norland: 'No sooner was his father's funeral over, than Mrs. John Dashwood, without sending any notice of her intention to her mother-in-law, arrived with her child and their attendants. No one could dispute her right to come; the house was her husband's from the moment of his father's decease . . . Mrs. John Dashwood now installed herself mistress of Norland; and her mother and sisters-in-law were degraded to the condition of visitors.'

If a man and woman separated, it was the man who retained control over any children and could prevent his wife having access to them. The Prince of Wales himself exerted this right: as his daughter was approaching marriageable age, the prince wanted to keep her away from her mother, whom he considered to be a bad influence. By 1812 it became public knowledge that he had refused to allow them to see each other, except for dinner once a week in the company of people carefully selected by him. This measure was more effective in giving the prince a bad press than all his greed, extravagance and infidelity.

The farce of the prince's marriage had begun in 1795, when he had agreed to wed as long as his debts were paid and his income from the Civil List more than doubled. The King wanted his eldest son to produce an heir, and since the prince was £630,000 in debt – an extraordinary sum in those days – the deal was done. He had already gone through a marriage ceremony with Mrs Fitzherbert in 1785 and they had lived together as man and wife

MRS FITZHERBERT. AN ENGRAVING
BY RICHARD COSWAY, 1792

for many years. However, this match was deemed illegal on the grounds that any marriage contracted by a
member of the Royal Family under twenty-five years
old and without the King's consent was invalid.
Furthermore, the Act of Settlement decreed that any
heir to the throne who married a Catholic forfeited all
right to the crown. Despite these obstacles, Mrs
Fitzherbert remained loyal to the prince until 1803,
when she finally broke with him because he placed her
low down the table at an official dinner at Carlton
House.

The Regent officially married his cousin
Caroline, the daughter of the King's sister Augusta
and the Duke of Brunswick. They met for the first
time on their wedding day, 5 April 1795, and took an
immediate dislike to each other. The prince said to

QUEEN CAROLINE. AN ENGRAVING
BY R. PAGE, 1818

James Harris, Lord Malmesbury, who accompanied him, 'Harris, I am not well;
pray get me a glass of brandy.' Caroline was twenty-seven, blonde, short and
sturdy, and said to be quite pretty with nice eyes. However, she was also inelegant,
vulgar and loud, and was already thought a wild and eccentric character by her own
family. Furthermore, she was said to have a strong aversion to all forms of personal
hygiene, which must have been off-putting indeed for the fastidious prince.
Despite their mutual loathing (she thought the prince fat), they managed to over-
come their differences enough to produce a daughter within nine months of getting married. By this time they had already agreed to live separately, initially within
his household and later at different residences. The prince ran back to Mrs
Fitzherbert, who celebrated his return with an opulent public breakfast for the
fashionable world.

Caroline was no shrinking violet, however, and she made sure that she got her
due when it was important. When the crowned heads of Russia and Prussia visited
England in 1814 after Napoleon's abdication to Elba, she was not invited to any of
the official engagements. However, when her husband and his fellow monarchs
were at the opera, she made an exquisitely timed entrance into her own box,

receiving applause from the audience and bows from all three rulers. Soon after this she left England to tour the Continent (much to the annoyance of her daughter, who was having difficulty with her father over whom she should marry and wanted an ally). Caroline took up with an Italian called Pergami and, according to rumour, they became lovers. She was clearly enjoying herself – dancing, eating, drinking and carousing and taking great pleasure in annoying her husband, who had sent spies to check up on her every move. Lady Bessborough wrote of the moment when she bumped into the princess at a ball in Genoa:

> The first thing I saw in the room was a short, very fat, elderly woman, with an extremely red face (owing, I suppose, to the heat) in a girl's white frock-looking dress, but with shoulder, back and neck quite low (disgustingly so), down to the middle of her stomach . . . I was staring at her from the oddity of her appearance, when suddenly she nodded and smiled at me, and not recollecting her, I was convinc'd she was mad, till William push'd me, saying, 'Do you not see the Princess of Wales nodding to you?'.

The uneasy truce between the prince and princess was shattered by the death of George III on 29 January 1820. The King's death brought the Regency to a close and George IV was proclaimed monarch on 31 January 1820, as he lay in bed suffering from pleurisy. A few days before his father's death, his younger brother the Duke of Kent had died suddenly (leaving behind an infant daughter who was later to become Queen of England). After letting his blue blood, his doctors announced the new King cured; but his heart was heavy. He was deeply troubled that the wife whom he loathed now had the right to be his queen. Determined that she should not be crowned, nor enjoy the prayers of the faithful every week in the liturgy, he embarked on the most disastrous escapade of his error-strewn career – to try to divorce her.

The house-party guests decided that they would mark the end of the Regency, the proclamation of George's ascent to the throne and the end of their incredible Regency experiment by staging a pageant on the theme of George IV's coronation, to be followed by a spectacular masquerade ball. Rehearsals began immediately.

The coronation was a morality tale for anyone skipping their way lightly towards matrimony. The philandering, scheming prince, whose love of plump older women made him a figure of ridicule and contempt, was hardly the most ele-vating exemplar for the young men of Kentchurch. Nor was his attention-seeking, indiscreet wife the ideal role model for the young ladies.

Determined to take up her rightful position as Queen, Caroline arrived back in England in June 1820. She became the focus of great national support, partly out of sympathy for her situation as a wronged wife but also out of a desire to show her despised husband the extent of his unpopularity. Caroline appeared regularly before her enthusiastic public, and across the country firework displays, bonfires and meetings were held in honour of this German woman who had previously paid no attention to the people who were now screaming for her cause.

The King, infuriated by Caroline's popularity, sent the infamous 'green bag' to the Cabinet, in which he had collected evidence of her infidelity. The dustiest recesses of the law were swept for some clause that would allow the King to divorce his wife, and the Bill of Pains and Penalties was dredged up. The Queen was then put on trial by the whole House of Lords, who were to decide whether or not she had committed adultery. The trial lasted for three months, during which time, according to Hobhouse (Byron's old travelling companion), the entire governing body of the country was 'sent to pry into foul clothes bags and pore over the con-tents of chamber utensils'. Public opinion remained loyal to the Queen throughout the process. As Lady Cowper wrote: 'The Queen has a strange good luck in her favour; the worse she behaves, the more it rebounds to her credit . . . She says it is true she did commit adultery once, but it was with the husband of Mrs Fitzherbert.'

On 10 November the bill was thrown out, not because the peers believed the Queen to be innocent but because they disapproved of the bill as a political meas-ure. 'Nobody cares for me in this business,' declared Caroline. The King did not get his divorce, but Caroline was kept away from the Coronation. On the day of the ceremony (which cost the nation four times that of Queen Victoria's) she turned up at the doors of Westminster Abbey demanding entry. She had constantly petitioned the Prime Minister about attending formally, but her missives were ignored or rebuffed. She banged on the doors, shouting, 'The Queen . . . open!' One confused page did so, only for an official to yell, 'Do your duty . . . shut the door!' The door was slammed in her face and within a few days she had fallen ill with what was probably an intestinal obstruction. 'I know I am dying – they have killed me at last!' she said. She died on 7 August 1821 at the age of fifty-three, less than three weeks after her attempt to be crowned. She was buried in Brunswick and on her coffin was the inscription CAROLINE THE INJURED QUEEN OF ENGLAND. Whether the women and men of Kentchurch Court would heed this moral tale or whether they would stumble blindly into a 'misalliance' with an unsuitable partner in their last, heady week of the house party remained to be seen.

In between rehearsals, the chaperones sounded out their charges' views on whom they wished to be coupled with. Mrs Rogers' interview with the countess was overshadowed by the fact that that week's newspaper had uncovered the secret of her poverty. Would she still have the audacity to aim for the high-ranking host? 'In some people's eyes her eligibility has plummeted,' admitted Mrs Rogers, 'but in those days status was very much more important than money. If you had a good title but were poor you were still smarter than someone with no title and masses of money. Because her title is in the female line it does not go to any offspring, nor to the husband, but none the less on invitations it would still be Mr X and the Countess Whoever, so everyone's still aware that Mr X has married a countess. That still happens today.'

Lady Devonport and Miss Hopkins found a moment of privacy on horseback, and it was as they were riding through the deer park together that Miss Hopkins revealed her decision. It was almost enough to make Lady Devonport fall off her horse. The results of all these conversations were kept secret and the chaperones did not even discuss their charges among themselves. The young ladies were rivals, and it would put them at a disadvantage to have the secrets of their hearts broadcast to the others' chaperones.

The guests were also considering what their parting gestures to the house would be. Miss Hopkins had asked to have a picnic to commemorate the one she had so enjoyed at the beginning of their stay, 'because that was when I really felt like I had become one with my inner feminine side'. Miss Conick and Sir Jeremy had both decided to plant trees. Miss Conick chose to plant hers in the woods to the east of the house, the place where she had found most solitude and peace. Sir Jeremy dug his into the deer park, the spot where he had learned how to be a real 'gentleman', able both to express love and to sabre a melon!

Mr Everett's parting gesture, the construction of a spectacular maze using around seven hundred stakes and two thousand metres of twine, was such a huge project that Miss Braund was drafted in to help. The friendship that grew between them during the many hours of shared toil kept the other house-guests guessing about the possibility of a last-minute romance between them; and the chaperones realised that they could use the maze in their match-making schemes. Before leaving the house, the prospective couples could make their way through the maze together; this would afford them the opportunity to work as a team and would be an ideal context for them to express their feelings towards each other through their body language. The chaperones could use this as a dress rehearsal and halt any disastrous liaisons before it was too late.

Following the discussions with the girls, it was the men's turn to be grilled. However, before they could be put through their paces by the chaperones, a cat appeared among the pigeons. As the guests filed into dinner that evening, they noticed that there was one place too many. Halfway through the soup course, uproar was caused by the surprise return of Captain Robinson! To cheers, applause, hugs and even tears, he was heartily welcomed back into the fold. A few surreptitious eyes turned towards Miss Francesca to gauge her reaction. When last seen with the captain, she was wishing him a tearful goodbye and promising to write daily. Within hours of his departure, however, she was overheard pronouncing favourably on the looks of the hermit, whom she had just met. Their friendship had blossomed into passion and at some point she would need to explain this situation to the captain.

At breakfast the next morning there was yet another disruption to the social order, in the form of a message for Mrs Enright, who was discreetly informed that her charge, Miss Conick, had won the lottery. 'When I came in here I was worth thirty-five pounds,' said Miss Conick, pulling a few pound notes from her cleavage. Reaching down to the floor, she picked up a great wad of notes and exclaimed with delight, 'I am now worth eight thousand pounds!' Overnight, Miss Conick had become the wealthiest woman in the house. Since the countess had been revealed to be a pauper, Miss Conick was now a better catch than her rival, despite their difference in status. And rivals they most certainly were (albeit courteous ones) for the attention of Mr Gorell Barnes. Both women had expressed an

interest in him (and him alone) during the weeks at the house. Were they aware of each other's feelings? Was this the cause of Miss Conick's unease in the countess's company? After all, the countess herself had said that she was 'never beaten in love by prettier girls', and perhaps the coolness she had displayed to Miss Conick was to warn her off? It was also true that the only woman Mr Gorell Barnes had shown much interest in, other than the countess, was Miss Conick. 'I was talking to GB in the gazebo the other night,' confided Miss Conick, 'and he said:

'Well, why don't you marry me, darling?' And I replied, 'Because you've been set up with the countess,' and he was like, 'No, I haven't, no, no, no, sweet girl. We're just friends.' So I don't know what's going on in his head, but the next night he asked Mrs Enright what was to stop him leaving with Miss Conick. What's he playing at? I don't know if he was joking, I don't know if he was half serious. I would be happy to leave here with Gorell Barnes. It would be shame if he ends up with the countess just because it's been engineered. Doesn't he realise he's being set up? Open your eyes! I wonder what he meant by asking me to marry him?

Mrs Enright had in fact frequently attempted to position her charge beside the host at dinner, sometimes successfully. She observed:

Miss Conick is a young woman of immense dignity and self-reliance, but I think it has been of use to her that I have challenged some of the protocol in this house. It was me who stood up to Mrs Rogers about this dreary seating plan which meant that the countess and Lady Devonport sat next to our host every single night, with inevitable consequences for the rest of us. I couldn't say whether she's grateful or not – why on earth should she be? It was boring me as much as her. Proximity and availability is persuasive with men who are emotionally a bit idle. If someone is sat next to them at dinner night after night after night, they'll make friends with them, it's the easiest thing to do; and if they're remotely attractive they may think it will be convenient at this moment to fall in love.

Miss Conick's lottery win now entitled her to occupy the best room in the house, to order new dresses, to ride, fence, sit at the top of the table next to the host and generally flaunt and enjoy her new status. 'I'm certainly not going to pull rank,' she declared.

I hate it when people do that. It's very insensitive to those below you in the social ladder who can't swan around doing whatever they like. Having money does not make you a better person, it doesn't automatically give you a right to be treated better and I feel that really strongly. I don't want to behave like some people have behaved in here. The only real difference this is going to make is that I don't have to get married. The sole purpose of you being taken on as a wife in the Regency was to produce heirs and to get all your assets, which a husband could then legally spend on mistresses and prostitutes while he raped and beat you every evening. I'm sorry, that doesn't sound like much fun, so I'm going to take my eight grand and run. Money equals independence in Regency times and, yeah, there will be a social stigma if I don't get married, but hey, stigma shmigma.

The chaperones gathered the following day in the library, an imposing wall of female wisdom and experience. With some trepidation, the men entered one by one. The first candidate to be scrutinised was Mr Foxsmith. When asked to name his chosen partner, he looked straight at Lady Devonport and declared, 'I want to be with you.' Lady Devonport dissolved into tears, pulled a ring off her finger which she handed to Mr Foxsmith, saying, 'This was my grandmother's and she was very happily married. She gave it to me before she died. I'd like you to give it to whoever you meet, because I know you'll make somebody very happy and they're a very lucky person whoever they are and I wish it could be me but it isn't.' Their love for each other was plain to see. They agreed to see each other after the house party ended, but for the immediate future Mr Foxsmith declared his intention to remain a bachelor. As he stood to leave, he bent down and planted a gentle kiss on her shoulder.

Next came Captain Robinson, whose return meant that there were enough young men to partner all six women. Always amiable and good-tempered, he answered the chaperones' questions readily and made it clear that Miss Francesca had told him about her relationship with the hermit. He was disappointed, but not desperately so, and declared his admiration for all the women at Kentchurch. Lady Devonport later revealed that he had said of Miss Samuel, 'If she had been here from the start, I never would have left.' So it was decided that they should accompany each other around the maze.

Mr Carrington was next in the hot seat. It had dawned on him that, unless he changed his ways, he would alienate the affections of Miss Hopkins and have to leave alone. On being questioned by the chaperones, he hurried to praise Miss Hopkins' and his suit was supported by Lady Devonport. She did, however, make it clear to him that her charge was very popular and there was no guarantee that he would be her partner. Looking less than anxious about his rivals, he saluted the chaperones, with whom he had always been very popular, and left.

Sir Jeremy was next to arrive, glass in hand and every inch the Regency gentleman. When asked whether he had particular feelings for any girl he replied, 'Yes, it would be Miss Braund.'

'We hoped that you would say that,' said Mrs Hammond.

'Has it been that obvious? I thought it was very subtle!' remarked Sir Jeremy with a smile.

Mrs Hammond replied, 'Since the beginning you have been extremely felicitous and solicitous to Miss Braund—'

'I feel a poem coming on!' interjected Sir Jeremy

' . . . and consistent. When you had little financially, your attentions to Miss Braund were no less than when you came into your money and title. That's what has impressed me the most and Miss Braund too. You crept up on her very slowly but she's become very fond of you as time has gone by.' The constancy of Sir

Jeremy's affections for Miss Braund was clear, and his desire to be her partner was quickly accepted. They had become close friends over the weeks and in the Regency might well have married, probably very happily, out of mutual respect and liking.

Miss Braund also got the nod of approval from the next arrival, Mr Everett, although everyone knew that this was because he had realised that his chances of winning Miss Hopkins' affections were slim. Not that he had given up hope altogether: 'She looked at me the other day and gave me a wink,' he said. 'My heart leaped into my mouth.' The chaperones hinted that Miss Hopkins might not be available to be his partner, and after he left they thought hard about who could accompany him around his beautiful maze but drew a blank. 'What about your charge, Mrs Enright?' enquired Mrs Hammond.

'Mine wants to live independently in Mayfair and set up a salon using your address book for a start, Lady Devonport,' Mrs Enright informed the others.

'She shall have it,' replied Lady Devonport promptly.

Miss Conick's independent spirit left the field clear for the countess to partner the host – but was his favour forthcoming? 'Mr Gorell Barnes,' said Mrs Hammond on the host's arrival. 'We are asking all the men the same question. Is there any particular lady in here that you favour above all the rest?'

'All the ladies are very fine,' he replied from the safety of the fence.

'Ah, you are always such a politician,' observed Lady Devonport; 'you never give anything away about what you are thinking. There must be someone you think of particularly highly.'

'Miss Braund.'

'Miss Braund?!' replied the chaperones with one voice. 'But you've never spoken to the girl,' exclaimed Lady Devonport.

'Exactly,' said Mr Gorell Barnes.

'So I trust you will accompany the countess around the maze, Mr Gorell Barnes?' said Mrs Hammond. Without saying yes or no, he inclined his head towards the chaperones.

'My attitude to the women has changed since I've been in the house,' admitted Mr Gorell Barnes later. 'In the twenty-first century you meet somebody and you might be pretty intimate with them in a few hours, whereas here it would take

MISS SAMUEL'S FINANCIAL INDEPENDENCE ALLOWED HER TO REMAIN AN OBSERVER OF THE MATCH-MAKING GAME

a lot longer. So in 1811 my attitude has changed but whether that will affect me in 2003, I'll have to wait and see.'

The following day the maze was finally ready, finished at the eleventh hour with the help of most of the house-guests. It was a beautiful sight, the myriad canes decorated with ribbons, flowers and *billets doux*. The first to find their way through it would win a bottle of champagne, generously offered by the host, but on the way they had to pick up three love tokens in the form of flowers – a rose, symbol of happiness in Mr Everett's rubric; lavender, symbol of wealth; and a sweet-pea, symbol of children.

That morning at breakfast, the couplings had been announced. Miss Samuel was to go with Captain Robinson, Miss Braund with Sir Jeremy, Miss Hopkins with Mr Carrington, the countess with Mr Gorell-Barnes and Miss Francesca with the hermit. Mr Foxsmith, Miss Conick and Mr Everett were to go alone. This order of play had not been achieved without some excitement. Miss Hopkins had initially informed her chaperone that she wished to be partnered by Mr Everett – hence Lady Devonport's near-tumble from her mount. Miss Hopkins had declared that it was more important to marry a man who was dependable and loving than one who was simply exciting. These sentiments her chaperone applauded in theory, though she doubted that they matched the realities of life. She was secretly pleased

LOVE TOKENS AND RIBBONS FLUTTER ATOP MR EVERETT'S MAZE

when Miss Hopkins changed her mind, the night before the couples were to be announced, following a charm campaign from Mr Carrington. Mr Everett was so upset by her decision, however, that the pleasure of going round the maze with Mr Carrington was considerably diminished for the caring Miss Hopkins. 'Two gentlemen were fighting for my affections and I had to make a decision between them,' she cried. 'It was absolutely horrible. Mr Everett sat on my right and kept looking at me and shaking his head. He walked off and I

MRS ENRIGHT TAKES A LAST LOOK
AROUND THE LANDSCAPE OF HER REGENCY SUMMER

had to go and find him but I couldn't and it broke my heart. Why should I have to choose between either of them? They both have fantastic attributes to offer to a young lady but they are so different. I followed the beat of my heart, but was it the right decision?'

Miss Samuel was trailed by Captain Robinson. 'He followed me around the maze like a little dog – it was very sweet and very funny,' she said fondly. Theirs was clearly just a friendship, and an embryonic one at that. And poor Mr Everett? Spurned once more, he wandered around the maze alone, looking a little forlorn.

The countess was very pleased with the outcome of the chaperones' machinations. In the light of her dire financial situation, she should have aimed for a wealthy man of lower status who might enjoy being married to a titled lady: Mr Everett, perhaps? However, the countess was adamant: her choice was Mr Gorell Barnes. If she could not have him, she would follow Miss Francesca's lead by retreating into the country and living the life of a hermit.

Miss Francesca had been inseparable from Mr Helm for the past two weeks and the couple now ambled around the maze together, picking up the love tokens they needed.

'I've got "children",' said the hermit.

'Put it back until we've found "happiness",' replied Miss Francesca. 'Ah, here's "money" at least!'

The hermit took the flower out of her hands and sprinkled its petals over her head. 'Here's the housekeeping!' he said.

The day following the adventures in the maze, the chaperones left Kentchurch to return to their former lives. The rift between Mrs Rogers and Mrs Enright had not been solved, but this had not blighted the whole experience for either of them. 'I will come away with some of my best memories,' said Mrs Rogers. 'The footmen in particular have been amazing and so was riding side-saddle up to the hermitage. I'm very proud of achieving that. My children said I was very brave for doing this and it has been remarkable.'

Mrs Hammond had learned a lot about herself through the experience. 'I'm an over-achiever', she explained, 'so I don't feel worthwhile unless I'm contributing something. Maybe after this I can just let go of the ropes a little bit sometimes, not for too long but occasionally. The thing I've realised most of all while I've been in here though is that I really want to write.'

Mrs Enright's thoughts were of her charge. 'I hope there will be a satisfactory outcome and that she will be happy with what happens. I should hate to leave feeling that the outcome was unforeseen, uncontrolled and perhaps not to her benefit.' (She need not have worried.)

Lady Devonport had mixed feelings: 'I hated loving this and I loved hating it,' she said. 'It's difficult to say how extraordinary this experience has been, how profound and how much it has meant to me (and how rubbish I've been at it), but I'm hugely grateful that I've been able to do it.'

Once they had gone, the atmosphere in the house changed completely. 'It's a remarkably different place,' said the host. 'I've been walking around the ladies' corridor, going into the girls' rooms and sitting on their beds talking to them, which I wouldn't dream of doing before – even though it's supposed to be my house. Everyone feels more at ease and happier now that the older generation aren't here any more. I think everyone's sort of relaxed, loosened up, and are completely being themselves. I didn't realise what effect they had over communication between the men and the women. Perhaps I let them have too much power, God knows.'

Mr Foxsmith did not, of course, share this feeling. Speaking through his tears, he said, 'I love Lady D. I love everything about her. She's so sorely missed in such a short time. The thing I really love is gone, she went away today. I have her golden ring. I just wish she was here. We were very, very good friends. Passionate friends.'

Having clad themselves in their finery, the young men and women of Kentchurch Court prepared for their final evening. In the gathering twilight, they walked across the gently sloping lawns to the laurel walk, the scene of so many private moments, quiet strolls and romantic assignations.

As the guests performed their pageant, it was appropriate that the man at the heart of the epoch they had been reliving should return to centre stage – the Prince Regent. The host played the part of the king-to-be-crowned; the countess was his estranged wife. The other guests danced and paraded their way through the Regency characters they had become familiar with over the past nine weeks – heiresses and mistresses, dandies and politicians, rebels and romantics. The pageant ended with Queen Caroline collapsed on the floor as the King walked into the night. Whereupon the countess stood up, brushed herself off, and followed him towards the music, twinkling lights and succulent food at the ball. The ladies donned masks and long black cloaks and remained silent so that the men had to try to guess who they were. They danced, drank and laughed, freed not just from the responsibilities of their Regency identities but also perhaps from their modern identities. The guests were keen to party. The freedom they all felt, released from the ever-present gaze of the chaperones, was intoxicating. Later on, with the masks

off, they caroused their way into the early hours of an exquisite summer's dawn. All pretence was abandoned and the men and women did as they pleased. As they stumbled to bed, many were not alone.

'Oh! I went to bed alone and now the countess seems to be in here with me! Good morning, Countess,' exclaimed Mr Gorell Barnes, after being woken by his footman the following morning. The happy couple breakfasted together in their dressing gowns and she curtsied to him as she left to get dressed. Mr Carrington and Miss Hopkins awoke to find themselves looking up at the canopied reaches of

Mrs Rogers' recently vacated bed, while Miss Francesca awoke to the sound of Hermit Originals (buttery biscuits of the hermit's own devising) being cooked over the fire at the hermitage. 'Finally got to bed at about 4 or 5. I got into Mrs Hammond's 4-poster, it was bliss,' confided Miss Braund to her diary. 'Sir Jeremy came and sat on my bed and wouldn't leave. I finally got him out about an hour and a half later. Don't know how I would have got through this whole experience without him though. Thank God for Sir Jeremy!'

It was their final day as inhabitants of the nineteenth century and they were ready to refamiliarise themselves with their twenty-first-century personas. But the unrestrained behaviour of the previous night left many questions unanswered. What is 'romantic', what is 'love' and how do you make a happy match? Can love and romance be found in the tokens, the surreptitious glances over dinner, the little notes and the stolen private conversations of the nineteenth century, or in the open, no-holds-barred, physically intimate, more egalitarian, contemporary behaviour seen at the ball? The experiment of the Regency House Party highlighted the myriad ways that 'romance', courtship and marriage have changed in two hundred years. Perhaps what the series revealed is that 'romance' is defined by the era in which it is expressed? Romance changes according to custom and taste, but love? That is surely today what it was two hundred years ago and will always be. Whether the strict conventions of the Regency allowed love to flourish any more than those of the relaxed and unconventional world we inhabit today, the reader must decide.

'Will you tell me how long you have loved him?' [asked Miss Bennet on being informed by her sister Elizabeth that she and Mr Darcy had become engaged.]

'It has been coming on so gradually, that I hardly know when it began. But I believe I must date it from my first seeing his beautiful grounds at Pemberley.'

Another intreaty that she would be serious, however, produced the desired effect; and she soon satisfied Jane by her solemn assurances of attachment. When convinced on that article, Miss Bennet had nothing farther to wish.

THE GAMES OF COURTSHIP AND ROMANCE DRAW TO A CLOSE

ENDWORD

'THIS EXPERIENCE has changed people's lives, it's been phenomenal,' said Mr Carrington as he was leaving. 'I've got a phrase running round my head that I won't forget. Gorell Barnes was asked the time and he said, "I don't know. A million o'clock?"'

The party broke up as the guests, singly or in couples, left for the twenty-first century. Although Miss Braund and Sir Jeremy had been more restrained than many of their companions at the ball, they left together in Sir Jeremy's coach the following morning, close friends and confidants. Miss Hopkins, however, left not with Mr Carrington but with Mr Everett. She was seen holding his hand as they set off in his carriage. 'I wanted him to know that his feelings did not fall on deaf ears,' she explained. 'Maybe this is a lesson I needed to learn in my life: don't always listen to your heart, sometimes listen to your head. I'm saying goodbye to the Regency Victoria – I came to quite like her and will take a part of her back with me, but I'm so glad to be a twenty-first-century woman. Freedom is indispensable and women have sacrificed a lot for that. But Regency, I'm going to miss you.'

GOOD-BYE TO KENTCHURCH COURT!
SADNESS AND RELIEF OVERWHELM THE GUESTS
AS THEY LEAVE THE EXQUISITE HOUSE

'This was the most beautiful, amazing, profound, emotional experience of my life and I am a better person for it. Now the future is rushing towards me,' said Mr Everett, with more than a hint of trepidation.

'It's been the happiest nine weeks of my life. I really needed it. Thank you,' said Miss Conick as her trunks were being packed.

'I'm going back to my life,' said Miss Francesca as she walked off towards the hermitage, 'and I know that I don't want to be a lady's companion any more. I want to get out and be myself again, do whatever I want and compete in an equal world.'

Miss Samuel left in her fine carriage, accompanied by Captain Robinson, who was still clearly overawed by her. Mr Carrington left on a velocipede – a Regency 'bicycle'; Mr Foxsmith on foot; and the others in their carriages. Many were in tears, but not the irrepressible Captain Robinson. 'I don't feel sad, I've been here before!' he said. 'I don't know if I will ever live like this again,' said Mr Foxsmith, 'but I hope my dead relatives look down on me and are proud that I made it as a gentleman.'

The countess left alone. Her parting thought in her diary was a nostalgic appreciation of the luxuries of Regency life: 'Imagine, if we ever meet up again we won't be in corsets, boots and breeches and there'll be no footman bringing booze on a silver tray.' Mr Gorell Barnes was last to leave. He cried when he said good-bye to his valet, Darren. 'The footmen have been my confidants, since talking to the guests is like Chinese whispers. Their professionalism has helped keep us on track. I'll miss them. The inspiration I will take from this place will be extensive and has made me feel humble.

The work of the footmen and maids at Kentchurch was universally praised.
As Caroline Ross Pirie explained: 'I needed to find young people who would be committed to this project and who would be prepared for the arduous tasks of a Regency servant, such as emptying chamber pots. The footmen and the maids never let us, or the guests, down, and I would give them a job anywhere, doing anything.'
Adela Kobic wrote and illustrated a diary of her experience as a lady's maid.

'It was fascinating to see how the Regency House Party experience changed the guests,' said Caroline Ross Pirie, the series producer, from her vantage point overseeing the whole experiment. 'The women, to survive in this world, had to become children. Their behaviour became increasingly infantile as their horizons shrank. Our feisty, twenty-first-century women became little girls in pretty frocks with puffed sleeves. One of them said that she rather enjoyed having no more responsibility than having to carry a parasol as she walked in the gardens. It was no wonder that so many Regency men had affairs with older women, as younger ones must have been quite unattractive because they were so confined. Yet while the women had to grow down to the Regency, the men had to grow up. They had to learn to have the posture and bearing of gentlemen, to be responsible for all their actions, and to maintain the position they were born to by the superiority of their conduct.'

The nine weeks also made the guests think about marriage, love and courtship. 'I remember', continued Caroline, 'Mr Gorell Barnes saying "I'm learning to love women for their minds," because their clothes didn't allow any insight into what their bodies looked like. But that's a lesson that won't do him or the other men any harm. And the love tokens that circulated around the house were also a source of great

FRIENDSHIP, AS WELL AS ROMANCE, WAS FORMED DURING THE REGENCY SUMMER

pleasure and so much more romantic than the average text message.

'The series highlighted the importance of spending time with people and not succumbing to the undignified pace of modern life. "We have to learn not to hurry," Mrs Enright said. "Manners are all about acknowledging other people and making them feel good about themselves, however busy we may be. It's time we relearned how to entertain each other instead of relying on the stereo, television and cinema." Even Lady Devonport, who found the female routine particularly frustrating, commented that "being constrained has taught me to rediscover my imagination and I am really grateful for that". After all, someone writing you a poem or singing you a song is so very much more gratifying than having someone flick a switch, plonk a glass of wine in your hand and ask you if you fancy a quick one,' concluded Caroline Ross Pirie.

Perhaps Sir Jeremy best summed up the profound, life-changing, roller-coaster ride of the Regency house experiment. 'I entered this house a hooligan. I am leaving it a gentleman.'

GAZETTEER

If the series has inspired you to redecorate your house and garden in the style of Kentchurch, you may find the following information helpful.

HOUSE

Hamilton Weston Ltd
Period wallpapers/fabrics, also retail shop and interior design service
info@hamiltonweston.com
www.hamiltonweston.com
T: 020 8940 4850

Zoffany
Fabrics, wallpapers, paints, carpets and furniture
sales@zoffany.uk.com
www.zoffany.co.uk
T: 08708 300 350

Context Weavers
Reproduction of historic fabrics and braids
T: 01706 220917

Watts of Westminster
Period decoration
sales@wattsofwestminster.co.uk
www.wattsofwestminster.com
T: 020 7376 4486

Sir William Bentley Billiards
Beautiful billiard tables
sales@billiards.co.uk
www.billiards.co.uk
T: 01488 681711

Branksome Antiques
Scientific, marine and medical items
branksome@antique-dealers-directory.co.uk
www.antique-dealers-directory.co.uk/branksome/
T: 01202 763324

The White House
Household linens, towels and accessories
sales@the-white-house.co.uk
T: 020 7629 3521

David Salmon Furniture
Fine English furniture
sales@davidsalmon.com
T: 020 7384 2223

Antique Musical Instruments
Early pianos and harpsichords; instrument sales and restorations
michaelcole@squarepianos.com
T: 01242 517192

Arthur Brett & Sons Ltd
Hand-crafted English furniture
sales@arthur-brett.com
T: 020 7730 7304

Isis Ceramics Ltd
Hand-painted ceramics
isisceram@aol.com
T: 01865 358000

The Classic Library
Decorative bound books and
library furniture
contact@markransom.co.uk
www.markransom.co.uk
T: 020 7376 7653

Candle Makers Supplies
Candles
candles@candlemakers.co.uk
T: 020 7602 4031

And So To Bed
An outstanding collection of
exclusive-design beds,
mattresses, furniture and
accessories
enquiries@andsotobed.co.uk
www.andsotobed.co.uk
T: 01372 460660/0808 144 4343

Seasons Textiles Ltd
Soft furnishing hire;
fabric/wallpaper sales
contact@seasonstextiles.
fsbusiness.co.uk
T: 020 8965 6161

Bespoke
Restoration of antique and
continental chandeliers and
lighting
T: 01684 572087

GARDEN

Cranborne Stone
A family firm that has
specialised in designing and
making high-quality cast-
stone garden and architectural
ornaments for over thirty
years
sales@cranbornestone.com
www.cranbornestone.com
T: 01258 472685

Chilstone
Hand-made traditional garden
ornaments, temples and
architectural stonework in
reconstituted stone.
ornaments@chilstone.com
T: 01892 740866

Allweather & Tubbs
Gothic gazebos and Chiswick
House round urns
www.allweatherandtubbs.co.uk
T: 01372 466106

The World Famous
Fireworks and pyrotechnic art
info@theworldfamous.co.uk
T: 020 7274 9000

Selected Reading

The following books have been useful in my research and I thoroughly recommend them to anyone interested in furthering their knowledge of the Regency period.

A Lady of Distinction, *The Mirror of the Graces*, Fort Bragg, CA, USA, R. L. Shep

Ashe, G., *The Hell-Fire Clubs: A History of Anti-Morality*, Stroud, Gloucestershire, Sutton Publishing, 2000

Colegate, I., *A Pelican in the Wilderness: Hermits, Solitaries and Recluses*, London, HarperCollins, 2002

Colley, L., *Britons: Forging the Nation 1707–1837*, London, Pimlico, 1992

Fryer, P., *Staying Power: The History of Black People in Britain*, London, Pluto Press, 1984

Girouard, M., *Life in the English Country House*, New Haven and London, Yale University Press, 1978

James, F. (ed.), *The Common Purposes of Life: Science and Society at the Royal Institution of Great Britain*, London, Ashgate, 2003

Jump, J. D., *Byron*, London and Boston, Routledge & Kegan Paul, 1972

Mandler, P., *The Fall and Rise of the Stately Home*, New Haven and London, Yale University Press, 1997

Mingay, G., *Mrs Hurst Dancing & Other Scenes From Regency Life 1812–1823*, London, Victor Gollancz, 1981

Murray, V., *High Society: A Social History of the Regency 1788–1830*, London, Viking, 1998

Priestley, J. B., *The Prince of Pleasure*, London, Heinemann, 1969

Radford, Peter, *The Celebrated Captain Barclay: Sport, Money and Fame in Regency Britain*, London, Headline, 2001

Stone, L., *Family, Sex and Marriage in England 1500–1800*, London, Weidenfeld & Nicolson, 1977

Uglow, J., *The Lunar Men*, London, Faber & Faber, 2002

Vickery, A., *The Gentleman's Daughter*, New Haven and London, Yale University Press, 1998

Von Hagens, G., *Bodyworlds*, exhibition catalogue, Institut für Plastination, Heidelberg, German, 2002

Watkins, S., *Jane Austen in Style*, London, Thames & Hudson, 1990

ACKNOWLEDGEMENTS

Author's Acknowledgements
Due to limited space, I can only list the names of people whom I wish to thank rather than give details of their contribution, but I hope they all know how much they have helped me in the writing of this book and how grateful I am for advice freely given, expertise generously imparted, grammar willingly corrected, baby-sitting lovingly executed and author-support unfailingly given.

Caroline Ross Pirie, the series producer, and her talented, committed and eternally helpful team at Wall to Wall and the guests, footmen and maids, housemaids, watchmen, grooms, gardeners and game-keeper, chef and cooks of Kentchurch Court, summer 2003 – you were amazing.

Dr Peter Mandler (principal historical consultant), Steve Bacon, Andrew Bampfield, David Bell, Dr Roberta Bivins, Sheila Bracewell, Timothy Dean, Ian Dowding, Ros Ebbutt, Truls Hansen, Professor Mervyn Heard, Austin Howard, Dr Kevin Ilsley, Dr Frank James, Dr Darryl Jones Rosanna Lucas-Scudamore, Hamish Macleod, Jo Manser, Kim Newman, Jacqueline Osei-Tutu, Professor Peter Radford, Alan Spalding, Lord Temple-Morris and the staff of Poole and Bournemouth Central Libraries and the London Library.

The editorial team at Time Warner Books: Viv Redman, Vicki Harris, Nick Ross, Filomena Wood, Linda Silverman; and Andrew Barron, the designer, Martin Thompson, the photographer, Julian Alexander at LAW Ltd and my agent Stephanie Cabot at William Morris Ltd. Robin Daly, Ellie Parker and family, Jackie Walker and Kay Brooks, Sally and Elliot Cass, Paula Webb and Crispin Swayne, Tiffany Farish, and my fabulous family: Anna, Robert, Camilla and especially my daughter Lily.

Producer's Acknowledgements
Mr and Mrs John and Jan Lucas-Scudamore, Joss and Rosanna Lucas-Scudamore, Alex Graham, Helen Hawken, Emma Willis, Rosemary Plum, Zoë Watkins, Tamsynne Westcott, Tim Carter, Sam Kingsley, Martin Johnson, Toby Farrell, Christine Pancott, Cate Hall, Mark Ball, Tom McDonald, Jonathan Francis, Daniel Read, Robin Daly, Aoife McArdle, Anthony Edey, Richard Wakefield, Alec Waterlow, Clare Wiltshire, Brian Read, Lesley Cross, Paul Halter, Tom McEwen, Emma Parsons, Ben Grist, Justin Morris, Rosalind Ebbutt, Sally Mason, Natalie Humphries, Sheelagh Wells, Mary Hillman, Daniel Pemberton, Daru Rooke, Ivan Day, Peter Radford, Judith Laske, Sam Bonham, Margaret Chance, Alan Tissington, Helen Brown, Janice Tissington, Jean Beech, Ella Gane, Jill Thomas, Linda Goodwin, Alex Woolfson, Sarah Williams, Ivan Day, Steve Sheppard, Hilary Miles, Cindy Morris, Eddie Powell, Kevin Smith, Ian Walker, Sam Costello, Helen Johnson, Adela Kobic, Christina Martin, Laura Salmon, Debbie Shepherd, Ollie Fishman, Matt Howley, Rob Hunt, Matt Jones, Tom Joseph, Alex McIntosh, Olly Mardling, A. Jackson Pentland, Jason Richards, Owen Rodd, Geoff Robbins, Darren Sher, Barry Collings, Dave Norman, Kevin Dawe, Maurice O'Donnell, Kentchurch Children's Trust, The Bridge Inn, Kentchurch, Chris Deakin, Ursula Adams, Jeremy Barlow, Professor Gunther von Hagens, Felicity Ruperti, The Right Honourable Clare Short, Matt Skelton, Steven Horn, Alistair Malloy, Tom Fortes Mayer, Graham Tobyn, John McCririck, Simon Armitage, Nick Foulkes, Jane Gibson, Venetia Murray, John White, John Styles, Professor Andrew Roberts, Dr Michael Neve, Dr John Casey, Dr Lawrence Klein, Dr Darryl Jones, Dr Richard Rathbone, Dr Jonathan Sleath, Rev. James Butterworth, The Working Class Movement Museum, Salford, The World Famous Fireworks Company, Hatched Brands, British Dental Association Museum, The National Army Museum, Chelsea

INDEX